TOP DISNEY

100 TOP TEN LISTS OF THE BEST
OF DISNEY, FROM THE MAN TO
THE MOUSE AND BEYOND

CHRISTOPHER LUCAS

LYONS
PRESS

Guilford, Connecticut

An imprint of The Rowman & Littlefield Publishing Group, Inc.
4501 Forbes Blvd., Ste. 200
Lanham, MD 20706
www.rowman.com

Distributed by NATIONAL BOOK NETWORK

British Library Cataloguing in Publication Information available

Library of Congress Cataloging-in-Publication Data

Names: Lucas, Christopher Patrick, 1968- author.
Title: Top Disney : 100 top ten lists of the best of Disney, from the man to the mouse and beyond / Christopher Lucas.
Description: Guilford, Connecticut : Lyons Press, [2019].
Identifiers: LCCN 2018055792 (print) | LCCN 2018059922 (ebook) | ISBN 9781493037728 (ebook) | ISBN 9781493037711 (pbk. : alk. paper)
Subjects: LCSH: Walt Disney Company—Miscellanea. | Disney, Walt, 1901-1966—Miscellanea.
Classification: LCC PN1999.W27 (ebook) | LCC PN1999.W27 L83 2019 (print) | DDC 791.430973—dc23
LC record available at https://lccn.loc.gov/2018055792

♾️™ The paper used in this publication meets the minimum requirements of American National Standard for Information Sciences—Permanence of Paper for Printed Library Materials, ANSI/NISO Z39.48-1992.

Printed in the United States of America

CONTENTS

LISTS ABOUT DISNEY CHARACTERS   103

CONTENTS

INTRODUCTION

Disney is a company that is familiar to almost everyone. In 2017, more than two hundred million people visited a Disney park; Disney films sold more than seven billion dollars' worth of tickets worldwide; thirty million viewers watched Disney TV programs, accounting for three billion dollars in video sales and downloads; and consumers spent more than thirty billion dollars on Disney merchandise.

With a library of ninety-plus years' worth of film and television characters and profitable in-house franchises like Star Wars, Marvel, the Muppets, and Pixar, Disney remains one of the most recognizable and beloved companies on the planet.

That's the reason I wrote this book. I am a lifelong fan of all things Disney, yet each day I discover something new about Walt and his company.

There's so much history that it's hard to keep track of it, or even to remember which classic characters and moments came when. That was the origin of this book, compiling a personal series of lists to put all these things in one easily accessible place. My lists and entries will be familiar to both longtime Disney fans and newcomers, yet will also include enough original material to enlighten even the most dedicated devotee. My aim is to tell the story of Walt and the Disney Company in an easy-to-follow way, through lists of their greatest milestones and achievements.

Each of the one hundred lists in the book is self-contained. You can read the book straight through, jump in at random spots, or simply pick and choose among your favorite subjects.

Some of the book's topics and entries are also designed to surprise. For instance, even the most stalwart Disney fans may not be familiar with *Miracle of the White Stallions*, Disney Legend Jack Wagner, or Disneyland's Mickey Mouse Club Circus. These are three of the many fascinating yet often overlooked entrants on the lists of Disney history included.

Finally, these lists were compiled by me based on years of Disney research. Though there are films that are my personal favorites (*Robin Hood*, *Superdad*, and *The Boatniks*), I could not justify putting them on a list when they were not a consensus top ten in their category according to the experts and fans. In the end, these lists are still just my sole opinion. I hope that if you disagree with some of my choices, this book will encourage you to design your own top ten lists, creating conversation and debate among you and your Disney-loving friends.

If you have any comments or suggestions, you can email me at MouseTopTen@gmail.com. For updated lists and new topics, please visit www.MouseTopTen.com.

Enjoy!

—Christopher Lucas

RULES FOR THE LISTS

The lists included in this book are based on my own research, selected by me after considering the opinions of several Disney experts, fans, and publications. I am aware that readers will disagree, and wonder why favorites are left out or why the items are ranked as they are.

I came up with some ground rules for the lists that might answer those questions:

1) While the ten items in each list have been selected as the top ten in their own category, they are not ranked within the list itself. When I could, I ordered them chronologically to avoid any notion of one item or person being greater than another. For instance, while *Mary Poppins* would certainly be front and center on the top ten live-action musicals list, it actually comes later on the list, according to its release date.

2) Since there are almost one hundred years of Disney history to sort through, I broke some of the lists into two parts: "classic" and "modern." For the purposes of this book, the "classic" Disney era is defined as the sixty-five-year span from the founding of the Disney Studios in 1923 (and Walt's own work before that) until 1988, when the last of Walt's old guard of animators retired. The "modern" era then runs from 1989 to the end of 2017.

3) I deliberately omitted films, characters, and television shows that were created and/or produced—or coproduced—with other companies (such as 1980's *Popeye*, with Paramount, or 2014's *Lincoln*, with DreamWorks); were created before Disney acquired the brand (like Kermit from the Muppets, Spider-Man from Marvel, or Darth Vader from Star Wars); were only distributed but not created by Disney (the Studio Ghibli films); or were produced by brands and companies that Disney is no longer associated with (*Shakespeare in Love* from Miramax). Pixar is the only exception to this rule, as its characters were associated with Disney long before Disney fully acquired the brand.

4) I used *Disney A to Z*—a comprehensive guide compiled by Dave Smith, *the* biggest Disney expert and the man who literally created the company's archival system—as the ultimate reference authority for the items in this book. If there was a question as to whether something was "Disney," I cross-referenced and checked it with *Disney A to Z* and the Disney Archives before including or omitting it.

5) With so much Disney history and so many great choices (it was really hard to leave some films, songs, and characters out), I tried, whenever possible, not to duplicate items on separate lists. For instance, while Lady and the Tramp would be logical additions to the list of Disney's top ten couples, I believe they are a better fit for Disney's top ten canines, so I placed them there, since they are—arguably—the two most famous Disney dogs and the couples list has so many other potential candidates to choose from.

LISTS ABOUT WALT DISNEY HIMSELF

GREATEST INFLUENCES ON WALT

HIS PARENTS

Walt Disney developed his can-do attitude, relentless work ethic, and keen sense of humor from his parents, Elias and Flora. Elias was a Canadian immigrant who moved to the plains of Kansas as a young man. He was a self-taught handyman and contractor, who was clean-living, devout, and no-nonsense. He fell in love with his next-door neighbor, Flora Call, and followed her family when they moved to Florida, not too far from where Walt Disney World is now located. They married in 1888 and tried their hand at Florida orange growing and cattle farming before moving to Chicago, where Walt was born in 1901, in a house that Elias built nine years before. Walt's family spent years moving from place to place as Elias tried to find steady work. Though he was kindhearted, his often dour and stoic attitude was in direct contrast to Flora's cheerfulness, optimism, and extroverted personality. Walt absorbed a lot of his mother's charm, and that shows, but he also learned valuable lessons from his dad. Elias gave Walt his first job at an early age, ensuring that he understood the rewards of working at something until the task is complete, striving for quality, and honoring promises made, no matter how difficult.

HIS FAMILY

Though they moved around quite a bit, Walt's family was extremely close. He had three older brothers, Herbert, Ray, and Roy, and a younger sister, Ruth, all of whom stayed in touch with each other their entire lives. In addition, Walt's extended family of grandparents, uncles, aunts, and cousins would pay him visits when he was a child, sharing family stories and encouraging him in his artistic pursuits and dreams, even when such support was lacking from his parents. His wife, Lillian Bounds Disney, whom he married in 1925, was Walt's rock. Lilly was his partner and confidante, encouraging him through his many ups and downs, making certain that the balance between Walt's life at home and his life at his studio was equal. They raised two girls, Diane and Sharon, who were a constant joy to Walt. In his later years, his grandchildren increased the amount of love and laughter. Walt's closest familial relationship, however, was with his brother Roy. Born eight years before Walt, Roy was Walt's best friend and business partner. Though they bickered from time to time—mostly about financial issues, as Roy handled the business side of the Disney Studios while Walt took care of the creative—Walt idolized his older brother. Their love and mutual respect were evident. The ultimate example of this was Roy's insistence on delaying his retirement for five years after Walt's unexpected death in 1966 to oversee the completion of his kid brother's final dream, Walt Disney World.

MISSOURI

In 1906, Elias moved his family from Chicago to a small farm in the town of Marceline, Missouri. As a young boy, Walt fell in love with the bucolic rural life, and it stayed with him. Chicago may have been his birthplace, but Missouri was home. As Walt said on a return visit there in 1956, "More things of importance happened to me in Marceline than have happened since, or are likely to happen in the future." Missouri's own Mark Twain was one of Walt's childhood idols. His tales of Tom Sawyer, Huck Finn, and their adventures in Hannibal inspired Walt to seek similar adventures in his little corner of the Show-Me State. Entire days were spent fishing, exploring, or just sitting under a tree on the farm dreaming. Soon after Herbert and Ray moved away, Elias got sick. The burden of work then fell on Roy and eight-year-old Walt. Elias was forced to sell the farm in 1911, and the Disney family moved to Kansas City. Life in a metropolis didn't hold much appeal for Walt, but he was exposed to the many cinemas and theaters that populated Kansas City, feeding his dreams of a career in the arts. Kansas City was also where Walt opened his very first cartoon studio, in 1920. In the early 1960s, Walt planned to build a Disney attraction in Marceline—a working farm and museum—and a second Disneyland on the banks of the Mississippi River in St. Louis. Both projects were canceled after his death. Several of Walt's films and many of the places in his parks (Main Street, U.S.A.; Tom Sawyer Island) reflect the fond memories of his days as a boy in the state he was always proud to call his own.

The Carnegie Library in Marceline, Missouri. (Wikimedia Commons)

FAILURE/DOUBTERS

Throughout his life, Walt had to overcome crushing defeats and naysayers who doubted his abilities, his business sense, and his dreams. He never let it stop him. Instead, it drove him to achieve even more. Walt was no stranger to adversity. His first attempt at a cartoon studio ended in bankruptcy.

He was left with nothing. Sensible minds told him to abandon his dreams and to get a reliable job somewhere in Kansas City. That would've been the rational game plan. Walt chose the riskier option and—undaunted by the setback—followed his dreams to California. As he recalled, "I think it's important to have a good hard failure when you're young. You may not realize it when it happens, but a kick in the teeth might be the best thing in the world for you." Even after he had some success in Hollywood, failure and doubt plagued Walt. His first cartoon superstar, Oswald, was stolen away from him. His choices to experiment with sound and color were mocked. The idea to create the first feature-length animated film was referred to as "Disney's Folly." *Fantasia* and other ambitious projects flopped commercially. Disneyland couldn't find any financial backing. (Lilly herself thought it was crazy to build a theme park.) Walt patiently listened to their comments, usually ignored them, and persisted. His courage to resist the peer pressure, placing absolute faith in his dreams, changed the world.

AMERICA

As proud as he was of his home state, Walt was even prouder of his country. He once said in an interview, "If you could see in my eyes, the American flag is waving in both of them and my spine is growing this red, white and blue stripe." Walt's patriotism inspired him to join the American war effort in 1917. He was a year too young to enlist in the military, so he served in France with the Red Cross Ambulance Corps. In the early 1940s, President Roosevelt chose Walt to be the State Department's goodwill ambassador to our neighbors in South and Central America. When the Second World War interrupted production at his studio, Walt offered to make training films for the U.S. government at cost, at a time when others were making a profit doing the same thing. Walt felt this was his patriotic obligation. He was passionate about preserving and telling stories of American history and folklore,

Mark Twain, whose tales of life on the frontier waterways of America inspired much of Disney's creative output both on film and in his theme parks. (Library of Congress)

as many of his popular movies and TV shows demonstrated. In the parks, Walt included moments and symbols of American history and achievement, the culmination of which was the audio-animatronic figure of his childhood idol, Abraham Lincoln. Walt brought the sixteenth president to life for modern audiences. In 1964, for his promotion of the values and ideals of American culture, Walt was awarded the Presidential Medal of Freedom, the highest civilian honor granted in the United States.

RAILROADS

When Walt was young, he would often run down to Marceline's railroad station, a mile from his farm, just to wave at passing trains. The Atchison, Topeka and Santa Fe Railroad line ran directly through Marceline. Walt's uncle Mike worked for the railroad and would stop by to see his nephew, telling him stories about life on the tracks and bringing him souvenirs. That helped to nourish Walt's love affair with trains, which became a recurring theme in his life and in his work. As a teen, Walt got a job selling candy on the railroad. Never much of a businessman, he would often leave his supplies unattended and take a loss of profit, but he didn't care because he was riding the rails on a daily basis. When he went bankrupt in 1923, his last purchase after settling with creditors was a train ticket from Kansas City to Hollywood. When he'd earned enough in the 1950s to buy a house in the upscale Holmby Hills section of Los Angeles, one of the first things Walt did was to install a small-scale passenger train and tracks that would run around the property. He even built a workshop modeled after his beloved family barn from Marceline. Walt's passion for trains culminated with the refurbishment of classic steam locomotives for Disneyland. They're now a fixture in almost all of the Disney parks, a fitting tribute to their founder.

SHOW BUSINESS

A born entertainer, Walt had his passion for telling stories nurtured by seeing stories performed, on stage and on screen. Two of the more notable ones that he recalled seeing in Kansas City as a child were an early silent film version of *Snow White and the Seven Dwarfs* and a traveling theatrical production of *Peter Pan*, performed by Maude Adams. The pantomimed antics of silent film superstar Charlie Chaplin also enthralled Walt. Spurred on by these experiences, Walt teamed with a school chum—Walt Pfeiffer—to dress up in costumes and put on their own shows re-creating some of Chaplin's routines, as well as delivering famous speeches like the Gettysburg Address. They called themselves "The Two Walts." Disney relished the opportunity to make audiences laugh, cry, or just be moved in some way. It gave him a map to follow in his career path. Hollywood was still in its infancy when Walt arrived. Always curious and eager to learn, he studied the work of his fellow artists and learned from their triumphs and failures. Walt was a lifelong student of the arts, believing that modern show business could bring culture to the masses. Chaplin and Disney became friends. Walt emulated Charlie's philosophy of bringing a personality to characters to increase the audience's involvement, rather than just trying to go from gag to gag and scene to scene. It was also Chaplin's transition from short films to features that inspired Walt to do the same with his cartoons. Disneyland was the result of Walt's channeling everything he learned about show business into a three-dimensional reality. Through it all, Walt never forgot what it was like to be a member of the audience. As he put it, "I've never called my work art, it's part of show business, the business of building entertainment. We are not trying to entertain the critics. I'll take my chances with the public. I don't like to kid myself about the intelligence and taste of our audiences. They are made up of my neighbors, people I know and meet every day. Folks I trade with, go to church with, vote with, compete in business with, help build and preserve a nation with. I just make what I'd like to see, warm and human stories, about historic characters and events and about animals . . . family entertainment."

NATURE

As a farm boy, Walt had lots of experience with animals. They were his childhood companions. He viewed them more as characters with personalities than as just livestock. Walt expressed his feelings on the matter to a reporter once: "Sometimes we can recognize ourselves in animals—that's what makes them so interesting. The spontaneity of an animal, you also find it in children." Anthropomorphic animals were a big part of Walt's cartoons (Mickey Mouse being the most prominent example). His studio's early animation efforts also featured awe-inspiring natural landscapes. With each film, Walt sought to bring more realism. That led to his studio's invention of the multiplane camera, to give a better sense of dimension. He also had live animals brought to the studio so that his animators could sketch them and see how they reacted in different situations. In the 1950s, Walt sent film crews out to capture live-action documentary footage of animals in their natural habitats. These *True-Life Adventures* won a number of Oscars and solidified Disney's reputation as one of America's great naturalists and stewards of the environment.

In such films as *Charlie, the Lonesome Cougar* (1967) Disney expressed his fascination with the natural world. (Buena Vista Distribution Company/Photofest)

TECHNOLOGY

Walt said the following in the 1960s, but it just as easily could apply to 2018: "It is a curious thing that the more the world shrinks because of electronic communications, the more limitless becomes the province of the storytelling entertainer." Disney knew that, as a showman, he had to use all the tools available to him in service to the story, and when those weren't enough to develop some more. He was a lifelong tinkerer who was inspired by inventors like Thomas Edison and Henry Ford, and his curiosity led him to explore new horizons. In the process, he set the standards for the use of sound, depth, and color in animation. Not afraid of new technology, Disney was the first studio head to embrace television when all the others were avoiding it as a direct competitor to films. Walt utilized television to great success in the 1950s, and the others quickly followed. The last decade of Walt's life saw some of his greatest technological achievements, as he partnered with major corporations to develop advances in—among other things—computers, communications, robotics, and energy conservation, many of which we are still benefiting from.

THE FUTURE

The phrase "optimistic futurist" is often used to describe Walt Disney. It's perfect for him. While other artists of his generation saw a future filled with bleak cityscapes, overpopulation, war, famine, and blight, Walt envisioned one that was brighter. That motivated him. Throughout his life, while he kept his feet in the present working on the day-to-day operations of a major corporation, Walt kept his eyes on the future. Many of his films and television shows dealt with the topic of what twenty-first-century life would be like, and they all gave a rosy forecast. Walt even christened one of the major areas of his theme park Tomorrowland, declaring that it would be ever-changing to keep up with mankind's greatest advances. His final project was the Experimental Prototype Community of Tomorrow. Walt spent years educating himself on the subject of urban planning and hoped to tackle some of the problems that had befallen big cities in the 1960s. Just as he did with his theme park, Walt was going to will this new dream for an optimistic future into a reality. Unfortunately, he passed away before this happened. One of the last things Walt did before he died was to explain his cheery vision of the future, EPCOT, to his brother Roy, using the ceiling tiles above his hospital bed as a makeshift map.

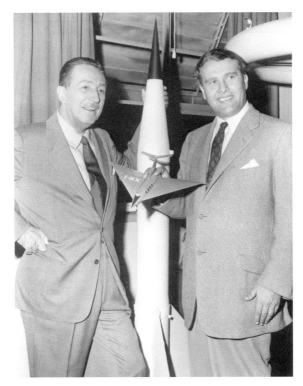

Walt Disney with Dr. Werner von Braun. Von Braun contributed to the 1955 Disney program *Man in Space*, a show partially credited with the establishment of NASA. (NASA)

KEY MOMENTS IN WALT'S LIFE

GETTING PAID FOR A DRAWING AT AGE NINE

Walt loved the people in his hometown of Marceline. He was a curious child and would spend hours chatting with some of the locals, like an eccentric Civil War veteran and raconteur everyone called "Grandpa Taylor." Inspired by these fantastic stories, Walt would often daydream and doodle. One day in school, the teacher asked the students to draw flowers and trees. Walt drew his with faces and arms, and was immediately reprimanded. He was instructed not to use his imagination, that it wouldn't be productive. That still didn't discourage the aspiring artist in Walt. He was fortunate that another friend from town, a retired physician, Doc Sherwood, knew just the right tonic to nurture Walt's dreams. Walt brought a sketch pad and crayons to Sherwood's barn one day and drew a picture of the doctor's prized horse, Rupert. When he was done, the kindly doctor surprised Walt by offering him a quarter for the work. As Walt recalled, "All the way home I walked on air, squeezing that quarter so tight it hurt. A wonderful thing had happened. Someone liked a drawing of mine enough to buy it. I knew that perhaps I would succeed in my ambition to be a cartoonist. Many honors and rewards have come my way since then, but none quite measures up to the thrill I felt on that day."

FORGING HIS BIRTH CERTIFICATE TO JOIN THE WAR EFFORT

An average student at Chicago's McKinley High School, Walt longed for adventure and the world beyond Missouri. When the United States entered World War I in 1917, he saw an opportunity—forging his birth certificate to appear a year older so that he could join the Red Cross Ambulance Corps and be shipped to France. While in Europe, he was exposed to different cultures and languages, often having to communicate using pantomime. The end of the war, and a bout with influenza, made Walt homesick, so he returned to the United States shortly after he got to Europe. As the song of that era stated, "How are you gonna keep 'em down on the farm after they've seen Paris?" This brief postwar experience overseas changed Walt. It broadened his moral compass, sharpened his storytelling instincts, and heightened his appreciation and respect for other viewpoints and cultural traditions.

CHECKING OUT LIBRARY BOOKS IN KANSAS CITY

When Walt returned to the United States, now an adult, he discovered that his father had squandered much of the money that he'd sent back home on an investment in the O-Zell Jelly Company. Elias wanted Walt to work there, but the place soon closed. Instead, using a portfolio of drawings he did in high school and in Paris, Walt found employment at a commercial art studio close to home. He had ambitions of becoming a newspaper cartoonist, but knew instinctively that there might also be other options for him. With limited resources, Walt visited the free public library in Kansas City for inspiration and discovered two books about the burgeoning art of film animation. He immediately checked them out and then pored over every single page of those books again and again. He knew that he'd found his niche. Soon after, Walt opened his own studio with some friends, and together by trial and error—they taught themselves to be animators. After bankruptcy and failure in Kansas City, Walt headed to Hollywood, bringing every lesson he'd learned about animation with him.

HIS 1928 TRIP TO NEW YORK CITY

In 1923, the Disney Brothers Studio was established as the first full-time animation studio in Hollywood. They had some success with a series of short comedies based on *Alice in Wonderland*, blending live action and animation. In 1927, Walt and his crew came up with a new character—Oswald the Lucky Rabbit—which was distributed by Universal. Audiences fell in love with Oswald. The Disney reputation was growing. In 1928, Walt traveled to New York City to meet with Charles Mintz, the distribution representative, ostensibly to negotiate a new deal. To his horror, what Walt learned when he got to the Big Apple was that Mintz had double-crossed him. Since the rights to Oswald technically belonged to Universal, Mintz was able to claim the character as his own. He then secretly hired away much of Disney's animation staff. Walt was stunned, and then angry. Instead of falling into depression, he channeled his anger. He sent a telegram to Roy saying not to worry, they'd figure something out. According to Disney mythology, on the train ride back to Los Angeles, Walt took out his sketch pad and created a new character for his studio, a variation on Oswald, this time with the features of a mouse. Walt supposedly wanted to name it Mortimer, but it was Lilly who suggested calling him Mickey Mouse. Walt, Ub Iwerks, and a few other loyal Disney animators worked in secret on three new Mickey Mouse films. When they debuted later that year, Mickey was on his way to becoming an international superstar, leaving Oswald in the dust.

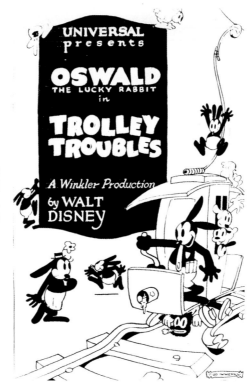

Oswald the Lucky Rabbit was Disney's first successful animated character. (Wikimedia Commons)

THE BIRTH OF HIS FIRST CHILD

Mickey Mouse and a series of cartoons called the *Silly Symphonies* made Disney a household name by 1933. Walt had trouble dealing with the stress of rapidly going from struggling artist to big-time Hollywood producer. The Great Depression that gripped the world, affecting bottom lines, also took its toll on Walt. He'd hoped to start a family with Lilly, but she suffered a series of miscarriages, which added to their angst. Walt took time off to deal with his frazzled nerves. After a relaxing hiatus, he and Lilly came back to L.A. refreshed. On December 18, 1933, their first child, Diane, was born. Walt's life changed forever. His family then became the relaxing center of his world. Even when he had to spend extra hours at the studio, Diane and her sister, Sharon—who was adopted by Walt and Lilly in 1937—joined their father. The studio was their playground. Walt would often take his girls to nearby Griffith Park to ride the merry-go-round. As he sat on a bench nearby watching them have fun, Walt wondered why there wasn't a place where the whole family could spend time together having fun on rides and attractions. The seeds of Disneyland were planted on those "daddy/daughter days."

From left to right, Lillian, Sharon, Diane, and Walt Disney at Schiphol Airport in Amsterdam, Netherlands in 1951. (National Archive of the Netherlands)

MEETING WITH HIS ANIMATORS TO TELL THEM THE STORY OF SNOW WHITE

One evening in 1934, Walt sent his staff out for dinner with instructions to return to the studio afterward. When they arrived, they discovered Walt on an empty soundstage surrounded by chairs. For the next three hours, alone in the spotlight, Walt proceeded to tell the story of Snow White and the Seven Dwarfs, inhabiting each and every role with a showman's flair. By the time he was done, every single person in the room was captivated, eager to follow Walt down the road to his craziest dream, the first feature-length animated film. After that meeting, knowing that the studio workload was going to increase, Walt hired three hundred more artists. He also started bringing in instructors from L.A.'s famed Chouinard Art Studio to teach classes to his animators in the studio itself. This led directly to Walt's vision of a college campus especially for artists, performers, and animators, which resulted in the incorporation of the California Institute of the Arts in 1961. Many future Disney employees graduated from CalArts, fulfilling Walt's dreams.

BUYING HIS PARENTS A HOUSE IN 1938

Flora and Elias Disney celebrated fifty years of marriage in 1938. Walt and Roy threw a big party for them, at which the whole extended Disney family gathered. The success of *Snow White* the previous year allowed the brothers to buy a house in Los Angeles as a gift for their parents, so that they could be closer to their grandchildren (Roy's son, Roy E. Disney, had recently been born). As the cooler fall weather approached, the furnace in the house started acting up. Elias tried to repair it; then Walt sent workers from the studio over to fix it. On the night of November 26, 1938, carbon monoxide fumes from the faulty furnace filled the home. Flora was overcome and died of asphyxiation and carbon monoxide poisoning. Elias barely escaped with his life. Walt was, naturally, devastated by this. Flora was the one who'd given him his sense of humor and spark of creativity. She was gone, and he blamed himself—in part—for it. It left a mark on him. Walt never spoke publicly about this tragedy after that.

HIS THIRTIETH WEDDING ANNIVERSARY PARTY

Walt and Lilly had gone through a lot in their three decades together. They experienced many highs and lows, personally and professionally. After the Great Depression, the death of his parents (Elias died in 1941), a strike at the studio, the war years, and a postwar loss of profits, Walt was back on top, with a new home for their family in Holmby Hills; success with *Cinderella* and *Peter Pan*, the live-action films, and his TV show; and the completion in less than a year of his dream park. He and Lilly deserved a big celebration. A few nights before Disneyland opened to the public, Walt and Lilly invited all their friends and family to a party at the park in honor of their thirtieth wedding anniversary. It was held in Frontierland. Guests took rides on the newly christened steamboat before heading over to the Golden Horseshoe for dinner and a show. Every picture from that night shows Walt and Lilly with huge smiles on their faces. His daughter Diane said on many occasions that this special evening spending time with the people closest to them in a place that was his unique vision was the happiest she'd ever seen her father.

HIS TRIP TO NEW ORLEANS IN 1946

By the end of the 1950s, Walt's theme park exceeded attendance expectations. Ever the tinkerer, Walt had his sights set on the latest technology and how to use it to improve his park. To that end, he'd formed several new companies to separate himself and his outside projects from the

New Orleans Square in Disneyland, inspired by Walt's visit to New Orleans in 1946. (Wikimedia Commons)

publicly owned Disney film studio and production company. These were Retlaw Enterprises, WED Enterprises, and MAPO. The first was to protect his family interest; the latter two were focused on mechanical design, research, and development (later to be known as Imagineering). In 1946 Walt and Lilly had visited New Orleans. Browsing a curio shop in the French Quarter, Walt happened upon a small mechanical bird in a cage, which moved in a lifelike way, thanks to tubes and wires. He knew that someday he'd like to update this primitive technology and make it bigger. Thus was born the idea of audio-animatronics, which became a trademark for Disney in the 1960s and a distinguishing feature of their theme parks. Walt was also inspired by this trip to add the first major area to Disneyland since its opening, New Orleans Square. That tiny place tucked into a bend at the Rivers of America gave Disneyland a bit of southern charm and Cajun flavor and became home to both Pirates of the Caribbean and the Haunted Mansion.

HIS 1965 MEETING WITH REPORTER EMILY BAVAR

In the summer of 1965, to celebrate the "Tencennial" (a word coined by Disney publicist Charles Ridgway) of Disneyland, reporters from around the world were invited to California to meet with Walt. These were just supposed to be fluff pieces about the history of Disneyland, Walt's additions to his park, and his recent involvement in the 1964 World's Fair. One of these reporters, Emily Bavar of the *Orlando Sentinel*, had a different agenda. After some pleasantries and small talk, she got right to the point and caught Walt by surprise by asking him to confirm or deny rumors that he was the mysterious person who was buying thousands of acres of land in central Florida. Walt stumbled for an answer, then spent a few minutes explaining to Bavar why central Florida wouldn't be a suitable location at all for development. He cited detailed weather reports, land appraisals, and highway studies, among other things. Walt thought he was throwing her off the track, but Bavar smiled, knowing that she'd gotten her confirmation. Her conclusion? Why would Walt know so much about central Florida unless Disney actually was buying land there for future development? The *Orlando Sentinel* ran with the story. Walt was then forced to call a hastily organized press conference in Florida to reveal his secret plans, long before he wanted to. This actually turned out to be a blessing in disguise, as Walt's health started declining and he died the following year. The premature reveal led him to make one last film, detailing his vision for the land in Florida. His Experimental Prototype Community of Tomorrow gave Imagineers a template when building Walt Disney World.

WALT DISNEY QUOTES

The following quotes have all been verified by the Disney Archives and appear in their book *The Quotable Walt Disney*.

If you're wondering why I don't include some popular sayings attributed to Walt that you'll find on the internet, like "Laughter is timeless, imagination has no age and dreams are forever" or "If you can dream it, you can do it!," it's because they were not—in fact—uttered by Walt. They sound like something he might have said, but no documentation exists to be certain.

The "If you can dream it . . ." false quote is probably the most reproduced one. The confusion comes from the fact that it was included as part of a popular 1980s Disney attraction, EPCOT Center's Horizons. Nowhere did it claim that Walt was the author; it was actually written by an Imagineer to capture the spirit of Walt. People just assumed it was a direct quote.

Here are ten that did come from Walt's own mouth, in context.

1) "**I only hope that we never lose sight of one thing that it was all started by a mouse.** The life and ventures of Mickey Mouse have been closely bound up with my own personal and professional life. . . . He speaks for me, and I speak for him."

2) "When you're curious, you find lots of interesting things to do. I can never stand still. I must explore and experiment. I am never satisfied with my work. I resent the limitations of my own imagination. . . . There's really no secret about our approach. **We keep moving forward opening up new doors and doing new things because we're curious.** Curiosity keeps leading us down new paths. We're always exploring and experimenting. We call it Imagineering."

3) "People often ask me if I know the secret of success and if I could tell others how to make their dreams come true. My answer is, you do it by working. **Get a good idea, and stay with it. Dog it and work at it until it's done, and done right. . . . The way to get started is to quit talking and begin doing.** . . . When we go into a new project, we believe in it all the way."

4) "**You can dream, create, design, and build the most wonderful place in the world . . . but it requires people to make it a reality.**"

5) "**Disneyland is something that will never be finished.** It's something I can keep developing, keep plussing and adding to. . . . It will be a living, breathing thing that will need change. . . . It will continue to grow as long as there is imagination in the world. . . . It will be a place for people to find happiness and knowledge. It will be a place for parents and children to share pleasant times in one another's company."

6) "Everyone has been remarkably influenced by a book. . . . **There is more treasure in books than in all the pirates' loot on Treasure Island and at the bottom of the Spanish Main.** Best of all, you can enjoy these riches every day of your life."

7) "**Animation can explain whatever the mind of man can conceive.** This facility makes it the most versatile and explicit means of communication yet devised for quick mass appreciation."

8) "I don't believe in talking down to children. I like to kind of just talk in a general way to the audience. . . . **I do not make films primarily for children. I make them for the child in all of us, whether we be six or sixty.**"

9) "Music has always had a prominent part in all of our products, from the early cartoon days. I cannot think of the pictorial story without thinking about the complementary music which will fulfill it. **Often the musical themes come first. . . . They show us the value of telling a story through song.**"

10) "**The special secret of making dreams come true can be summarized in four C's. They are Curiosity, Confidence, Courage and Constancy.** The greatest of these is confidence."

MOST INFORMATIVE BOOKS ABOUT WALT DISNEY

Walt, a modest man, never published his own autobiography. More than a thousand books have been written about him and his life, covering almost every angle. Here are ten of the best.

THE STORY OF WALT DISNEY (1957) by Diane Disney Miller as Told to Pete Martin

The closest thing we have to an autobiography. Though Diane's name is on the cover, Martin interviewed Walt extensively, and it's assumed that many of the thoughts in the book were expressed by the creative genius himself, through his daughter.

WALT DISNEY: AN AMERICAN ORIGINAL (1976) by Bob Thomas

Thomas, a journalist by trade, never actually worked for Disney. His scholarly work was so well received, however, that he was offered Disney Legend status (which he graciously declined).

WALT DISNEY'S RAILROAD STORY (1998) by Michael Broggie

Written by the son of Disney Legend Roger Broggie, who helped to set up Walt's backyard railroad, this book blends personal memories and interviews with those closest to Walt to tell the story of how his lifelong love for trains helped shape his character.

INSIDE THE DREAM: THE PERSONAL STORY OF WALT DISNEY (2001) by Katherine and Richard Greene

Beautifully illustrated with some family photos never seen before, the Greenes' book includes interviews with almost eighty friends, family members, associates, and employees of Walt to provide the most fully rounded portrait of the man yet. Released for Walt's one hundredth birthday.

WALT DISNEY'S MISSOURI (2002) by Brian Burnes, Robert W. Butler, and Dan Viets

A comprehensive look at the places and people Walt encountered in the state where he spent the first third of his life. It goes a long way toward explaining how Walt became the man he did.

HOW TO BE LIKE WALT (2004) by Pat Williams

The former GM and cofounder of the NBA's Orlando Magic, Pat Williams is also a big admirer of Walt Disney. He wrote this book as a tribute to Walt, using episodes from Disney's life to show readers how they, too, can live a life that has a positive impact on themselves and others.

WALT DISNEY: TRIUMPH OF THE AMERICAN IMAGINATION (2006) by Neal Gabler

Though some leaps are taken to speculate about Walt's inner thoughts, there's no denying that Gabler's comprehensive modern biography fits right in with the best of them.

THE VAULT OF WALT (2010) by Jim Korkis

In this first in a series of *Vault of Walt* books, Disney historian Korkis combines oral histories with research to find hidden and previously unpublished stories about Walt and his company. Diane Disney Miller gave her official endorsement to this book, which rarely happened.

THE WISDOM OF WALT/BEYOND THE WISDOM OF WALT (2015/2017) by Jeffrey A. Barnes

Barnes, a PhD who teaches the very first accredited college course on the history of Disneyland, is known as "Doctor Disneyland." These two excellent books mix Walt's history with successful strategies and philosophies that others can use to improve their own lives.

EAT LIKE WALT: THE WONDERFUL WORLD OF DISNEY FOOD (2017) by Marcy Carriker Smothers

One of the most unique books ever written about Walt Disney. Smothers takes us on a journey through Walt's life through the foods he loved, and explores how they impacted his work and legacy. Part cookbook, part travelogue, part biography, it's entertaining from cover to cover.

HONORABLE MENTION

DISCOVERING WALT: THE MAGICAL LIFE OF WALT DISNEY (2001) by Jean-Pierre Isbouts
The best children's book ever written about the life of Walt Disney. It not only gives his history from his childhood to his death but also provides inspirational passages.

MOST INFORMATIVE FILMS ABOUT WALT DISNEY

PROJECT FLORIDA: WALT DISNEY'S VISION FOR EPCOT (1971) directed by James Algar

Filmed shortly before Walt's death in 1966, this documentary features him describing his vision for the twenty-seven thousand acres in Florida. Many of Walt's plans never came to fruition, but it is fascinating to see him in front of a gigantic map laying out his final dream in detail.

THE WALT DISNEY STORY (1973) no director listed

Made to be shown repeatedly in the Disneyland Opera House before *Great Moments with Mr. Lincoln*, this half-hour documentary—which was later shown at Walt Disney World and then released on home video for fans—is mostly made up of short film clips and personal interviews with Walt. It's narrated by Walt, his story told by him in his own voice.

WALT DISNEY: ONE MAN'S DREAM (1981) directed by Phil May

Originally produced as a TV special to help promote the opening of EPCOT Center in Florida (still a year away), it covers Walt's life from childhood to his death, with musical vignettes hosted by Mac Davis, Ben Vereen, Julie Andrews, Michael Landon, Marie Osmond, and Dick Van Dyke. Child actor Christian Hoff, who plays Walt at age ten, was the very first person to portray Disney in something produced by the company. Carl Reiner plays "the doubter," a voice who pops up throughout the film to tell Walt that his ideas and dreams will never work.

A DREAM IS A WISH YOUR HEART MAKES (1995) directed by Bill Corcoran

This life story of Disney Legend Annette Funicello was produced as a television movie by another company. It features award-winning actor Len Cariou as Walt Disney. Throughout Annette's life, Walt is shown as an advisor and mentor to her. She follows his plan for her career even after his death.

WALT: THE MAN BEHIND THE MYTH (2001) directed by Jean-Pierre Isbouts

Commissioned by Walt's family foundation and narrated by Dick Van Dyke, this biography of Walt features interviews with those closest to him and rare footage never before seen of Walt's home life. It also doesn't shy away from controversial topics and urban legends linked to Walt. It tells his story in a straightforward, honest manner. The best Walt bio of them all.

DISNEYLAND: SECRETS, STORIES AND MAGIC (2007) various directors

Released as part of the *Disney Treasures* limited edition DVD line, this series of documentaries collected from the 1950s to the 2000s tells the story of Walt's vision for his dream park, the effects its opening and success had on his family and his company, and the ways he and his Imagineers continually strived to make it better.

WALT & EL GRUPO (2010) written and directed by Theodore Thomas

The son of legendary "Nine Old Men" animator Frank Thomas uses home movies and archival footage to tell the story of Walt's ten-week goodwill tour of South American countries in 1941.

SAVING MR. BANKS (2013) directed by John Lee Hancock

The mostly true story of the making of *Mary Poppins* and Walt's struggles with her creator, P. L. Travers (Emma Thompson). This was the first Disney film to feature an actor (Tom Hanks) playing Walt as an adult. It was also one of the few movies ever to be filmed at Disneyland.

Tom Hanks as Walt Disney and Emma Thompson as *Mary Poppins* author P. L. Travers in *Saving Mr. Banks* (2013). (Walt Disney Studio Pictures/Photofest)

WALT BEFORE MICKEY (2015) directed by Khoa Lee

An independent film headlined by notable names (Thomas Ian Nicholas as Walt, Jon Heder as Roy), it covers the struggles of the Disney brothers at the beginning of their professional journeys, both in Missouri and California.

A GREAT BIG BEAUTIFUL TOMORROW: THE FUTURISM OF DISNEY (2016) directed by Christian Moran

An incredible documentary, released on streaming services and YouTube, and made independently by Moran. This film perfectly captures and explains the spirit of optimistic futurism that defined Walt, and most of his creations and projects in his later years.

HONORABLE MENTION

PBS AMERICAN EXPERIENCE: WALT DISNEY (2017) directed by Sarah Colt

This documentary is based largely on Neal Gabler's biography of Walt. Like the book, it takes speculative leaps into Walt's psychology. Still, it's filled with great Disney clips and insights from some of the best animation historians in the world.

EXPERTS ON WALT DISNEY'S LIFE

DAVE SMITH

The founder of the Disney Archives in 1970, Dave Smith knows more about Walt and his company than almost anyone else alive. He made cataloging the history of Disney his life's work. The author of many books about Disney, Smith was named a Disney Legend in 2007 and retired shortly after that.

JIM HILL

A journalist and theme park historian who is so well plugged in to what's going on with Disney that he's often able to get scoops about the company before others do, Jim Hill is also the host of a few Disney podcasts and has a series of articles about Walt at jimhillmedia.com.

DIDIER GHEZ

A Disney researcher and historian, Ghez has conducted personal interviews with almost everyone who knew or had associations with Walt himself. These interviews were compiled in a long-running series of books called *Walt's People* and on the website didierghez.com.

JIM KORKIS

The author of more than forty books about Walt Disney, Jim Korkis has made it his mission to clear up some of the urban legends, myths, and misunderstandings about the man. Second only to Dave Smith, Korkis is the go-to guy for questions about Walt.

BILL COTTER

A Disney employee from 1976 to 1982, Cotter was tasked with compiling the history of television shows produced by Walt and his company. The author of more than two hundred articles and books about Disney, Cotter also is an expert on the various World's Fair expositions.

LEONARD MALTIN

One of the most well-respected and knowledgeable film critics in the world, Leonard Maltin is also an unabashed Disney fan and expert. He created the *Walt Disney Treasures* home video series in conjunction with the hundredth-anniversary celebration of Walt's birth in 2001. He currently hosts the *Treasures from the Disney Vault* series on Turner Classic Movies.

DON HAHN

Hahn began his career as an animator with Disney in the 1970s and quickly moved up the ladder. By the 1990s, he was producing films like *Beauty and the Beast* and *The Lion King*. He moved on to live action as the executive producer of the Disneynature series of films, and is an award-winning documentarian. He has also written some of the best books about Walt and the art of animation. The Walt Disney Family Museum, by request of Walt's daughter Diane, brought Hahn on to create a special documentary about the Disney family's Christmas celebrations.

JOHN CANEMAKER

If you listen to the audio commentary track on most Disney home video releases of their classic animated films, you are likely to hear the voice of John Canemaker. An animator, author, and historian, he has penned several articles about Walt Disney for the *New York Times* and has written books about Walt's "Nine Old Men" of animators and artist Mary Blair.

JEFF KURTTI

The Walt Disney Family Museum in San Francisco owes a great debt to Jeff Kurtti. A Disney fan since childhood, he wound up working for the company in 1986 and has since written more than twenty books about it. After leaving Disney, Kurtti worked closely with Walt's daughter Diane, spending five years as creative director, content consultant, and media producer for the Walt Disney Family Museum, helping it become a reality in 2009.

TOM SITO

One of the most influential people in animation, Tom Sito has spent time working alongside many of the luminaries of the field. In addition to his accomplished work as an animator, he is also a historian, lecturer, and union leader for the former Motion Picture Screen Cartoonists Guild, of which he is president emeritus. Sito is one of the foremost experts on Walt Disney, especially the period of Walt's career when Disney Studios was gripped by labor disputes.

HONORABLE MENTION

DAVID SKIPPER

A member of the prestigious Chautauqua lecture circuit, Skipper has traveled the world for the past thirty years performing in one-person shows as famous authors and showmen like H. G. Wells, Edgar Allan Poe, Charles Dickens, and L. Frank Baum. One of his most dynamic roles is as Walt Disney. Skipper has done exhaustive research on his subject and brings Walt to life each time, using props that Walt himself would have used to enhance the presentation. Audiences young and old are always delighted by Skipper's interpretation of Walt, as they feel that they are in the same room with the man himself.

IMPORTANT PLACES TO VISIT
RELATED TO WALT'S LIFE
(OTHER THAN THE THEME PARKS)

SAN FRANCISCO, CA

The Walt Disney Family Museum, a fun and in-depth look at the life of one of the twentieth century's most influential figures, was opened by Walt's descendants at the Presidio in San Francisco. From the museum you have a tremendous view of San Francisco Bay and the Golden Gate Bridge. The headquarters for Lucasfilm, with its Yoda-themed fountain, are also located nearby.
www.waltdisney.org

The Disney Family Museum in San Francisco. (Wikimedia Commons)

CHICAGO, IL

Walt and Roy's birthplace, at 2156 Tripp, was designed by their mother, Flora, and built by their father, Elias, in 1892. It is still standing. Preservationists are currently restoring it.
www.thewaltdisneybirthplace.org

MARCELINE, MO

The Walt Disney Hometown Museum and Farm are both located in Marceline. A visit there will give you a sense of what made Walt tick and inspired him more than almost any place.
www.waltdisneymuseum.org

KANSAS CITY, MO

Several places related to Walt's teenage years and time as a young entrepreneur still exist in Kansas City. Preservationists are working to keep them around.
https://thankyouwaltdisney.org

GARDEN GROVE, CA

When Walt moved to California in 1923, he initially lived with his uncle, Robert Disney, in North Hollywood. The garage next to Robert's house was used by Walt as his first studio. It was saved from demolition in 1984 by the Friends of Walt Disney, who generously donated the historical building to the Stanley Ranch Museum, located at 12174 Euclid Street in Garden Grove.
https://garden-grove-historical-society-museum.business.site

THE TAM O'SHANTER, LOS ANGELES, CA

Walt's favorite restaurant, very close to the Disney Studios and Walt's first homes on Kingswell Avenue and Woking Way. Many of Disney's animators also frequented this restaurant (and still do). Its Tudor cottage style was said to inspire the look of several early Disney films like *Snow White* and *Pinocchio*. Walt's preferred table is still there.
www.TamOShanter.com

GRIFFITH PARK, LOS ANGELES, CA

The park where Walt took his daughters to ride the merry-go-round, and was inspired to create a family-friendly park while he sat watching them. It's also home to Walt Disney's actual backyard barn and the Carolwood Pacific Railroad Museum, dedicated to Walt and the fellow railroad enthusiasts, like Ward Kimball, who worked for him. The railroad museum is the only free Disney-related attraction in the world.

www.carolwood.org

PALM SPRINGS, CA

The Smoke Tree Ranch in Palm Springs was Walt's second home. He often wore an "STR" tie.

www.smoketreeranch.com

CALIFORNIA INSTITUTE OF THE ARTS, VALENCIA, CA

The school Walt helped found and fund. Many Disney animators graduated from there.

www.calarts.edu

NEW YORK CITY, NY

Though Walt didn't spend too much time in the Big Apple, several sites, like the World's Fair grounds in Queens and the Broadway Theater—where Mickey made his debut in 1928—are still around. New York City Vacation packages offers a special Disney-themed tour of New York.

www.nycvp.com

LISTS ABOUT THE DISNEY COMPANY

MILESTONES IN DISNEY COMPANY HISTORY

1923—THE FOUNDING

When Walt arrived in Hollywood in 1923, he tried his best to find work at all of the studios in town, to no avail. He then visited Roy, who was recuperating from an illness at a nearby veteran's hospital, and pitched him on opening their own studio together. After much back-and-forth, Roy agreed. They borrowed five hundred dollars from their uncle Robert and set up shop on Kingswell Avenue in Los Angeles, calling their new venture the Disney Brothers Cartoon Studio. With just a handful of employees, Walt and Roy began producing *Alice* comedies for a New York distributor named Margaret Winkler, on their way to revolutionizing the animation business.

1926 TO 1929—THE EARLY YEARS

By 1926, the name of the business had changed to the Walt Disney Studios and it had moved to a bigger location nearby, on Hyperion Avenue. It was there that a character named Oswald the Lucky Rabbit was created. He was a success and brought modest profits for Disney. They didn't take the proper legal precautions to fully own the rights to Oswald, so he was taken away by Winkler's husband, Charles Mintz, and then Universal Studios. Mickey Mouse—whom the brothers did secure as their own—came from Walt's head as a result of that debacle. The Walt Disney Studios started making cartoons with sound, a first for Hollywood. The success of the Mickey films brought great profits. In 1929, Walt Disney Productions Ltd. was formed, enabling the company to create separate in-house arms for publishing, music licensing, merchandise, and real estate acquisition, with Roy guiding the financial wheel of the Disney ship while Walt focused on the creative side.

Walt Disney Studios.
(Library of Congress)

1932—THE EXPERIMENTATION ERA BEGINS

The tremendous profits from Mickey's cartoons gave Walt the freedom to explore. He began a series of shorts called the *Silly Symphonies*, with no main character, that his staff could use for experimentation in their medium. In 1932, a cartoon called *Flowers and Trees* was pretty much complete. It was, as the previous ones had been, in black-and-white. Walt thought they could do better, so he struck an exclusive deal to license the new Technicolor process for Disney cartoons, and started again—at great expense—with *Flowers and Trees*. The gamble paid off. Not only did his deal with Technicolor give Walt the jump on every other animation studio at the time, the short won Disney his first Oscar, the start of an amazing streak. At one point, Disney Studios monopolized the Best Short category at the Academy Awards. In all, through 2017, Disney has won more than one hundred Oscars, with Walt himself holding the unbreakable record of thirty-two Academy Awards, the most ever given to one person.

1940—THE NEW STUDIO OPENS

With the profits from *Snow White and the Seven Dwarfs*, Walt and Roy were able to purchase more than forty acres of land in the Los Angeles suburb of Burbank. There they built a studio that opened in 1940 and was meant to feel like a college campus, with buildings for each of the departments, cafeterias, gymnasiums, recreation halls, and other fun things to foster a more laid-back atmosphere. It was unlike almost any other corporate complex in America. The place was Walt's pride and joy. He loved showing guests around. Disney's corporate headquarters, and its studios, are still located there today.

1940—THE INITIAL STOCK OFFERINGS

What had been a company privately owned by two brothers (Walt held a 60 percent stake; Roy had the rest) was opened to outsiders on April 2, 1940. An initial public offering of 155,000 shares of preferred Disney stock was created. It was an immediate success, netting almost four million dollars. While Walt was happy for the influx of capital, it also caused him some headaches as he now had to answer not just to one person—his older brother—but also to a board of directors and shareholders, who often cared more about the bottom line than his latest dreams. He often bristled at their repeated financial vetoes of his ideas. On November 12, 1957, Disney stock was listed for the first time on the New York Stock Exchange, where it remains one of the most followed and traded, with shares valued at more than one hundred dollars each.

1941 TO 1945—THE STRIKE AND THE WAR YEARS

Walt always tried to treat his employees like family, greeting each other on an informal, first-name basis. He also gave generous bonuses and privileges to those he thought worked the hardest to make Disney succeed. The back-to-back failures of *Pinocchio* and *Fantasia*, combined with the cost of the new studio, wiped away all the profits from *Snow White* and the stock sales. Walt was forced to lay off and cut the salaries of many people. This started a ripple of employee resentment that culminated in a strike at the studio on May 29, 1941. It lasted five weeks, resulted in the Disney employee count being cut in half, and shook Walt to his core. While he wasn't completely blameless, and many of the demands asked of him by the union were fair, when work resumed Walt was no longer the same type of freewheeling boss he'd been in the 1930s. He now had some trust issues with even his most loyal employees. Toward the end of the strike, Walt left the studio and Hollywood for a bit to take his goodwill tour of Central and South America, where he was showing our neighbors why they should stay aligned with the United States should we enter the World War. After the attack on Pearl Harbor in December 1941, work at the Disney Studios halted. Not only did many of Walt's staff have to join the war effort, the studio campus itself was taken over by the U.S. Army in the interests of national security, since a Lockheed airplane manufacturing plant was nearby in Burbank. Walt eventually made a deal with the government to keep the studio open during the war in exchange for making training and morale films and other items to help the war effort. Both the strike and the war had long-term effects on Disney. The studio didn't fully recover from them until the 1950s.

1950 TO 1965—THE REBOUND ERA

Following the old adage of not putting all your eggs in one basket, Walt and Roy realized that if Disney was going to pull itself out of their postwar slump, and show profits to their shareholders, they needed other streams of income besides animated films, educational films, and shorts. The first step was live-action movies, necessitated because the British had frozen Disney's profits made in the United Kingdom, insisting that they be spent there. Live-action films like *Treasure Island*, made in Great Britain, were less expensive and quicker to make than animated films, earning bigger returns. That led to the transition into more live-action Disney films being produced in the United States. The next step was television, which every other Hollywood studio was avoiding. The Disney brothers embraced the new medium, using it to advertise their films and reignite interest in the Disney brand and Disney merchandise. The only place where the brothers differed was on Walt's vision of a Disney theme park, which Roy felt would never work. This led Walt to put his own personal assets on the line to establish his own private companies, Retlaw Enterprises, WED, Walt Disney Inc., and MAPO, which all fell outside of the purview of Roy and of Disney's shareholders. Eventually they came around to Walt when his park was a proven success. These independent companies, with the exception of the one controlling Walt's family's assets, were all folded into the main Disney Corporation by 1965.

1966—THE FOUNDER'S DEATH

People knew that Walt wasn't feeling well as 1966 wore on, but nobody guessed how serious things were. On December 15, 1966, Walt passed away, in a hospital just across the street from his studio in Burbank. The line of succession went to Roy—who saw the plans for Walt Disney World through to completion until his own death in 1971—but the Disney Company lost its footing for a while, not sure how to proceed. Despite a few hits here and there, and the valiant efforts of folks like Walt's son-in-law, Ron Miller, Disney's output was lagging in the 1970s. This dithering caused the corporate world to take notice. By the 1980s, the wolves were at the door, with raiders poised to make a run on Disney's stock, scheming to take control of the company and sell off the assets. An internal shakeup by Disney's own board of directors set a new course, saving the company.

1984 TO 2000—THE RENAISSANCE ERA

In 1984, Michael Eisner was brought over from Paramount to head Disney. He shared Walt's showmanship flair and entertainment instincts. Frank Wells, his chief operating officer, was the financial whiz. The two of them guided Disney to a major comeback, dominating in film, television, music, theater, publishing, retail, tourism, sports, and several other areas. By the 1990s, Eisner's touch was golden, with the triumphs outnumbering the failures. By the start of the new millennium, though, Eisner's remarkable run at Disney was coming to a close.

2004—THE ACQUISITIONS ERA

In 2005, Bob Iger was named the successor to the recently retired Eisner. The year before, Eisner had negotiated a deal to acquire Jim Henson's Muppets for Disney, as he'd done in 1996 when he made ABC and ESPN part of Disney. That's how Iger, a former ABC executive, arrived there in the first place. Iger has since continued Disney's acquisition mode, adding Pixar in 2006, Marvel Comics in 2009, Lucasfilm in 2012, and a blockbuster proposed deal to acquire FOX and its film and TV franchises and assets by the end of 2018. Most of these deals have cost billions, but the return on them has been tremendous, setting up the Disney Corporation for continued growth and prosperity as it nears its hundredth anniversary in 2023.

DISNEY CORPORATE ICONS

Major corporations are lucky if they have one identifiable icon that the general public can immediately recognize and associate with their brand. Disney has been blessed to have so many of them that each generation for the last ninety years can claim one as their own. Here are ten that have been the face of Disney at different periods in its history.

WALT DISNEY HIMSELF

At the beginning of his journey to Hollywood in the early 1920s, this midwestern dreamer had aspirations of being a cartoonist or director. His subsequent career led to so much more. Walt Disney's name itself became shorthand for quality family entertainment. Most people know "Uncle Walt" through his role as the avuncular television host of the mid-'50s and/or as the creator of Disneyland, but he was already an accomplished producer and innovator by then. At the time of his untimely death in 1966,

Walt Disney was just as much a part of the Disney Company's image as any of the characters his studio created. Sadly, today's generation seems to only know the name Walt Disney, not necessarily the man. Walt's daughter Diane, along with his grandchildren, remedied that by opening the Walt Disney Family Museum at the Presidio in San Francisco in 2009. This fantastic museum has as its mission telling twenty-first-century audiences the inspiring story of the man behind the mouse.

"THE FAB FIVE" (1928 TO 1935)

When **Mickey Mouse** made his debut in 1928, not even Walt could have imagined that three concentric circles would become instantly identifiable as the symbol of all things Disney. Mickey, Walt's brainchild and alter ego, saved the Disney studio from certain financial ruin in the 1920s and remains the heart and soul of Disney.

Though he's Disney's biggest star, Mickey can't carry the load himself.

Four other characters—Minnie Mouse, Pluto, Goofy, and Donald Duck—have become, along with Mickey, the top characters in Disney's canon, known affectionately as "the Fab Five."

Minnie Mouse made her debut in 1928, alongside Mickey, in *Steamboat Willie*. Early on, she was portrayed as a damsel in distress, always having to be rescued by Mickey. She eventually developed an independent personality and became a popular figure with her own theme song ("Minnie's Yoo Hoo"). When asked about the nature of Mickey and Minnie's relationship (Are they married? Boyfriend/girlfriend?), Walt almost always coyly replied that Minnie was simply Mickey's "leading lady" and left it at that.

Pluto was created because Walt's writers wanted to give Mickey a pet. He first appeared on-screen in 1930's *The Chain Gang* as an unnamed bloodhound following Mickey's scent, and then as Minnie's dog Rover in *The Picnic* that same year. He was soon christened Pluto (after the recently discovered planet) and spun off into his own series of forty-eight shorts. Unlike other anthropomorphic Disney characters, Pluto has always retained his animal qualities and has acted and behaved just as a real dog would.

The other famous Disney dog has not.

Walt introducing Mickey to his cat. (Library of Congress)

Disney surrounded by his best-known characters. (Walt Disney Pictures/ Photofest)

Goofy also began as an unnamed canine background character in *Mickey's Revue*. Moviegoers took notice of his infectious laugh, and he was elevated to a starring role as "Dippy the Goofy Dawg," with his own theme song ("Oh, the World Owes Me a Livin'") Eventually the writers just began referring to him as Goofy. He is genetically a dog, but has been written and drawn as a human/dog hybrid wearing a vest, turtleneck, and hat. Goofy's world, as seen in forty-nine of his own short films and a few features, is inhabited with characters who look just like him, so there is no noticeable dog comparison. In a 2005 survey conducted by Disney, 25 percent of Americans said that they identified with Goofy more than any of their other characters.

Donald Duck is Mickey's polar opposite.

From his very first appearance as a supporting player in 1934's *The Wise Little Hen*, Donald captured the public's fancy. He was roughly drawn then, but had many of the same irascible, hotheaded characteristics that we see today, as well as the trademark sailor suit and hat. Animators were free to have Donald do things that the sweet-natured Mickey could not. By the mid-1940s, Donald was Disney's biggest star, appearing in 128 of his own cartoons and getting hundreds of fan letters a week, more than Mickey or Walt.

There's no way to separate this quintet of characters. They are the core group of Disney icons.

JIMINY CRICKET (1940)

When Walt Disney was working with his creative team on their 1940 film version of Italian author Carlo Collodi's book *Pinocchio*, he had a problem with the main character. As written, Pinocchio was a mean-spirited juvenile delinquent. Walt had his animators and writers soften Pinocchio's edges, but it still wasn't enough. Disney finally hit on the solution after rereading the book. There was a small unnamed cricket who makes a fleeting appearance. Walt gave him the moniker Jiminy Cricket and asked Ward Kimball to shape the character into the conscience of Pinocchio. Kimball gave the cricket human features, clothing him in a top hat and spats and giving him an umbrella. Jiminy was the heart of *Pinocchio* and its breakout star. Walt knew that he had to use him beyond that one film. In 1947, Jiminy was cast as the host of Disney's musical feature *Fun and Fancy Free*. Beginning in 1955, he also hosted segments of *The Mickey Mouse Club*. In the 1950s and '60s, Disney made a series of popular educational cartoons starring Jiminy called *I'm No Fool*. They've been shown at school assemblies for decades. In recent years, Jiminy has become the face of the environmental/recycling effort in Disney parks. He gently reminds guests that Disney has "gone green." He remains to this day the embodiment of the conscience of Disney.

TINKER BELL (1953)

J. M. Barrie's 1904 play *Peter Pan: The Boy Who Wouldn't Grow Up* featured Peter's friend Tinker Bell, a small fairy. Her traditional onstage depiction was as a tiny spotlight, accompanied by tinkling bells. Disney broke that tradition with his 1953 animated version of *Peter Pan*, showing Tinker Bell for the first time as a full character. He also changed her from a fairy to a pixie, trailed by pixie dust. Contrary to popular belief, Tinker Bell's shapely figure was NOT modeled after Marilyn Monroe. Walt hired Hollywood veteran Margaret Kerry, who'd co-starred in the *Our Gang/Little Rascals* films, for the role. She acted out Tink's scenes on film as a reference for the animators. When Walt began building his dream park in 1954, he wasn't completely sure that the public would embrace it. He was reluctant to use Mickey Mouse as a mascot for the TV show tied to Disneyland, just in case it failed. He chose Tinker Bell instead. By 1961, she and the park were both so popular that Tink began the nightly fireworks by flying over Sleeping Beauty Castle in real life, as she did on the show. Just like Jiminy Cricket, Tink was elevated to iconic status beyond her one screen appearance. To this day, Tinker Bell's magic wand spreads pixie dust on almost all Disney products (though she's never actually used a wand in any of her film or stage appearances).

DAVY CROCKETT (1954)

When Walt Disney was planning on adding a series of stories about American folk heroes to the Frontierland portion of his weekly Disneyland anthology show, he was stumped as to which one to choose

Fess Parker (right) starred as Davy Crockett in the TV series *Davy Crockett: King of the Wild Frontier*. (Wikimedia Commons)

first. After much deliberation, he asked his staff to draw a name from a hat. The name they chose changed American pop culture history. Davy Crockett was a nineteenth-century folk hero, frontiersman, and former U.S. congressman from Tennessee. His exploits had been embellished over the years, making him a natural fit for TV audiences in the early days of the medium. Nobody, including Walt, expected Davy to take the country by storm the way he did. On December 15, 1954, more than half of America tuned in to watch the first of three episodes of *Davy Crockett*. It is credited with giving birth to the modern television miniseries. Within weeks, everyone was caught up in the "Crockett Craze." Fess Parker, who played Davy, became an overnight megastar, the theme song hit the top of the charts, and demand for coonskin caps was more than Disney merchandisers could handle. As with all fads, enthusiasm for Davy Crockett dimmed, but not before he made a permanent mark on the consciousness of the nation. To this day, grown men and women can sing "The Ballad of Davy Crockett" by heart and Davy's coonskin cap remains as recognizable a piece of Disneyana as the mouse ears.

WINNIE THE POOH (1966)

In 1961, Walt Disney licensed the rights to the beloved British storybook character Winnie the Pooh and his Hundred Acre Wood friends, who had debuted in books by A. A. Milne in 1923. With a delightful musical score by the Sherman Brothers and the perfect casting of Sterling Holloway as the voice of Pooh, the first short—*Winnie the Pooh and the Honey Tree*—premiered in 1966. It was the last animated short to be directly supervised by Walt. After Walt's death, the studio's feature animation output dwindled somewhat, yet production on Winnie the Pooh shorts continued, with each more popular than the last. The bear with the red shirt and rumbly tummy had become another savior for Disney during a fallow period. If you visited Disney parks in the 1970s or early '80s, Winnie the Pooh was front and center with Mickey. His popularity lifted the merchandising division

Winnie the Pooh was one of several classic children's book characters recast by Disney films. (Wikimedia Commons)

of a company by then relying mostly on nostalgia and rereleases of classic films. Even in 2018, Pooh remains a stalwart favorite with old and new fans.

ARIEL AND BELLE (1989 AND 1991)

After a string of live-action flops in the 1970s and '80s and an average of five years between new animated films, Disney was in danger of being taken over by corporate raiders. A powerhouse Hollywood executive trio, consisting of Michael Eisner, Frank Wells, and Jeffrey Katzenberg, was brought in to revive the Disney brand. They got back to basics, developing the types of films that made Disney popular in the first place. The new bosses especially wanted to find fairy tale princesses who would take their place among the Disney greats, but with a modern sensibility. A musical adaptation of Hans Christian Andersen's "The Little Mermaid" came first, in 1989. It featured a headstrong, red-haired mermaid princess named Ariel, who yearns for the world beyond the ocean floor. She was an immediate sensation and a critical darling, putting Disney animation back on top. Ariel also began a second golden age of animation at the studio. Two years later, *Beauty and the Beast* was released. The heroine in that film, Belle, was even more independent. Her story resonated with audiences of all ages and catapulted the film to heights even Walt never reached, becoming the very first animated film to earn an Oscar nomination for Best Picture. Ariel and Belle quickly became the new faces of Disney in the 1990s, appearing at the parks, freshening up their cast of characters, and ushering in an age of strong-willed female Disney characters. Without these two, there'd likely be no Lilo, Rapunzel, Tiana, Elsa, Anna, or Moana in the new millennium.

BUZZ AND WOODY (1995)

Shortly after Ariel and Belle helped turn things around for hand-drawn animation, Disney began a collaboration with Pixar on computer-animated films. In 1995, they co-released a film about the

Woody, Buzz, and all the other animated toys from the Toy Story trilogy are shown here in a poster for *Toy Story* 3. (Disney/Pixar/Photofest)

secret life of toys. It would go on to become one of the biggest box office successes in history and launch a franchise worth billions for Disney. *Toy Story* had as its main stars a duo designed to appeal primarily to young boys, who were not likely to be interested in the traditional roster of Disney princesses. Buzz Lightyear is a space ranger, a type A personality who is always seeking adventure. He carries the DNA of swashbuckling on-screen space heroes like Captain Kirk, Han Solo, and Buck Rogers, as well as the name of a real-life astronaut hero, Buzz Aldrin. Sheriff Woody is a stuffed cowboy doll, in constant danger of being tossed aside by his owner for newer and flashier toys like Buzz. In this Disney take on the "buddy comedy," Buzz and Woody start out as heated rivals and wind up becoming best friends. Just as Ariel and Belle brought young girls back to Disney, Buzz and Woody did so for boys. They led the way for other male-centric Disney duos like Lightning McQueen and Mater from *Cars* and Hiro and Baymax from *Big Hero Six*, all integral parts of Disney's plans to appeal to a new generation of fans and to introduce all-new attractions, merchandise, and sequels.

HANNAH MONTANA (2006)

Disney has had plenty of experience minting young female superstars. From Annette Funicello, Hayley Mills, and Julie Andrews in Walt's era to more-recent Disney Channel teen idols like Christy Carlson Romano, Raven-Symoné, and Hilary Duff, they have been a well-oiled hit-making machine. These were just warmup acts for the biggest teen star of them all. When thirteen-year-old Destiny Hope "Miley" Cyrus—the daughter of country superstar Billy Ray Cyrus—auditioned for a new Disney Channel show in early 2005, she had no idea that she'd be altering the musical and television landscapes in less than a year. *Hannah Montana* became an instant ratings hit on the Disney Channel in spring 2006. This sitcom about a typical schoolgirl who leads a double life as a pop star struck a nerve in little girls transitioning from preteens to adolescents. Like no other female Disney TV character before her, Hannah Montana was a true international sensation. At its peak, Hannah's show attracted two hundred million viewers in the United States alone, with millions more around the world. Live concert tours broke box office records, her albums topped the charts, and merchandise sales were in the billions. Cyrus reinvented Disney's playbook for grooming young stars and paved the way for Disney to break through the Top 40 radio market in a way they hadn't done in decades. Other highly successful Disney Channel franchises like *High School Musical*, *Camp Rock*, and *The Descendants* and performers like Demi Lovato, the Jonas Brothers, and Selena Gomez quickly followed.

CAPTAIN JACK SPARROW (2003)

When Disney announced plans to turn its popular ride Pirates of the Caribbean into a feature film, many people scoffed at the notion. The screenwriters and director did a great job with this unusual task, but it was the lead actor who actually made *Pirates* a hit. As written, Captain Jack Sparrow is your typical roguish scalawag of a pirate, in the tradition of Robert Newton's Long John Silver. In the hands of any seasoned performer, this would be a great character, but Johnny Depp made it so much better. Depp decided to deliver a fresh take on the pirate portrayal. He gave a foppish, devil-may-care tint to Jack Sparrow, taking as inspiration the idea of the pirate as a rock star. Depp even cited the Rolling Stones' Keith Richards as a role model. You're never quite sure whether Captain Jack Sparrow is a good guy or a bad guy. He is a prankster, quick on his feet and always ready with a quip. He is morally ambiguous, though he does cling to a code of pirate ethics and a sense of core values that he lives by. The *Pirates of the Caribbean* brand has gone on to be *the* most successful in

Disney history. A recent magazine poll placed Captain Jack Sparrow second only to Indiana Jones in the list of most-admired film heroes. Not bad for a character who started as a spin-off from a ride.

DISNEY EXECUTIVES
(CLASSIC ERA, 1923 TO 1988)

ROY O. DISNEY

Walt's older brother, best friend, partner, and confidant, Roy was mostly unknown to the general public, yet he kept the financial wheels of the Disney empire going and growing. If Walt was a creative genius, the same could be said about Roy when it came to business. His astute fiscal moves helped to fuel Walt's dreams and innovations. The brothers often came to an impasse when Walt wanted to do something that seemed beyond the studio's budget, but Roy always found a way, and the company usually benefited from it. He postponed his retirement to take over as head of the company after Walt's death in 1966. The unassuming Roy made his most public appearance at the October 1971 opening of Walt Disney World, dedicating it to the memory of his brother. Roy passed away two months later. In 1999, a Blaine Gibson statue of Roy sitting on a bench with Minnie was installed in the Magic Kingdom's town square.

Roy Disney shares a bench with Minnie Mouse in this sculpture at Disney Studios. (Wikimedia Commons)

DONN B. TATUM

The president of Walt Disney Productions from 1968 to 1971, Donn Tatum started out in 1956 as a production business manager. After Roy died in 1971, Tatum took over as Disney's CEO and chairman of the board, titles he held until 1980. He was on Disney's board of directors until 1992. He passed away a year later and was immediately named a Disney Legend.

CARDON "CARD" WALKER

It's a classic tale of working your way up in a company from humble beginnings to great heights. Card Walker started as a mail clerk at Disney in 1938 and eventually became one of its most powerful executives. As president of the company from 1971 to 1980 and chairman of the board from 1980 to 1983, it was Walker who made sure that EPCOT Center was completed, as Walt intended, on the Florida property. Opened in 1982, EPCOT Center differed from Walt's original plans of a futuristic city of tomorrow, but Walker kept the innovative spirit of it. Walker retired soon after EPCOT opened but remained on Disney's board of directors until 1999.

RON MILLER

When twenty-one-year-old Ron Miller married Diane Disney in 1954, he fully intended to pursue a career in professional football. He did indeed play for the Los Angeles Rams, until Walt saw him knocked unconscious during a game and offered him a job at the studio. Miller accepted. He began as an assistant director and eventually became coproducer of films. Walt was grooming him for the top job. After Walt passed away, Miller became executive producer of most of Disney's films and TV shows. He was named president of Walt Disney Productions in 1980 and weathered four years of corporate tumult before leaving the company. Like his father-in-law, Miller was a visionary who set the wheels in motion for exciting new projects, many of which came to fruition only after his departure and for which he, sadly, receives little credit.

BILL COTTRELL

An employee at Disney starting in 1929, Bill Cottrell held several jobs, from cameraman to animation director and story man. His most important role came in 1952, when he was named vice president of the newly formed WED Enterprises, developing TV shows and designing Disneyland. In 1964, he was named president of Retlaw Enterprises, the corporation that controlled the Disney family's personal assets. Cottrell retired in 1982.

BOB MOORE

A talented artist who began as an animator for Disney in 1940, Bob Moore had his skills put to different use when he transitioned into the marketing department. He took over as the art director of Disney's advertising division in 1951 and stayed there until 1981, designing marketing material and several classic movie posters. The U.S. postage stamp that honors Walt Disney, released in 1968, was codesigned by Moore. A little Disney secret: Walt himself got so many requests for autographs that some of his artists were authorized to sign his name for him. Moore was one of those people.

JOE FOWLER AND JOE POTTER

Two former military men who were hired by Walt to carry out his innovative plans for the parks, Fowler and Potter had similar career tracks. Fowler was an ex-Navy admiral brought in by Walt in 1954 to oversee the entire construction of Disneyland in less than twelve months. He stayed on in a similar position for Walt Disney World, retiring in 1972, one year after its completion. Potter was a major general in the U.S. Army who'd been a governor of the Panama Canal. Since Potter had experience in tropical climate construction, Walt personally enlisted him to oversee the swamp dredging and subsequent infrastructure completion of the massive project in Florida. Potter retired shortly after that job was done, in 1974.

DICK NUNIS

Just before the opening of Disneyland in 1955, twenty-three-year-old Dick Nunis—acting on the advice of his college classmate Ron Miller—took a summer job as an assistant trainer at the park.

At the time, there were six hundred cast members. He moved up the ranks and by 1968 was vice president of operations. He was such a great worker that Walt made him one of the few confidants he trusted with the secret plans for "Project X" in Florida. That would pay off a few years later, in 1971, when Nunis was named executive vice president of the Walt Disney World resort. In 1980, he became president of both Disneyland and Walt Disney World. When Nunis retired in 1999, Disneyland had more than thirteen thousand cast members, with fifty thousand more in Florida.

CHARLIE RIDGWAY

From 1963 to 1994, if you heard or saw anything about a Disney park in the media, chances are it was because of Charlie Ridgway. He began as a publicist for Disneyland in 1963 and then moved on to Walt Disney World. During the course of his career, he orchestrated more than 150 big events related to the parks, staying on until just after the opening of Euro Disney in 1992. In later years, he consulted on various publicity projects for Animal Kingdom and the Disney Cruises.

RICHARD F. "DICK" IRVINE

He started out as an art director with Disney in the 1940s, but Dick Irvine's talents were soon put to better use at WED. He was named the head of the new division in 1953, overseeing the design and development of Disneyland. He also worked on the 1964 World's Fair and at Walt Disney World before retiring in 1973. A steamboat and ferryboat at Walt Disney World were both named in his honor.

DISNEY EXECUTIVES (MODERN ERA, 1989 TO PRESENT)

ROY E. DISNEY

The only son of Roy O. Disney, Roy E. joined the family business at the age of twenty-four. He specialized in nature films and shows, working on the *True-Life Adventures* as editor and then writer, director, and producer. After the deaths of his uncle and father, Roy E. joined Disney's board of directors. In 1984, he became head of the animation department just as the new crop of executives, led by Michael Eisner, whom he recommended for the top job, came in. Roy E. was at the forefront of Disney's 1990s animation renaissance. In 2003, he left Disney, but he was so beloved by the staff that he was dubbed director emeritus and had the animation building named in his honor. His untimely death in 2009 marked the end of an era for the Disney Company.

MICHAEL EISNER

In September 1984, after the departure of Ron Miller, at a time when the company was under siege from corporate raiders, Michael Eisner was named Disney's chairman of the board and CEO. His steady hand at the wheel helped calm the storms and get Disney through the tough mid-1980s period. As former vice president of entertainment at ABC and chief operating officer of Paramount Pictures, Eisner possessed extremely sharp skills in picking film and TV projects with audience appeal. Starting in the late '80s, he put together a string of hits that was unrivaled in company

Michael Eisner.
(Wikimedia Commons)

history. His attention to and expansion of the parks and resorts in the 1990s lifted their sagging revenue. Eisner's enthusiasm, humor, imagination, and dedication to continuing Walt's mission of "plussing" Disney properties made him the perfect person to fill the founder's shoes. After twenty-one years with Disney, Eisner retired in 2005.

FRANK WELLS

If Walt was the role model for Michael Eisner, then Roy was the prototype for Frank Wells, who joined the company as president on the same day that Eisner took over. Wells and Eisner were the perfect team, just as Walt and Roy were. Wells was astute in business and would try to rein in some of Eisner's more ambitious plans, or to at least try to get them under budget. It worked, and together they helped bring Disney to incredible heights (which was fitting for Wells, who had climbed to the top of the tallest mountains on each continent, with the exception of Mount Everest). Sadly, the sixty-two-year-old Wells was killed in 1994 in a helicopter crash. He was only with Disney for a decade, but his mark on the company endures.

JEFFREY KATZENBERG

Brought over from Paramount by Eisner in 1984 to be chairman of the studio division, Jeffrey Katzenberg was the whiz kid who could do no wrong. For ten years, he cranked out hit film after hit film, taking chances on risky projects like *Pretty Woman*, *Good Morning, Vietnam*, *The Nightmare before Christmas*, and *The Lion King*. In 1994, Katzenberg left Disney to start his own studio—DreamWorks SKG—with Steven Spielberg and David Geffen.

Jeffrey Katzenberg.
(Wikimedia Commons)

ROBERT IGER

When Disney acquired Capital Cities/ABC in 1995, the president of ABC at the time, Robert Iger, stayed on as the new chairman of the ABC group. After Eisner's retirement in 2005, Iger was named CEO. His conservative management style is closer to that of Roy Disney and Frank Wells, but Iger has been at the helm for such bold Disney moves as the acquisitions of Pixar, Marvel, Lucasfilm, and FOX; the creation of a streaming service to rival Netflix and Hulu; and the building of a resort in Shanghai.

MARTY SKLAR

Like Roy E. Disney, Marty Sklar began working at Disney while Walt was still alive, so technically they should both be on the classic era list. Since most of their greatest accomplishments with the company came later in their careers, I'm placing them here. Sklar, who passed away in 2017, was the dean of Imagineers. He is the only man to have played a part in the opening of every single Disney park from 1955 to 2016. He was a cast member at Disneyland, while still a student at UCLA, when it debuted in 1955 and began as a writer for a Disney magazine in 1956. He moved over to WED five years later to assist in the development of attractions for the 1964 World's Fair, continuing as a key person in the creation of the Walt Disney World Resort, EPCOT Center, Tokyo Disneyland, Euro Disney, and others. Sklar rose through the ranks and by the 1980s was named vice chairman of Imagineering, acting as the international ambassador and spokesman for Imagineers. It was a position he held until his retirement in 2009, eight years after being named a Disney Legend.

AL WEISS

Walt Disney World takes in a tremendous amount of money each day. In 1972, it was mostly cash transactions. That meant that registers had to be continually swapped out and accounted for during peak times. Al Weiss, an eighteen-year-old Florida college student with a talent for numbers, was among the few given this enormous task. He excelled at it, and moved up the cast member ladder until being named executive vice president of Walt Disney World in 1994, under Dick Nunis. He then succeeded Nunis as president in 1999, and was eventually named president of worldwide operations for all Walt Disney Parks and Resorts in 2005. Weiss retired from the company in 2011, after thirty-two years of service.

MEG CROFTON

When Weiss moved up to his position overseeing worldwide operations, his protégé—Meg Crofton—was named president of the Walt Disney World Resort, which by then was the most popular vacation destination on the planet. Crofton's career track was unusual. She started out in 1981 as an employee of one of Disney's subsidiaries, Vista United, which provided telecommunications services for Walt Disney World. In 1984, she began managing Shades of Green, the resort hotel built on the property for military families, run by the U.S. Department of Defense. After that, Crofton transferred to Disney World's human resources department, which she helped run until becoming the resort's president in 2006. She retired in 2015, succeeded by the current resort president, George Kalogridis.

THOMAS SCHUMACHER

When Thomas Schumacher, who has an extensive theater background, joined the Disney Feature Animation team in 1988, they were just starting to find their stride. He eventually became executive vice president and then president of the division, overseeing twenty-one films (bringing a bit of Broadway razzle-dazzle to them) and then blending Pixar seamlessly into the Disney animation program. His success continued as he moved over to Disney's Theatrical Division in 2003, in charge of mega Broadway hits like *The Lion King*, *Mary Poppins*, and *Aladdin*.

HONORABLE MENTION

SENATOR GEORGE MITCHELL

One of the most distinguished and accomplished politicians to ever serve in the United States Senate, George Mitchell represented his home state of Maine from 1980 to 1995. He was Senate Majority Leader for the last six of those years. Senator Mitchell joined Disney's board of directors in 1995, after his time in Washington was done. When Michael Eisner retired in 2004, Senator Mitchell was named as Disney's chairman of the board, a title he held for three years. Eisner often sought advice from Senator Mitchell, who is an expert negotiator. In addition to his post-Senate work with Disney, Mitchell brokered the 1998 Good Friday Peace Agreement in Northern Ireland, authored a 2007 investigative report on steroid abuse in baseball, and was President Obama's special envoy for Middle East peace from 2009 to 2011.

JOHN LASSETER

Already a huge Disney fan as a child in the 1960s, consuming as much information as he could about the company, John Lasseter knew early on which path he wanted his life to follow. In 1975, he enrolled at CalArts, training under some of Walt's "Nine Old Men" in the newly formed animation program. During the summer, he worked as a Jungle Cruise skipper at Disneyland. He was hired as a Disney animator in 1979, and soon showed his prowess for innovation, especially in the new area of computer animation. When he was let go by Disney in 1984, he joined Lucasfilm to work in a computer animation department that evolved into Pixar Films. He oversaw all of their productions. When Disney purchased Pixar in 2006, it named him executive producer of all Disney animated films and a consultant on all park designs. He left Disney in 2018.

DISNEY ARTISTS/ANIMATORS (CLASSIC ERA)

THE "NINE OLD MEN"

Walt chose to group these nine key animators and Disney Legends together (his name for them, the "Nine Old Men," was a play on President Franklin D. Roosevelt's "Nine Old Men" of the Supreme Court), so I will do the same.

Les Clark was the only one of the nine to have been there at the creation of Mickey Mouse. Clark joined Disney in 1927, one year before Mickey's debut. He was also one of the youngest ever to join, starting his job at Disney just a few days after he graduated high school. He was the key animator of Sorcerer's Apprentice Mickey, Wendy, and Alice. Les retired in 1975.

As work on *Snow White and the Seven Dwarfs* was getting under way, **Marc Davis** answered a want ad for an artist and was hired by Disney. He was so proficient that a few years later he was trained as an animator. Tinker Bell and the villains Maleficent and Cruella de Vil were some of his more famous designs. As an Imagineer, Davis also developed many of the concepts for Pirates of the Caribbean and the Haunted Mansion. He retired in 1978, but continued as an advisor and consultant for Disney parks and Imagineering.

A prolific author and teacher on the art of animation, **Ollie Johnston** began his Disney career in 1935. He worked on twenty-four of their animated features before retiring in 1978. Five of his most memorable creations were Thumper, Mr. Smee, Lady, Pongo, and Bagheera.

Often paired with his lifelong best friend Johnston (the two coauthored a popular book about the history of Disney animation), **Frank Thomas**—who came to the studio right out of college in 1934—was considered the most adept performer of the nine. He specialized in villains, using a mirror to capture his own facial expressions to draw classic comically evil characters like Captain Hook, Lady Tremaine, and the Queen of Hearts. He retired in 1978.

Another artist who worked on almost every animated film from *Snow White* to *The Rescuers*, often as directing animator, **Milt Kahl** was a Disney employee from 1934 to his death in 1987. The Fairy Godmother, Tramp, Peter Pan, and Shere Khan were four of the best-loved characters that he brought to life.

A mentor to the group of young artists who came to Disney in the 1970s and '80s, **Eric Larson** first worked with the studio as an animator on *The Three Little Pigs* in 1933. He created—among others—Figaro, Mr. Toad, and Peg. His last project before he died in 1988 was as a consultant on *The Great Mouse Detective*. Traces of his style can still be seen today, thanks to his work as a teacher of modern Disney animators.

Personally hired by Walt in 1935, **John Lounsbery** became one of his most trusted animators. He designed Gideon and J. Worthington Foulfellow, Tony, and Colonel Hathi and was the animation director on most of the classic feature films from the 1940s to the 1970s, eventually taking the director's chair for 1974's *Winnie the Pooh and Tigger Too*. He was working as codirector of *The Rescuers* before his death in 1976.

A specialist in action sequences, like Monstro the gigantic whale swallowing Gepetto and the ride of the Headless Horseman as he chases Ichabod Crane, **Wolfgang "Woolie" Reitherman** started as an animator with Disney in 1933 and transitioned to directing animated films with 1961's *101 Dalmatians*. He eventually helmed seven films. His young sons (Robert, Richard, and Bruce) provided voices for three of Disney's 1960s boy heroes (Wart, Mowgli, and Christopher Robin). After Walt's death in 1966, Woolie was named producer of all the animated films. He retired in 1980.

Ward Kimball marker at Disney Studios. (Wikimedia Commons)

The most fascinating of the nine was **Ward Kimball**—who worked at Disney from 1934 to 1973 and was a true renaissance man. In addition to his work as an animator, with some of the most unique and inventive designs (the Mad Hatter, Jiminy Cricket, and Gus and Jacques) ever seen in Disney films, Ward also played trombone and fronted the studio's Dixieland jazz band (the Firehouse Five Plus Two), directed innovative shorts, and produced episodes of Walt's anthology TV show. He was the only artist Walt ever called a genius. Like Walt, Kimball loved trains, installing a full-size steam engine with tracks in his backyard, and often spent time with the boss rhapsodizing about riding the rails.

All these "Nine Old Men" animators were terrific performers in their own right, using their pencils to bring comedy, drama, romance, slapstick, expression, and articulation to drawings on paper that made their characters as deep and believable as any that had appeared in Hollywood's live-action films. They defined Disney animation as we know it.

UB IWERKS

In 1918, Walt met Iwerks, a fellow artist, when they worked together at the Pesmen-Rubin Commercial Art Studio in Kansas City. When they were both laid off, the nineteen-year-olds opened their own studio together. The partnership failed, but when Walt established a second studio—Laugh-O-gram Films—in 1922, Ub was his first hire. Iwerks, one of the fastest and most skilled animators who ever lived, followed Walt to Hollywood and became Disney's chief animator, working closely with him on the creation of Mickey. A Disney animator who predates the Nine Old Men, Ub was not grouped with them by Walt because he left Disney in 1930 to start his own studio. Iwerks returned to Disney in 1940 to begin a second successful career as an Oscar-winning innovator in motion picture technology. Both of his sons also worked for Disney.

Jack Frost, one of Ub Iwerks animations. (Wikimedia Commons)

FREDDIE MOORE

With very little formal training as an artist, Moore joined Disney in 1930. He was a natural, taking to animation right away, designing the Three Little Pigs, Timothy Q. Mouse, and Lampwick from *Pinocchio* (which was done as a self-portrait). He's best known for implementing the "squash and stretch" style of animation, which added personality to characters, and for updating Mickey Mouse's look, in 1938. He changed Mickey from a pie-eyed caricature of a mouse to the modern icon resembling a person. Moore passed away in 1952.

NORM FERGUSON

He began as a cameraman for Disney in 1929, but Ferguson transferred to the animation department and soon rose through the ranks. He designed some of the earliest Disney villains, like Peg-Leg Pete, the Big Bad Wolf, and the Old Hag/Witch from Snow White. His greatest contribution was

Pluto, whose personality traits—all displayed mostly without a word being spoken by Pluto—were imbued by Ferguson's pencil. He left Disney in 1953.

HAMILTON "HAM" LUSKE

An animator on many of the short films and *Silly Symphonies* from his hiring in 1931, Luske helped create Snow White and then moved on to directing the Disney military training films and corporate films in the 1940s, before transitioning to directing Disney features. He won an Oscar for his visual work on *Mary Poppins*, just a few years before his death in 1968. His son, Tommy Luske, provided the voice for Michael in *Peter Pan*.

BEN SHARPSTEEN

One of Disney's core of animators in the earliest years (1929 to 1930) when they were just blossoming, Sharpsteen was relied on by Walt more than almost any other employee. He soon transitioned into directing. He stayed with the company for thirty years and won an Oscar.

VLADIMIR "BILL" TYTLA

With less than ten years at Disney, 1934 to 1943, Tytla had one of the shortest tenures of all the golden age animators. His talent for capturing feelings in his work was greatly admired by Walt, who assigned him some classic villains. He created the evil puppet master Stromboli in *Pinocchio* and one of the most terrifying screen villains of them all, Chernabog the demon from the "Night on Bald Mountain" sequence in *Fantasia*.

MARY BLAIR

A multitalented artist, Blair was selected by Walt above several of his longtime male staffers to join Disney's goodwill group that toured Latin America. The motion pictures that evolved from the trip,

HONORABLE MENTION

CARL BARKS AND FLOYD GOTTFREDSON

In 1935, Barks started as an in-betweener artist and writer at Disney. In 1942, Walt moved him over to writing and drawing the popular Donald Duck comic books and newspaper strips. He continued doing that until 1966, expanding Donald's world with a big family tree and cast of Duckburg characters, the most famous of which was Uncle Scrooge McDuck. Barks died in 2000, and his artwork is still in demand all over the world. Floyd Gottfredson had a similar career track as Barks. He also began as an in-betweener, taking over Mickey's daily comic strip at the request of Walt in 1930. It was a job Gottfredson held until he retired in 1975. Most of the canon surrounding Mickey Mouse and his extended universe comes from Gottfredson's comics.

Saludos Amigos and *The Three Caballeros*, highlighted Blair's astonishing concept art and led to Walt bringing her on board at WED. There she designed many beloved attractions, including It's a Small World, which is considered the epitome of the "Mary Blair style."

PETER ELLENSHAW

Specifically chosen by Walt to paint background mattes for the live-action Disney films made in his native Great Britain, Peter Ellenshaw moved to the United States in the 1950s to work full-time for Disney. Ellenshaw continued in the matte department, with an inventive visual artistic flair that won him an Oscar. He also did artwork for the Disney parks. His son, Harrison Ellenshaw, worked for Disney as vice president of visual effects and won an Oscar himself.

EYVIND EARLE

A world-renowned artist whose paintings had already been displayed at prestigious museums like the Metropolitan in New York City, Earle was hired by Disney to do backgrounds for several films in the 1950s. He's best known for his contributions to *Sleeping Beauty*, some of the finest artwork ever to be seen in a motion picture. It's influenced many animated films since.

Eyvind Earle's painterly backdrops to *Sleeping Beauty* represented some of the finest artwork ever to appear in an animated film. (Walt Disney Pictures/ Photofest)

DISNEY ARTISTS / ANIMATORS (MODERN ERA)

TONY AND TOM BANCROFT

In a unique situation, these twin brothers grew up not too far from Disneyland in Orange County, with dreams of being artists, and then joined Disney's animation department together in the late 1980s. They stayed until the early 2000s, working on most of the classics of the renaissance era. Tony was responsible for Pumbaa in *The Lion King*, and Tom for Mushu in *Mulan*. Tony was also the codirector of *Mulan*. They now host an animation history podcast together and offer online animation courses (at a reasonable price) at taughtbyapro.com.

BRAD BIRD

A graduate of CalArts in the same class as John Lasseter and Tim Burton, Brad Bird is one of the most creative visionaries the animation world has ever seen. As an eleven-year-old, he made a short animated film that he sent to Disney. It so impressed Milt Kahl that they began a correspondence and Kahl became Bird's mentor. After being hired by Disney and working on *The Fox and the Hound* and *The Black Cauldron*, Bird left the company. He transitioned to television production, helping to bring *The Simpsons*, *King of the Hill*, and *Rugrats* to life, before moving on to write and direct his own animated features. In 1999, his film *The Iron Giant* was released by Warner Brothers to critical acclaim. It's since become a classic. He was then brought over to Pixar by Lasseter, where he wrote and directed *The Incredibles* and *Ratatouille*. Both films won Bird the Academy Award for Best Animated Feature. In 2005, Bird cowrote and directed the live-action Disney feature *Tomorrowland*, starring George Clooney.

RON CLEMENTS

An apprentice to Frank Thomas in the 1970s, Ron Clements rose to supervising animator of *The Fox and the Hound* in 1981. When Michael Eisner asked his animation staff to come up with ideas for new films, it was Clements who reread Hans Christian Andersen's "The Little Mermaid" and pitched it as a possible film. He was named as codirector of that movie. After it became a box office phenomenon, he continued on as codirector (with John Musker) of films like *Aladdin*, *Hercules*, *The Princess and the Frog*, and *Moana*.

ANDREAS DEJA

In 1980, twenty-three-year-old Andreas Deja was hired by Eric Larson, with whom he'd started a correspondence, to work at Disney on the development of *The Black Cauldron*. Deja stayed on and became one of the key animators of the Disney films of the 1990s and 2000s. He is most famous for his design of the villains Gaston and Scar as well as the creation of Roger Rabbit. Deja is passionate about preserving the history of the Nine Old Men, writing books about their work and operating a blog, *Deja View*, in which he shares information about their methods.

MARK DINDAL

Fresh out of the CalArts animation program, Dindal came aboard Disney in 1980 and worked on all the early 1980s projects until leaving Disney for a few years to do his own freelance work. He came back just in time to work on *The Little Mermaid* and to be the head animator for *The Rescuers Down Under*. In 2000, he directed *The Emperor's New Groove*, turning it from an epic Disney musical to a smaller-scale comedy. His last Disney feature was 2005's *Chicken Little*.

ERIC GOLDBERG

A producer of animated commercials, Eric Goldberg closed his own studio in the early 1990s to join Disney, just as it was beginning to dominate again. He was responsible for the animation of Genie in *Aladdin* and Philoctetes in *Hercules*. Goldberg's passion project was an animated sequence set to George Gershwin's "Rhapsody in Blue." The short—a love letter to New York City, set in the 1930s and featuring a caricature of Goldberg himself—made its way into *Fantasia 2000* and was one of the highlights of that movie. In recent years, Goldberg animated Louis in *The Princess and the Frog* and Maui's living tattoos in *Moana*.

MARK HENN

Like Dindal, Henn, a graduate of the CalArts animation program, joined Disney in 1980. His first big project was animating Mickey in *Mickey's Christmas Carol*. Later, mostly working out of Disney's Florida animation studio campus, he was the animator for Princess Jasmine, young Simba, and Princess Tiana. He also directed the award-winning short *John Henry* in 2000.

GLEN KEANE

Arguably the best known of all the animators on this list, Glen Keane was in the public eye (sort of) long before he joined Disney in 1974. His father was Bil Keane, the cartoonist and creator of the long-running comic strip *Family Circus*. Glen was the inspiration for Little Billy, one of the stars of the strip. Trained by several of the Nine Old Men, Keane himself became a mentor and supervising animator to the new crop of artists who joined Disney after him. He retired in 2012 and was named a Disney Legend in 2013. His legacy includes the looks of such diverse characters as Elliott the Dragon, Ariel, Beast, Aladdin, and Tarzan. In 2017, he collaborated with basketball star Kobe Bryant on an animated short that won an Oscar.

Glen Keane storyboarding for an audience. (Wikimedia Commons)

JOHN MUSKER

Often paired with Clements because the duo directed so many films together, Musker became a Disney employee around the same time and worked as an animator on *The Rescuers*, *The Fox and the Hound*, *The Black Cauldron*, and *The Great Mouse Detective*. His passion project, even in the late 1980s, was an animated adaptation of *Treasure Island* set in space. It took almost two decades, but Musker was finally able to see *Treasure Planet* completed in 2002. He's since developed and codirected—with Clements—*The Princess and the Frog* and *Moana*.

BRUCE W. SMITH

Yet another CalArts graduate, Smith started with Disney working on *Who Framed Roger Rabbit* and then on the Roger Rabbit shorts. He left Disney for a brief time to cocreate and direct the hit animated film *Bebe's Kids*, and then came back to develop *The Proud Family*, a TV show that ran on the Disney Channel for four years. Smith was the supervising animator for Kerchak in *Tarzan*, Pacha in *The Emperor's New Groove*, and Dr. Facilier in *The Princess and the Frog*.

MOST INFORMATIVE BOOKS ABOUT THE DISNEY COMPANY

DISNEY A TO Z: THE OFFICIAL ENCYCLOPEDIA (2016) by Dave Smith

Now in its fifth edition, this is *the* best reference book ever written about all things Disney.

THE WONDERFUL WORLD OF DISNEY TELEVISION: A COMPLETE HISTORY (1997) by Bill Cotter

A comprehensive book, covering each episode of Walt's anthology show and more.

BUILDING A COMPANY: ROY O. DISNEY AND THE CREATION OF AN ENTERTAINMENT EMPIRE (1998) by Bob Thomas

The best biographer of Walt tackles the Disney Company's story from Roy's point of view.

WALT'S TIME: FROM BEFORE TO BEYOND (1998) by Robert B. Sherman and Richard M. Sherman

The official autobiography of the Sherman Brothers, filled with anecdotes and rare photos.

THE DISNEY FILMS (2000) by Leonard Maltin

One of America's great film critics explores every feature film made during Walt's lifetime.

THE DISNEY TREASURES/THE DISNEY KEEPSAKES (2003) by Robert Tieman

Reprinted items from the Disney Archives fill out this history of the Disney Company.

TODAY IN HISTORY: DISNEY (2006) by Eve Zibart

Each day of the calendar filled with Disney trivia and information.

THE WALT'S PEOPLE SERIES (2014 TO 2018) by Didier Ghez

Oral histories of Disney employees, collected and transcribed by Disney expert Ghez.

INK & PAINT: THE WOMEN OF WALT DISNEY'S ANIMATION (2017) by Mindy Johnson

A detailed history of the legions of female artists who toiled for decades in anonymity to help create Disney's most famous films. A great tribute to their legacy.

YESTERDAY'S TOMORROW: DISNEY'S MAGICAL MID-CENTURY (2017) by Don Hahn

A look at how the Disney Company influenced the look and style of America in the 1950s and '60s.

MOST INFORMATIVE FILMS ABOUT THE DISNEY COMPANY

THE RELUCTANT DRAGON (1941) directed by Alfred L. Werker and Ham Luske

An inside look at how Disney films are made, as humorist Robert Benchley searches for Walt at the new Disney Studios in Burbank to pitch his cartoon version of *The Reluctant Dragon*. Features cameos by many of the famous Disney animators and vocal artists.

Scene from *The Reluctant Dragon* (1941). (Walt Disney Pictures/Photofest)

FROM FANTASIA TO FANTASYLAND (1978) various directors

A documentary produced by Thames Television in England, it features direct interviews with many of Walt's classic animators, who were nearing the end of their careers at Disney.

FRANK AND OLLIE (1995) directed by Theodore Thomas

A loving retrospective about two of Disney's greatest animators, Frank Thomas and Ollie Johnston, told in their own voices.

THE HAND BEHIND THE MOUSE: THE UB IWERKS STORY (1999) directed by Leslie Iwerks

Created by the granddaughter of the Disney Legend; Kelsey Grammer narrates this look at the life of Walt's trusted friend and his on-again, off-again relationship with the boss and company.

THE SWEATBOX (2002) directed by Trudie Styler and John-Paul Davidson

Filmmaker Styler, the wife of Grammy Award–winning musician Sting, originally set out to document the creation of *The Emperor's New Groove*, but wound up with a fascinating look at behind-the-scenes chaos as Disney changed the concept from epic musical to smaller comedy.

DISNEY ON THE FRONT LINES (2004) various directors

Part of the *Disney Treasures* DVD series, this collection of shorts and features from the early 1940s also contains stories about life and work at the Disney Studios during World War II.

THE AGE OF BELIEVING: THE DISNEY LIVE ACTION CLASSICS (2008) directed by Peter Fitzgerald

Produced for Turner Classic Movies, this documentary chronicles the history of Walt's successful move into live-action films in the 1950s and beyond.

WAKING SLEEPING BEAUTY (2009) directed by Don Hahn

Written by noted film and theater expert Patrick Pacheco, this documentary details the decade (1984 to 1994) that saw Disney's animation department change from the old guard to the new.

THE BOYS: THE SHERMAN BROTHERS' STORY (2009) directed by Gregg Sherman and Jeff Sherman

Made by the sons of the two legendary songwriting brothers, this film details their family's long history in the music business and how they defined the sound of Disney for generations.

FLOYD NORMAN: AN ANIMATED LIFE (2016) directed by Michael Fiore and Erik Sharkey

The life story of the first African American animator at Disney, a groundbreaker forced by the company to retire at age sixty-five but who is still active in animation.

In 1987, Disney began its own in-house Hall of Fame, giving out Disney Legends awards to those who have made a significant contribution to the company and to its culture. More than 250 people have been given this high honor in the last three decades. Most of the names you'll find listed in this book of top tens are already Disney Legends. The following two lists covers those who should be better known and those who haven't been named Legends yet but should be.

DISNEY LEGENDS WHO SHOULD BE BETTER KNOWN

BILL GARITY

One of the most technically proficient people who ever worked for Walt, Garity revolutionized the use of sound on film when he began with Disney in 1928. In the 1930s, he helped create the multiplane camera and then design Walt's Fantasound system, one of the first uses of stereo in movie theaters. His last act with Disney before leaving was to oversee the construction of the new studio in Burbank. He died in 1971 and was named a Legend in 1999.

BECKY FALLBERG AND RUTHIE THOMPSON

Without the Ink & Paint Department, which meticulously hand painted the thousands and thousands of cels that went into making the work of the animators look great on-screen, Disney films would not look as stunning as they do. The workers in this department, mostly women, were largely unknown to the public, but their painstaking labor, using custom-made shades of color designed for their exclusive use, contributed largely to the success and style of Disney. Fallberg joined this department in 1942 and became its manager in 1975. Disney honored her as a Legend in 2000, along with Thompson, who started at Ink & Paint in 1927 and eventually became supervisor of Disney's scene planning department, responsible for storyboards.

JOE GRANT

With an expert eye for character design, Joe Grant was put in charge of approving all character model sheets at Disney in the 1940s. *Lady and the Tramp* was largely Grant's idea, as he wouldn't give up until Walt approved it. He worked with the studio until *Alice in Wonderland* and then took an extended leave. Remarkably, he returned to Disney while in his eighties to consult on design and story for such modern classics as *Beauty and the Beast*, *Pocahontas*, and *Tarzan*. He's also the only person to have done major work on both *Fantasia* and *Fantasia 2000*, sixty years apart. Even after he became a Disney Legend in 1992, Grant kept working. The last film he took part in before he died in 2005 at age ninety-seven was 2004's *Home on the Range*.

BURNY MATTINSON

In 2013, eight years after he joined the ranks of the other Disney Legends, Burny Mattinson celebrated his sixtieth anniversary as a staffer at the Disney Studios with a big party there, making him the very last full-timer to have worked directly with Walt. Mattinson was a mail room clerk in 1953, and was eventually promoted to the animation department. In the early 1980s, he came up with the idea to bring Mickey Mouse back to the big screen in a short based on Dickens's *A Christmas Carol*. After the project was approved, Mattinson wrote, produced, and directed it. He did the same with *The Great Mouse Detective* a few years later.

RON DOMINGUEZ

Born on the Anaheim property that eventually became Disneyland (his family's home, purchased by Disney, stood roughly where the Rivers of America are now), Dominguez joined the park as a ticket taker when it opened in 1955 and moved all the way up to vice president before he retired in 1994. He was given Disney Legend status in 2000.

ALFRED AND ELMA MILOTTE AND WINSTON HIBLER

Walt sent the Milottes, a team of married cinematographers, to Alaska in the 1950s to capture hours of footage of animals in the wild. It was another bold experiment on Disney's part, which resulted in the Academy Award–winning series of *True-Life Adventures* films. The Milottes, who both passed away in 1989 and were named Disney Legends in 1998, stayed on to shoot many of the *True-Life Adventures*, often spending months at a time filming on location in remote areas. When Walt was faced with a shortage of staff in 1942 due to World War II and needed writers and directors for his military training films, Winston Hibler was hired. After the war, he transitioned to dialogue director. Hibler—who was posthumously named a Legend fifty years after his hire—has as his biggest claim to Disney fame the fact that he was the stoic narrator of Walt's *True-Life Adventures* films, which endeared him to a generation of fans.

BILL WALSH

In 1950, as Walt was contemplating a move into television, he called on longtime employee Bill Walsh—a writer on the *Mickey Mouse* comic strips—and convinced him to write and produce the first Disney television show, *One Hour in Wonderland*. That led to Walsh being Walt's lead producer for all of the Disney TV shows. He then moved into feature films, with his name at the front of the credits, right after Walt's, for most of the great live-action films, until his death in 1975. Walsh was named a Disney Legend in 1991.

DON DaGRADI

DaGradi, who worked closely with both Walt and Walsh, started with Disney in the 1930s as a writer on the shorts, then progressed to writing the feature films. He cowrote *Mary Poppins* and many of the other great live-action films of the 1950s and 1960s. DaGradi was named a Disney Legend in 1991, the same year he passed away.

ROBERT STEVENSON

While he's not listed with folks like Hitchcock, Lucas, Spielberg, or Scorsese, Robert Stevenson is one of the most successful Hollywood directors ever. His string of more than twenty live-action Disney hits stretches from *Johnny Tremain* to *The Shaggy D.A.*, with 1964's *Mary Poppins* as his crowning achievement. Stevenson died in 1986 and was named a Disney Legend in 2002.

JACK WAGNER

You may not know the name, but you most definitely know the voice. Starting in 1970, Jack Wagner, a Los Angeles radio host and 2005 Disney Legend, began recording announcements for the American Disney parks, a task he continued with Disneyland Tokyo and Paris. Many rides and attractions feature his narration and safety spiels, but the one that's most familiar to those who have visited Disneyland or the Walt Disney World Resort in Florida is "Please stand clear of the doors . . . Por favor manténgase alejado de las puertas," played during each and every monorail ride. He passed away in 1995, but his dulcet tones can still be heard, not only at Disney but at the Orlando and Houston International Airports, too.

FOLKS WHO ARE OVERDUE FOR RECOGNITION AS DISNEY LEGENDS

RON MILLER

According to sources inside the company, Ron Miller has been offered Disney Legend status several times but has repeatedly declined. He definitely deserves the honor. Miller was the one who kept

Walt's creative vision and ambition alive when others wanted to play it safe and stick to old formulas. As Disney's president from 1980 to 1984, Ron Miller took many bold chances in green-lighting projects. Some of them paid off in big ways (Disney Channel, Touchstone Pictures, and CAPS computer animation), while others fizzled, but Miller was not afraid of sticking to Walt's mantra of "Keep moving forward." Disney fans everywhere owe Ron Miller a tremendous amount of gratitude. Hopefully, he will one day accept the invitation to join his fellow Disney Legends.

VERNA FELTON

This is a head-scratching omission. Verna Felton played so many classic Disney animated characters that it's easy to lose count. Her excellent acting abilities, using just her voice, brought depth, humor, and warmth to Mrs. Jumbo, *Cinderella*'s Fairy Godmother, and *Sleeping Beauty*'s Flora as well as cold, genuine menace to villains like *Alice*'s Queen of Hearts and Aunt Sarah from *Lady and the Tramp*. Felton, who died in 1966, should be inducted as a Disney Legend as soon as possible.

T. HEE

When folks would see this name on credits in a Disney cartoon, they'd assume it was some sort of joke by the animators. Thornton "T." Hee was indeed a real person, whose contributions to Disney started in 1938. He codirected sequences in *Pinocchio* and *Fantasia* and was renowned for his skill in caricature. Later on, he joined WED and worked on the 1964 World's Fair. Many of his peers from both divisions are now Disney Legends, as T. Hee should be.

HAZEL GEORGE

An old polo injury kept Walt in constant pain. He relied on daily visits from the studio's nurse, Hazel George, to apply hot packs to relieve the agony. This usually happened at the end of the day, so Walt would use the opportunity to unwind and talk with George about the stresses of running his company. She quickly became one of his closest confidantes. She was also much more than that. George was encouraged by Walt in the 1940s to put her writing talents to good use. Using the pseudonym of "Gil George," she worked with the musicians on Disney's staff and created the lyrics for more than one hundred Disney songs. It was also Hazel who organized the Disney employees to invest in Walt's dream of Disneyland when nobody else thought it would work. Most of the men who cowrote the songs with George are now Disney Legends. It's about time she joins the club. Walt would certainly be pleased with her inclusion.

MARGARET KERRY

Each of the actresses who played Disney princesses, and female heroes like Alice, in the golden era (and even some from the modern one) has been named a Disney Legend, save for one. Tinker Bell, as she appeared in 1953's *Peter Pan*, was voiceless. Yet she was played by an actress, Margaret Kerry, who was hired by Walt to perform the scenes on film so that the animators could have a reference. Tinker Bell's look was modeled on Kerry. Her Hollywood career was notable before Tink, and she continued afterward, with a co-starring role on TV's *Andy Griffith Show*. In recent years, Kerry has become a tireless ambassador for Disney, appearing at conventions and fan events. Margaret Kerry is one of the last links to the period when Walt still gave personal

Margaret Kerry, "the first Tinker Bell," is now a Disney ambassador. (Wikimedia Commons)

attention to making sure that every detail in his films was just right. She certainly has all the qualifications and history to be named a Disney Legend.

PHIL HARRIS

Jazz is one of the few original American art forms, and one of its best bandleaders in the 1940s was Phil Harris. He made an Academy Award–winning short film featuring jazz, and his wife Alice Faye starred with him on popular radio shows. When Disney was casting *The Jungle Book*, Harris was given the role of Baloo the Bear. He soon made it his own. The animators and writers were inspired by Harris's recording sessions to expand Baloo's role in the film, and his scat-singing bebop jazzy style added to songs like "The Bare Necessities." The film was so popular that Harris was brought back to voice two other characters, Thomas O'Malley and Little John, who also shared Harris's free-wheeling improvisational attitude. When Baloo was made the star of an animated TV series in 1989, Harris voiced him once again. He is one of the most recognizable of all Disney voices and should have been named a Legend by now.

THE McEVEETY BROTHERS

Bernard, Joe, and Vince McEveety all joined Disney as writers and directors in the 1950s. Between the three of them, the résumé of these talented and prolific brothers includes several live-action favorites from the 1960s and '70s like *The Bears and I, Napoleon and Samantha, Treasure of Matecumbe, Million Dollar Duck, The Barefoot Executive, The Apple Dumpling Gang, Superdad, Charley and the Angel*, and *One Little Indian*. Their names are all over that era of Disney history. If that's not grounds for being Disney Legends, I'm not sure what is.

NORMAN TOKAR

Like the McEveetys, Tokar is another workhorse live-action Disney director who surprisingly has been left out of the Disney Legends club. His first film for them was *Big Red*, in 1961. He followed that with such films as *Savage Sam*, *The Ugly Dachshund*, *The Cat from Outer Space*, *The Boatniks*, *The Horse in the Gray Flannel Suit*, and *Candleshoe*, before his death in 1979.

TOM HANKS

Tim Allen began his career with Disney. Most of his famous work has been with them, and Buzz Lightyear is an icon, so Allen was an easy selection for Disney Legend status. Tom Hanks has worked for every studio in Hollywood, so he's not exclusively "Disney" like Allen. However, it's hard to imagine anyone else playing Sheriff Woody, as Hanks has now done in several *Toy Story* films and shorts. He also started off Touchstone Pictures with a success (*Splash*) and was the first actor ever approved by Disney to portray Walt as an adult in one of their official projects (*Saving Mr. Banks*). No other modern-day actor would have been as perfect for the job as Hanks. That alone merits Disney Legend status for him.

HONORABLE MENTION

DIANE DISNEY MILLER

Walt's oldest daughter was a very reserved person. She definitely inherited the shyer side of his nature. Even when her husband, Ron Miller, ran the company that bore her family's name, Diane stayed out of the spotlight. After her mother, Lilly, passed away in 1997, and the hundredth anniversary of Walt's birth approached, Diane began to make more and more public appearances to remind the world that Walt was a person and not just some brand name. This drive led her to collaborate with her seven children on books and documentaries about Walt's life, using personal family photos and keepsakes, culminating with the opening of the Walt Disney Family Museum at the Presidio in San Francisco in 2009, not far from the place where she and Ron operated a successful winery. Diane passed away in 2013 at the age of seventy-nine. Though she never held a day-to-day executive role at Disney, she deserves to be on the Legends list simply for the fact that she and her sister Sharon (who also merits inclusion) inspired Walt's creativity many times, most notably with the idea for Disneyland.

FRANK WELKER

Another actor whose name you probably don't know, but whose voice is heard in some of the biggest box office earners of all time, Frank Welker has not only given life to classic Disney characters like Abu, Flit, Cri-Kee, and Pegasus (all of whom communicate through unique sounds without ever saying an actual word, no easy feat) but is also the voice of other iconic cartoon characters such as Fred on *Scooby-Doo*, Dr. Claw from *Inspector Gadget*, Megatron, Curious George, and Baby Kermit and Baby Beaker on *The Muppet Babies*. On film, he's provided vocal tracks for—among others—*Gremlins*, *Harry Potter* movies, *Night at the Museum*, *Raiders of the Lost Ark*, *The Smurfs*, and more than twenty Disney and Pixar movies from *Who Framed Roger Rabbit* to Tim Burton's *Alice in Wonderland*. His live-action film career also started at Disney, with 1969's *The Computer Wore Tennis Shoes*. For the sheer volume of work he's done for Disney alone, Welker should be on its list of Legends.

LISTS ABOUT DISNEY FILMS

DISNEY ANIMATED FILMS (CLASSIC)

THE "BIG FIVE": SNOW WHITE, PINOCCHIO, FANTASIA, DUMBO, AND BAMBI (1937 TO 1942)

Historians and movie critics consistently group these five films together as the apex of Disney's style and creativity. They were produced at a time when the majority of Walt's core team was still together and the dual impacts of the strike and World War II had not fully shaken the studio. The most interesting thing about the five is that they were finished in such a short time frame (1937 to 1942) by the same employees, yet all five of them are completely different in tone, story line, and look. It's one of the most remarkable accomplishments in productivity that Hollywood has ever seen.

Snow White (1937). (RKO Radio Pictures/ Photofest)

Walt took one of his biggest risks ever with the release of his very first animated feature film, **Snow White and the Seven Dwarfs**, a labor of love directed by David Hand. Years in the making and planning, it went down to the wire as his staff raced to get it finished before the star-studded December 1937 premiere at Hollywood's Carthay Circle Theater. Even as the lights dimmed at the screening and the picture started, Walt's doubters were certain that he'd made a big mistake. Ninety minutes later, the tears and cheers that filled the audience of notables in reaction to this beautifully animated story—performed through pencils and paintbrushes—of a princess in peril, her forest

Pinocchio ink and paint artist (1940). (Walt Disney Studios/Photofest)

friends, a team of diverse little helpers, an evil queen, and a dashing prince, proved that Walt was right. Big-screen animation would never be the same.

For the 1940 follow-up to his triumphant feature film debut, Walt chose **Pinocchio**, a tale of an easily distracted little wooden puppet who is brought to life and yearns to become a real boy. It was directed by Ben Sharpsteen and Ham Luske, with more characters and locations than *Snow White* (the film takes place in charming European villages, on an island filled with amusements, and on a raging ocean); the staff of 750 who labored on this film were tested but came through admirably. The use of the multiplane camera and more than fifteen hundred shades of paint created a look like no other animated film before or since.

Walt expanded the horizons of the motion picture industry in 1940 by creating a feature film combining classical music and animation. **Fantasia** was the first of Walt's "package" films, using different directors and animators for a series of musical vignettes, this time conducted by Leopold Stokowski. Walt wanted to use special stereophonic speakers (Fantasound) to enhance the audience's experience. That hampered efforts to release it nationwide, as few theaters were equipped to handle the film's technical demands. That, along with audience apathy to the concept, the onset of World War II, and rebuffs from musical purists who didn't like mixing cartoons with the work of classical composers, combined to kill the box office. It also put an end to Walt's vision of constantly adding and removing sequences from the film to keep it fresh upon rerelease. (The studio didn't get around to doing that until *Fantasia 2000*, which retained the Sorcerer's Apprentice sequence

"Dance of Hours" from *Fantasia* (1940). (Walt Disney Productions/ Photofest)

from the original but surrounded it with all new scenes.) *Fantasia*, like *Pinocchio*, was not a financial success when first released, but it has since become a certified cinematic landmark, and the most astonishing feat in early animation.

The costs for producing both *Pinocchio* and *Fantasia* were enormous, and the returns were minimal. That's why 1941's **Dumbo**, directed by Ben Sharpsteen, was such a relief to Walt and Roy. Painted in less expensive watercolors, it came in at under a million in budget and was a tremendous hit. While not as lavishly illustrated as the other four films, this short (64 minutes) but simple tale of an ostracized young circus elephant who triumphs against all odds held great appeal for audiences on edge with fears of an expanding World War.

Dumbo (1941). (Walt Disney Pictures/Photofest)

A coming-of-age tale set in the forest, 1942's **Bambi** was the first Disney feature to be entirely populated by animals (man is referred to, but never seen). Begun just after the completion of *Snow White*—and codirected by David Hand—*Bambi* took years to make, because the animators meticulously studied real-life animals by visiting zoos, consulting with experts, and bringing live deer in to the studio to watch them run and play. All of that work shows on-screen, as the natural world comes to life in a most realistic way. Nature is the star of this film, and fewer than a thousand words are spoken. Profits were low for Bambi, too. Walt was then forced to curtail his feature film efforts until the war was over. Disney never got back to this artistic level. *Bambi* marked the end of its amazing gold standard era.

Scene from
Bambi (1942).
(Wikimedia Commons)

CINDERELLA (1950) directed by Wilfred Jackson, Ham Luske, and Clyde Geronimi

For his postwar return to an animated feature concentrating on one story, Walt chose this timeless medieval tale of a poor girl who dreams of a better life and is magically transformed by a fairy godmother. He poured almost all of Disney's resources into it, a big risk. Audiences fell in love with *Cinderella*, with theaters selling out around the world. The film saved the Disney animation department, which had struggled to return to its great heights of a decade before.

PETER PAN (1953) directed by Wilfred Jackson, Ham Luske, and Clyde Geronimi

Walt had been planning to make this adaptation of J. M. Barrie's tale of eternal childhood since 1935, but didn't get it going until well after the war years. Though the character had been around for decades, Disney's version of Peter Pan soon became the iconic one. This boy who refused to grow up had great appeal to Walt, who shared a bit of that sentiment. Audiences agreed. *Peter Pan* was another triumph.

Actress Kathryn
Beaumont (voice
of Wendy Darling)
looks over a rough
storyboard for *Peter
Pan* (1953). (RKO
Radio Pictures Inc./
Photofest)

SLEEPING BEAUTY (1959) directed by Clyde Geronimi

Though it followed the classic Disney template of a princess in peril who finds herself and true love along the way, *Sleeping Beauty* was a box office dud when it debuted. Walt spent more money on this film (six million dollars) than on any other animated feature to that date and had high hopes for it, even naming the castle in Disneyland after the title princess before the film came out. It's since taken its place among the greats, thanks to a unique artistic and visual style that puts it close to the ranks of the "Big Five."

LADY AND THE TRAMP (1955) directed by Wilfred Jackson, Ham Luske, and Clyde Geronimi

There's a lot of nostalgia packed into this tale of dogs from different sides of the tracks who fall in love despite themselves. Set in the early 1900s, *Lady and the Tramp* evoked the time period that Walt was most fond of, and even had a scene inspired by something that happened to him in real life. He'd once presented Lilly a puppy in a hatbox as a gift, which made its way into the film. This was another big hit for the studio.

101 DALMATIANS (1961) directed by Wolfgang Reitherman, Ham Luske, and Clyde Geronimi

The first animated film to use the Xerox process to assist in production (can you imagine having to hand paint that many dots?), *101 Dalmatians* is a cute tale about two dog owners, and their dogs, who meet in London and fall in love. What really drives the film, one of the biggest of 1961, is the villain, Cruella de Vil. She is, as her name suggests, cruel and evil. Cruella's scheme to kidnap puppies to make them into fur coats was one of the most shocking ever put in a Disney cartoon, but it's portrayed with enough slapstick and an eventual comeuppance for the villain and her henchmen that the film is more fun than somber.

THE JUNGLE BOOK (1967) directed by Wolfgang Reitherman

Based on Rudyard Kipling's classic coming-of-age tale of a human child left as a baby in the jungle and raised by animals, *The Jungle Book* was lifted to classic territory by its bouncy Sherman Brothers score and a vocal cast composed primarily of jazz icons and enthusiasts like Phil Harris (Baloo)

Promotional poster for *The Jungle Book* (1967). (Disney/Photofest)

and bandleader Louis Prima (King Louie). While not as lavishly drawn as some of the earlier Disney films, *The Jungle Book* is a fun romp from beginning to end. It was the last animated film to be directly supervised by Walt and—as a testament to his instincts for a good story—was one of Disney's biggest financial successes.

THE RESCUERS (1977) directed by Wolfgang Reitherman, John Lounsbery, and Art Stevens

Based on two award-winning children's books by Margery Sharp, *The Rescuers* was long in development at Disney and marked the changing of the guard, as many of Walt's original staff began figuratively handing over the keys to the animation department to a new generation of artists. This tale of two intrepid mice working for the Rescue Aid Society on a mission to save a young orphan girl was a surprise hit at the box office and helped boost Disney's bottom line at a time when the company needed it the most.

THE FOX AND THE HOUND (1981) directed by Art Stevens, Ted Berman, and Richard Rich

This was the first film created mostly by Disney's new animation team. Some of the older animators were there to give advice and help move things along, but it was the young staffers who brought

HONORABLE MENTION

THE MUSICAL PACKAGE FILMS (1943 TO 1949)

When funds were low, Walt turned to making these feature films comprising shorts strung together, often with narration or hosts—like Edgar Bergen, Jiminy Cricket, or Luana Patten—bridging the gap between stories. They were pop culture spins on the idea of *Fantasia*, containing some classic Disney work (*Peter and the Wolf, Casey at the Bat, Johnny Appleseed, The Legend of Sleepy Hollow*, and *Mickey and the Beanstalk*) and inspirations for attractions (Mr. Toad's Wild Ride). Unfortunately, these films are not as beloved as the ones with complete story lines, and are often overlooked by fans when they think of the Disney animated features canon.

Saludos Amigos (1943)

The Three Caballeros (1945)

Make Mine Music (1946)

Melody Time (1948)

Fun and Fancy Free (1947)

The Adventures of Ichabod and Mr. Toad (1949)

this tale of two childhood best friends, Tod—a fox—and Copper—a hound dog—who don't realize that they should actually be on opposite sides according to the rules of hunting. It was a bittersweet story, but another bonanza for the company, taking its place among the classics in Disney's canon.

OLIVER & COMPANY (1988) directed by George Scribner

This Disney take on Charles Dickens's *Oliver Twist* set in modern-day New York City, told from a dog's point of view, was one of the last traditional hand-drawn feature films before computer animation started to dominate. More than three hundred artists worked on it. Computers were tested out as a way to create some backgrounds and objects, leaving animators free to focus on the characters. Featuring songs by Howard Ashman, Barry Manilow, and others, with a powerhouse voice cast consisting of Billy Joel (whose rendition of "Why Should I Worry?" from the soundtrack became a chart topper), Bette Midler, Cheech Marin, Joey Lawrence, Dom DeLuise, and Robert Loggia, *Oliver & Company* was loved by audiences and was—for a short time anyway—the highest-grossing animated film in history.

DISNEY ANIMATED FILMS (MODERN)

THE LITTLE MERMAID (1989) directed by John Musker and Ron Clements

A return to the formula that made the studio famous, this tale of an undersea princess who longs for life on land was the beginning of the modern golden era of Disney animation. Lavishly illustrated, with a cast of memorable characters and a score that rivals many Broadway shows.

Still from *The Little Mermaid 2* (2000). (Walt Disney Home Video/Photofest)

BEAUTY AND THE BEAST (1991) directed by Gary Trousdale and Kirk Wise

It's rare to top a perfect film, but the team at Disney animation did it with their second princess tale in a row, this time about an independent and intelligent woman who is held captive by a beast in his enchanted castle and falls in love with him, seeing through his outer shell. The movie stunned critics, who gave it five-star reviews. Audiences were just as enthralled, as was the Academy, which nominated it for Best Picture—the first time that had ever happened for an animated film. It set the standard in animation and storytelling for years to come.

ALADDIN (1992) directed by John Musker and Ron Clements

A change of pace after two blockbuster princess films, this retelling of the *Arabian Nights* stories, with a young protagonist who is a street urchin with a heart of gold, drew the crowds to cinemas once again. The songs, the villain, a headstrong princess, and a tour de force by Robin Williams as the Genie made this one a Disney classic almost as soon as it was released.

THE EMPEROR'S NEW GROOVE (2000) directed by Mark Dindal

After a few hits and misses following the films of the early '90s, Disney started the new millennium with this comic romp about a spoiled brat emperor who is transformed into a llama by an evil sorceress and learns humility along the way. Though it was originally meant to be an epic musical, the hipper, more sarcastic edge in this film signaled a benchmark for Disney animation.

LILO & STITCH (2002) directed by Chris Sanders and Dean DeBlois

A tale set in Hawaii, about a young girl who teams up with an alien to discover the true meaning of family. A curious mix of sci-fi and heartwarming drama, this film works on many levels. The soundtrack, a mix of island-themed music ("Hawaiian Roller Coaster Ride" is a fun one) and Elvis recordings, actually contains more Elvis songs than any of Presley's own films.

TANGLED (2010) directed by Byron Howard and Nathan Greno

After another dry patch, Disney animators returned to the princess genre with this tale of Rapunzel spiffed up for modern audiences. Instead of being a damsel waiting to be rescued, she proves that she can make her own way in the world, to the chagrin of her erstwhile rescuer.

WRECK-IT RALPH (2012) directed by Rich Moore

A clever film, set inside the world of video games. Several classic arcade characters make cameos. Ralph, who plays a bad guy in his own game but who longs to be seen as the good guy, goes on a journey to save his arcade pals. Entirely digitally animated by Disney.

FROZEN (2013) directed by Chris Buck and Jennifer Lee

The highest-grossing animated film of all time, this twenty-first-century interpretation of the classic Disney princess stories, based on Hans Christian Andersen's *The Snow Queen*, provided a mantra ("Let It Go!") for those facing obstacles, naysayers, or doubters in their life.

ZOOTOPIA (2016) directed by Byron Howard and Rich Moore

Like *The Emperor's New Groove*, this film had a sassier and hipper viewpoint than most Disney films. This comedy has achieved cult hit status. Its heroes, Nick Wilde and Officer Judy Hopps, team up to solve a case, providing commentary on modern office politics and the need for cooperation and understanding between people with different viewpoints.

The 2013 hit *Frozen* is the highest-grossing animated film of all time. (Walt Disney Studios Motion Pictures/Photofest)

MOANA (2016) directed by John Musker and Ron Clements

Almost like *The Little Mermaid* in reverse, an island princess dreams of life on the sea and sets out on an ocean adventure to restore balance in the universe by returning an ancient talisman.

HONORABLE MENTION

TIM BURTON'S THE NIGHTMARE BEFORE CHRISTMAS (1993) directed by Henry Selick

Originally released as a Touchstone film, it has since been brought under the Disney banner, thanks to fan support. The tale of the Pumpkin King, Jack, who discovers the magic of Christmas and wants to bring it back to Halloween Town, it's become a televised staple in two separate seasons. It's also caused a debate: Is it a Halloween movie, a Christmas movie, or both? The Haunted Mansion in Disneyland does an overlay featuring scenes from this film each year.

DISNEY LIVE-ACTION NON-MUSICAL FILMS (CLASSIC)

TREASURE ISLAND (1950) directed by Byron Haskin

Walt's first live-action film with no animation whatsoever, this retelling of Robert Louis Stevenson's classic 1881 swashbuckling pirate tale was a huge critical and commercial hit, setting the bar high for future live-action Disney films.

20,000 LEAGUES UNDER THE SEA (1954) directed by Richard Fleischer

The first fully live-action Disney film to be shot at its studios in Burbank, this CinemaScope spectacular captured the thrills of Jules Verne's nineteenth-century story of Captain Nemo and his futuristic submarine, the *Nautilus*. Big stars like Kirk Douglas, James Mason, and Peter Lorre boosted the box office, and the impressive visual effects earned the filmmakers three Oscar nominations, two of which they won—for special effects and set decoration.

The Nautilus submarine in *20,000 Leagues under the Sea* (1954) inspired a ride at Disneyland that operated for many years. (Wikimedia Commons/photo by Alex Reinhart)

OLD YELLER (1957) directed by Robert Stevenson

Walt once said that to tell a great story, you must include both laughter and tears. *Old Yeller* is one of the best examples of this. It's a film that many fans get emotional just thinking about. This tale of a family's life on a remote Texas ranch in the 1860s is centered around their pet—the title character—a stray dog who protects them and whom they grow to love. Sixty years later, the finale still packs an incredibly powerful punch.

THE SHAGGY DOG (1959) directed by Charles Barton

Originally pitched as a TV series to ABC, which rejected it, this film about a boy who magically transforms into a sheepdog was the first live-action comedy produced by Walt. It paved the way for all the successful comedies that followed. Fred MacMurray, one of Walt's favorite actors, was cast against type in this film. It also began his long association with Disney. This film was so well loved and remembered that it spawned a sequel in 1976 (without MacMurray), a TV movie in 1994, and a terrific feature film remake in 2006, starring Tim Allen.

POLLYANNA (1960) directed by David Swift

Walt again drew on Oscar-caliber Hollywood star power for this sentimental tale of an optimistic young girl (Hayley Mills) in early 1900s New England. Jane Wyman, Karl Malden, Agnes Moorehead, and Adolphe Menjou all appeared as townspeople who had their lives changed by meeting Pollyanna. Mills was given an Academy Award for her work. The movie was so popular and the character so indelible that the term "Pollyanna" became a popular phrase to describe someone who always has a sunny outlook on life.

SWISS FAMILY ROBINSON (1960) directed by Ken Annakin

Shot on location in the Caribbean, this chronicle of the adventures of a Swiss clan shipwrecked on a deserted island was one of Walt's most expensive live-action films to make. It paid off, and is still one of the highest-grossing films in Disney's history. It was so popular that the treehouse the family crafted in the film was re-created for the Disney parks.

THE ABSENT-MINDED PROFESSOR (1961) directed by Robert Stevenson

The world was introduced to a magical substance, Flubber, in this black-and-white comedy starring Fred MacMurray as the title character who works at Medfield College, Disney's favorite fictional school (the campus was actually the Disney studio property in Burbank), and invents a strange goo that helps the hapless Medfield basketball team to a winning streak. Audiences loved the film, which spawned a sequel and several remakes.

THE PARENT TRAP (1961) directed by David Swift

Another landmark for Disney's visual effects department, this comedy of errors about identical twin girls separated at birth and reunited at a summer camp required the technicians to seamlessly blend split-screen shots of the star, Hayley Mills, who played both roles. It worked, becoming one of Disney's most popular films, leading to three sequels and a remake.

Through the use of split-screen technology Hayley Mills was able to play identical sisters in *The Parent Trap* (1961). (Walt Disney Pictures/Photofest)

THE LOVE BUG (1969) directed by Robert Stevenson

This was the first big live-action hit for Disney after Walt's death. No film released in 1969 made more money than this one. Dean Jones played Jim Douglas, a race car driver and inheritor of a beat-up Volkswagen Beetle that turns out to have magical abilities. The car itself, nicknamed Herbie, is one of Disney's biggest nonhuman live-action stars. Herbie's iconic racing number—53—was supposedly inspired by the uniform number of L.A. Dodgers Hall of Fame pitcher Don Drysdale. Three sequels and several remakes followed.

FREAKY FRIDAY (1977) directed by Gary Nelson

A cult classic, this film follows a mother and daughter who each think the other's life is too easy, and then magically have their bodies switched for a day. It didn't stay in theaters long, but gained a following in later years and is still considered a favorite among Disney fans, leading to two separate remakes, in 1995 and again in 2003.

HONORABLE MENTION

THE DEXTER RILEY TRILOGY

Kurt Russell stars as Dexter Riley—a popular yet mischievous Medfield College student—in this trio of hit films. Dexter's easygoing charm and group of loyal friends, who help him thwart the bad guys and escape the wrath of the dean, made these three films quite appealing to the younger audiences that Disney so desperately sought in the 1970s.

The Computer Wore Tennis Shoes (1969)

Now You See Him, Now You Don't (1972)

The Strongest Man in the World (1975)

DISNEY LIVE-ACTION NON-MUSICAL FILMS (MODERN)

HONEY, I SHRUNK THE KIDS (1989) directed by Joe Johnston

Because it was released the same summer as blockbusters like *Batman*, *Indiana Jones and the Last Crusade*, *Lethal Weapon 2*, *Star Trek V*, and James Cameron's *Abyss*, nobody expected much from this little Disney comedy about an inventor whose children are accidentally zapped down to miniature size. It actually made more money than most of those other films and spawned a franchise, leading to more movies, a TV show, and even a theme park attraction.

HOCUS POCUS (1993) directed by Kenny Ortega

This story of a trio of daffy yet sinister seventeenth-century sister witches who return from the dead to terrorize twentieth-century Salem, Massachusetts, was met with lukewarm audience and critical response in theaters in summer 1993. It grew more popular when it was released on video and played repeatedly on TV. It's now become a Halloween staple.

THE SANTA CLAUSE TRILOGY (1994, 2002, 2006) directed by John Pasquin and Michael Lembeck

There have been so many stories told about Santa Claus that it seems hard to find fresh ground. Disney did it, not once but three times, with its series of films starring Tim Allen as Scott Calvin, a divorced dad who accidentally knocks Santa off of his roof on Christmas Eve and has to permanently take over the jolly old elf's duties. The sequel saw Calvin searching for a Mrs. Claus while battling evil North Pole robots. The final part of the trilogy cast Jack Frost as Calvin's nemesis, tricking him into giving up the title of Santa. All three are now holiday classics, with Allen becoming the face and definition of Santa for a generation of kids.

Martin Short was Jack Frost to Tim Allen's Santa in *Santa Clause 3: The Escape Clause* (2006). (Walt Disney Pictures/Photofest)

FLUBBER (1997) directed by Les Mayfield

Robin Williams took a big risk with this remake of *The Absent-Minded Professor*. He needn't have worried, as the title green goo, animated by computers, became the star of this movie. Its success, and that of the previous year's *101 Dalmatians*, set the stage for a series of remakes of Disney classics, both live-action and animated, that continues to this day.

THE PRINCESS DIARIES (2001) directed by Garry Marshall

An interesting flip of the genre that made Disney famous, featuring a princess who doesn't know she's a princess. Even when she discovers the truth that she's the heir to the throne of a small European monarchy, Princess Mia is reluctant to give up her "normal" life in San Francisco. Followed by a sequel which was just as well received.

HOLES (2003) directed by Andrew Davis

Based on a best-selling children's book by Louis Sachar, this story of young boys forced—because of trouble with the law—to continually dig holes in the scorching heat, under the direction of a cruel warden and her inept staff, was a surprise hit. A catchy song from the film, "Dig It," became a radio mainstay.

PIRATES OF THE CARIBBEAN SERIES (2003 TO 2017) directed by Gore Verbinski and Rob Marshall

Five films in all have been made about the continuing adventures of Captain Jack Sparrow. This series defined the style of Disney live-action films for the beginning of the twenty-first century.

Pirate Jack Sparrow (Johnny Depp) is strung up in this outtake from *Pirates of the Caribbean: Dead Men Tell No Tales* (2017). (Walt Disney Studios Motion Pictures/Photofest)

ALICE IN WONDERLAND (2010) directed by Tim Burton

Tim Burton returned to Disney to direct his own adaptation of Lewis Carroll's trippy story of a proper British girl lured into a weird parallel world. While it shares many elements and costume designs with the animated classic, this new version used Burton's trademark visual style and CGI to bring the tale into new directions. Dazzling in scope, it was nominated for several Oscars.

MALEFICENT (2014) directed by Robert Stromberg

Angelina Jolie brings heart and sympathy to a character previously viewed only as a Disney villain. The film deepens Maleficent's backstory, making her more of a tragic hero than anything else. This was part of a second wave of Disney trying to find new ways to interpret old tales.

THE JUNGLE BOOK (2016) directed by Jon Favreau

Astonishing in its use of digital animation to make animals realistically talk, this film is so well done that you almost forget you are watching fake images. It's also pretty faithful to the animated classic's story line, character portrayals, and musical score.

Even after it became known for feature animation, Disney continued to produce shorts. At first, each was part of a series with one particular character, but Walt expanded that in 1929 with the creation of the *Silly Symphonies*, seventy-five films with no central character. These pictures were filler material, run either before or after the main film. Use of shorts in theaters faded by the 1960s, so production on them largely stopped at Disney. A lot of Disney's Academy Award wins came from shorts. Here are some of the best. (*Note:* I did not include any Pixar shorts, as many of them were made independently, before the company was fully acquired by Disney.)

NOTABLE DISNEY SHORTS

TOMMY TUCKER'S TOOTH (1922)

Made by Walt for a dentist in Kansas City, it was the first Disney educational film.

TROLLEY TROUBLES (1927)

The madcap first appearance in theaters of Oswald the Lucky Rabbit.

LONESOME GHOSTS (1937)

Mickey, Donald, and Goofy team up to bust ghosts. Developed use of transparent paint.

ADVENTURES IN MUSIC: MELODY (1953)

First ever 3-D cartoon. Professor Owl teaches a class about the importance of melody.

TOOT, WHISTLE, PLUNK AND BOOM (1953)

Academy Award winner about the history of musical instruments, hosted by Professor Owl.

IT'S TOUGH TO BE A BIRD (1969)

Another Oscar winner, using comedy to explain why birds are so important to life on Earth.

FRANKENWEENIE (1984)

Young animator Tim Burton's live-action tribute to Frankenstein. Remade into a feature film.

TUMMY TROUBLE (1989)

The first Disney animated short in decades. Roger Rabbit and Baby Herman cause chaos.

PAPERMAN (2012)

An Oscar winner. A young man searches for a lady with whom he had a quick connection.

FEAST (2014)

Silent film about a dog observing his master's love life. Yet another Academy Award winner.

SILLY SYMPHONIES SHORTS

SKELETON DANCE (1929)
A depiction of skeletons frolicking, directed by Walt Disney. The very first *Silly Symphonies* film.

THE UGLY DUCKLING (1931/1939)
The classic Hans Christian Andersen tale was made once in black-and-white, then again in color.

FLOWERS AND TREES (1932)
The very first color cartoon, a milestone in Hollywood history. It won Disney's first Oscar.

Flowers and Trees, one of Disney's classic Silly Symphonies from 1932. (Walt Disney Pictures/ Photofest)

THE THREE LITTLE PIGS (1933)

The resilient title characters and theme song in this Oscar winner lifted Depression-era spirits.

THE GRASSHOPPER AND THE ANTS (1934)

A cautionary fable. The lazy Grasshopper was voiced by Pinto Colvig, better known as Goofy.

THE TORTOISE AND THE HARE (1935)

Another fable, about being too overconfident. Also won the Academy Award for best cartoon.

THE THREE ORPHAN KITTENS (1935)

Disney's fourth Oscar in a row went to this cartoon about three kittens exploring a warm house.

THE COUNTRY COUSIN (1936)

This small-town mouse in a big-city tale marked five consecutive Academy Awards for Disney.

THE OLD MILL (1937)

A stormy night is the backdrop in this double Oscar winner. First use of the multiplane camera.

MOTHER GOOSE GOES HOLLYWOOD (1938)

One of the last *Silly Symphonies*, featuring caricatures of stars like W. C. Fields and Eddie Cantor.

MICKEY MOUSE SHORTS

PLANE CRAZY (1928)

Mickey as a pilot trying to impress Minnie. The first finished Mickey cartoon, but released third.

Plane Crazy (1928) featuring Mickey and Minnie Mouse. (Walt Disney Pictures/Photofest)

THE KARNIVAL KID (1929)

Features the first words ever spoken by Mickey ("Hot dog!")—voiced by Walt.

THE BAND CONCERT (1935)

Mickey's debut in color, as a bandleader dealing with a cyclone and a feisty Donald.

ORPHAN'S BENEFIT (1934/1941)

Goofy and Donald join Mickey and a few others to put on a show for kids. Remade in color.

THRU THE MIRROR (1936)

A fantastic and surreal dream of Mickey's, based on Alice's adventures in the looking glass.

BRAVE LITTLE TAILOR (1938)

The most expensive Mickey cartoon. He saves Minnie, and a medieval town, from a giant.

THE POINTER (1939)

The first film to show Freddie Moore's redesigned Mickey, on a hunting trip with Pluto.

THE NIFTY NINETIES (1941)

Walt's homage to the 1890s and 1900s, with Mickey and Minnie attending a vaudeville show.

MICKEY'S CHRISTMAS CAROL (1983)

A triumphant return to the big screen after thirty years for Mickey, in this Dickens adaptation.

GET A HORSE! (2013)

Thirty years after *Mickey's Christmas Carol*, another hit, featuring a madcap wagon ride.

While Pluto had his own series of forty-eight shorts released between 1937 and 1951, and Donald became a big star in his own right, a few of the films on the following lists were actually first released as Mickey Mouse shorts. They are noted by asterisks.

HONORABLE MENTION

MICKEY'S POLO TEAM (1936)
Walt loved playing polo, as reflected in this cartoon with Hollywood and Disney stars as players.

PLUTO SHORTS

THE MOOSE HUNT (1931)*

The first time Pluto was given a name. Mickey is chased by a moose. Pluto saves them both.

PLUTO'S JUDGEMENT DAY (1935)*

Mickey yells at Pluto for chasing kittens. Pluto has a nightmare of facing a jury of cats.

Title lead for *Pluto's Judgement Day* (1935). (Walt Disney Pictures/Photofest)

BONE TROUBLE (1940)

The bulldog Butch—Pluto's nemesis—chases him into a hall of mirrors, with comic results.

LEND A PAW (1941)

An Oscar winner. Pluto struggles with his conscience, in the forms of Angel and Devil Pluto.

PLUTO'S PLAYMATE (1941)

A baby seal tangles with Pluto on a visit to the beach. They eventually become friends.

PLUTO JUNIOR (1942)

A puppy with boundless energy disturbs a very tired Pluto as he tries to sleep.

PRIVATE PLUTO (1943)

The debuts of Chip and Dale, not yet named, as they pester Pluto, who is on army guard duty.

PLUTO'S HEART THROB (1950)

Pluto and Butch compete for the attention of Dinah, whom they are both sweet on. Pluto wins.

PLUTO'S PARTY (1952)*

Mickey's nephews prevent Pluto from enjoying his own birthday cake.

PLUTO'S CHRISTMAS TREE (1952)*

Pluto discovers Chip and Dale living in his Christmas tree and tries to get them out.

GOOFY SHORTS

GOOFY AND WILBUR (1939)
The very first Goofy cartoon. He goes on a fishing trip with his pet grasshopper, Wilbur.

Originally part of *The Reluctant Dragon* (1941), the Goofy episode *How to Ride a Horse* was released as a Disney short in 1950. (Walt Disney Pictures/Photofest)

HOW TO PLAY BASEBALL (1942)
Created specifically to be released in theaters with Samuel Goldwyn's tear-jerking baseball drama *Pride of the Yankees*, this short was the first in the series of Goofy's *How to . . .* films.

CALIFORNY ER BUST (1945)
A comical look at covered wagons heading west in the 1800s. Goofy again plays every part.

KNIGHT FOR A DAY (1946)
Goofy plays every single role in this takeoff on medieval jousting tournaments.

FATHERS ARE PEOPLE (1951)
The first film to show Goofy's struggles as a dad, which would be a big theme in later cartoons.

HOW TO BE A DETECTIVE (1952)

An unusual film noir cartoon, where Goofy plays Johnny Eyeball, private eye.

FATHER'S DAY OFF (1953)

When his wife heads out, Goofy tries doing housework, and nearly destroys the place.

GOOFY'S FREEWAY TROUBLES (1965)

As Stupidus Ultimus, Goofy shows drivers the dangers of being careless behind the wheel.

A GOOFY LOOK AT VALENTINE'S DAY (1983)

An educational film where Goofy explains the history of the February holiday.

HOW TO HOOK UP YOUR HOME THEATER (2007)

A modern day *How to . . .* made in honor of Goofy's seventy-fifth anniversary; nominated for an Oscar.

DONALD DUCK SHORTS

Donald Duck's star on the Hollywood Walk of Fame. (Wikimedia Commons/photo by Shaka)

DON DONALD (1937)*

The first appearance of Daisy Duck, then known as "Donna." Donald tries to woo her in Mexico.

DONALD'S NEPHEWS (1938)

Huey, Dewey, and Louie appear for the first time on-screen. They constantly prank Donald.

THE AUTOGRAPH HOUND (1939)

Donald sneaks onto a movie lot to get autographs, but the Hollywood stars all want his.

THE NEW SPIRIT (1942)

This Treasury Department film has Donald dutifully paying taxes, convincing many to follow.

DER FUEHRER'S FACE (1943)

An Oscar winner. Donald has a nightmare of life as a Nazi. The title song was a huge hit.

DONALD'S DOUBLE TROUBLE (1946)

Donald meets his smooth-voiced lookalike, and the doppelgänger falls in love with Daisy.

CHIP AN' DALE (1947)

Donald accidentally chops down Chip and Dale's treehouse, and they try to save it.

DONALD'S DREAM VOICE (1948)

Trying to get away from his grating quack, Donald takes pills to change it. Things go wrong fast.

TRICK OR TREAT (1952)

Donald plays Halloween pranks on his nephews, who team up with Witch Hazel to get back.

DONALD IN MATHMAGIC LAND (1959)

This short did the impossible. Donald made learning about math both entertaining and fun.

HONORABLE MENTION

WORKING FOR PEANUTS (1953)
Chip and Dale steal peanuts from zookeeper Donald's elephant. Filmed in 3-D, and later shown in 3-D theaters at both Disneyland and Walt Disney World.

TOUCHSTONE FILMS

SPLASH (1984) directed by Ron Howard

The very first Touchstone film, reinventing the mermaid mythology and setting it in New York City. It introduced Darryl Hannah to audiences and made Tom Hanks a bona fide movie star.

THE COLOR OF MONEY (1986) directed by Martin Scorsese

A sequel to 1961's *The Hustler*, with Tom Cruise as a pool-playing hotshot facing off against Paul Newman's Fast Eddie Felson from the earlier film. It won Newman his only Academy Award.

ADVENTURES IN BABYSITTING (1987) directed by Chris Columbus

Elisabeth Shue is a babysitter trying to keep her three charges safe on a crazy night in Chicago.

THREE MEN AND A BABY (1987) directed by Leonard Nimoy

One of Disney's biggest live-action hits ever, about three bachelors (Ted Danson, Steve Guttenberg, and Tom Selleck) trying to take care of a baby left at the door of their lavish Upper West Side NYC apartment. It spawned a sequel, with talk of a third film in the works.

GOOD MORNING, VIETNAM (1988) directed by Barry Levinson

Perfect casting of Robin Williams as an unconventional military radio host during wartime.

WHO FRAMED ROGER RABBIT (1988) directed by Robert Zemeckis

A Hollywood milestone, coproduced with Steven Spielberg. A mix of live action and animation, this tale of trouble in Toontown briefly brought two of the most famous cartoon characters (Mickey Mouse and Bugs Bunny) together on the big screen for the first time.

Who Framed Roger Rabbit skillfully combined live action with animation. (Touchstone Pictures/Photofest)

DEAD POETS SOCIETY (1989) directed by Peter Weir

Robin Williams plays mostly against his own type, as an inspirational teacher at a rigid prep school for boys. It won the Oscar for best screenplay and was a sleeper summer hit.

PRETTY WOMAN (1990) directed by Garry Marshall

The movie that rocketed Julia Roberts to superstardom. Audiences fell in love with this modern-day Cinderella story with a decidedly adult theme.

FATHER OF THE BRIDE (1991) directed by Charles Shyer

In this remake of the 1950 Spencer Tracy film, Steve Martin put his own spin on the role, starring opposite Diane Keaton. The sequel is just as beloved.

ED WOOD (1994) directed by Tim Burton

The true story of one of the most unusual directors to ever work in Hollywood. Johnny Depp plays the cross-dressing, offbeat Wood with charm and enthusiasm. It's some of Burton's best work, and earned Martin Landau the Oscar for his portrayal of Bela Lugosi.

HONORABLE MENTION

THE ERNEST COMEDIES (1987 TO 1991) directed by John Cherry III

Jim Varney's highly popular "Ernest" character was created in the early 1980s for local TV commercials. Disney took notice, creating a series of films featuring the hapless but good-natured handyman. Made on extremely low budgets, they took in a tidy profit for the studio. Varney, who died at the age of fifty in 2000, did other things for Disney, including appearances in the parks and on TV specials, as well as originating the role of Slinky Dog in the *Toy Story* films.

HOLLYWOOD PICTURES FILMS

ARACHNOPHOBIA (1990) directed by Frank Marshall

The first Hollywood Pictures film, a comic thriller about killer spiders invading a small town.

THE HAND THAT ROCKS THE CRADLE (1992) directed by Curtis Hanson

A hit film about a crazed nanny seeking revenge on the family by whom she's employed.

THE JOY LUCK CLUB (1993) directed by Wayne Wang

Four pairs of Chinese American mothers and daughters explore their family histories.

QUIZ SHOW (1994) directed by Robert Redford

An Oscar-nominated film, exploring the scandals surrounding TV quiz shows in the 1950s.

DANGEROUS MINDS (1995) directed by John N. Smith

Michelle Pfeiffer plays a former Marine turned teacher in a tough Los Angeles neighborhood trying to break through to her students in a school plagued by violence.

CRIMSON TIDE (1995) directed by Tony Scott

A blockbuster film, with Gene Hackman and Denzel Washington co-starring as naval commanders facing off in a battle for control of a nuclear submarine during a crisis.

THE ROCK (1996) directed by Michael Bay

Another blockbuster, this time with Nicolas Cage trying to stop rogue U.S. Army personnel from launching a deadly nerve gas attack on San Francisco from their base on Alcatraz Island.

MR. HOLLAND'S OPUS (1996) directed by Stephen Herek

In this tearjerker, with Richard Dreyfuss playing the title character, a small-town teacher with big dreams realizes at the end of a long career just how many lives he's impacted.

10 THINGS I HATE ABOUT YOU (1999) directed by Gil Junger

An adaptation of Shakespeare's *The Taming of the Shrew*, set in a high school.

THE SIXTH SENSE (1999) directed by M. Night Shyamalan

One of Disney's biggest hits ever. It was nominated for six Oscars, including Best Picture—a rarity for horror films. Hayley Joel Osment's line, "I see dead people," was ranked forty-fourth in the top hundred movie quotes of all time by the American Film Institute.

PIXAR FILMS

THE TOY STORY TRILOGY (1995, 1999, 2010) directed by John Lasseter and Lee Unkrich

The first Pixar feature film, made in conjunction with Disney, was *Toy Story*. It was groundbreaking, and it changed the way audiences perceived animation. Four years later, the sequel was released. It introduced the character of Jessie the Yodeling Cowgirl (voice of Joan Cusack), who had a heart-breaking, showstopping song, "When She Loved Me," about the loss a toy feels when it is abandoned by its owner. The third film in the trilogy reached the level of masterpiece, reducing audiences to tears as the toys realize that they are family, no matter what fate befalls them. It's one of only four animated films to be nominated for Best Picture. A fourth film in the series debuts in 2019.

MONSTERS, INC./MONSTERS UNIVERSITY (2001/2013) directed by Pete Docter/Dan Scanlon

Pixar turned the classic "scary monster in the closet" story upside down, telling it from the perspective of the monsters themselves. The two heroes, Mike (voice of Billy Crystal) and Sulley (voice of John Goodman), work together to save a human child who has accidentally wandered into their world of Monstropolis. In the process, they discover that there are better ways of doing the jobs they were trained for their whole lives. The sequel, *Monsters University*, was actually a prequel, taking place during Mike and Sulley's college years.

FINDING NEMO/FINDING DORY (2003/2016) directed by Andrew Stanton

The bond between a father and his son is the theme of *Finding Nemo*, which sees Marlin (voice of Albert Brooks) searching the ocean for his son, Nemo (voice of Alexander Gould), who was caught by an Australian dentist for the tank in his Sydney office. The breakout character was Dory (voice of Ellen DeGeneres), who accompanies Marlin on his quest. Dory was so popular that she became the focus of the sequel, *Finding Dory*, which was as big a success as the first film.

THE INCREDIBLES (2004) directed by Brad Bird

What would happen if superheroes weren't allowed to be super anymore, and had regular jobs and families, blending in with the rest of society? That is the interesting premise of this film, which sees Bob Parr, aka Mr. Incredible (voice of Craig T. Nelson), lead his superhero family and friends out of retirement to face off against a supervillain. A sequel was released in 2018.

THE CARS TRILOGY (2006, 2011, 2017) directed by John Lasseter, Brad Lewis, and Brian Fee

The California car culture that many of Pixar's staff experienced growing up was the inspiration for this series of hits about anthropomorphic cars living in a world without humans. The mythology of old Route 66 as it winds through small-town America, and how one should slow down a bit on the road of life to enjoy it, is the theme of the first film. The sequel went in an entirely different direction, more of a James Bond spy theme, and wasn't as well received by critics or fans. The third film went back to the roots while introducing a popular female rookie.

WALL-E (2008) directed by Andrew Stanton

A story told almost purely through visuals, with barely any dialogue until almost an hour into the movie. The title character is a robot who communicates only through electronic noises that sometimes sound like words. It was nominated for six Academy Awards.

UP (2009) directed by Pete Docter and Bob Peterson

The montage seen in the first fifteen minutes of *Up* is one of the most beautiful and touching ever to appear in a film—animated or otherwise. Grown men and women were reduced to tears. The rest of

Both heartbreaking and heart-warming, the Pixar animated film *Up* (2009) received five Academy Award nominations, including Best Picture. (Buena Vista Pictures/Photofest)

the film, about a senior citizen trying to honor his wife's dreams and the young boy who accompanies him on that quest, are just as delightful. This was only the second animated film in history –after *Beauty and the Beast*–to be nominated for Best Picture.

BRAVE (2012) directed by Mark Andrews, Brenda Chapman, and Steve Purcell

Brave—a tale of a princess in medieval Scotland who dreams of being a great warrior and leader, instead of just a figurehead married off to some prince—was a change of pace for Disney and for Pixar, which had never made a film set entirely in the distant past.

INSIDE OUT (2015) drected by Pete Docter and Ronnie Del Carmen

An animated look into the brain of a preteen girl as she struggles with a big change in her family's life. Emotions work in tandem and apart to help the girl navigate the inner turbulence and help her sort out her feelings. It's an interesting mix of scenes set in the real world, in the protagonist's mind, and through her eyes in a first-person perspective. It made close to a billion dollars for Disney.

COCO (2017) directed by Lee Unkrich and Adrian Molina

The animators spent years in Mexico, trying to get the look and feel of the country just right for this tale of a young boy who crosses over to the spirit world on the festive Day of the Dead and encounters his ancestors. Their work shows, as this is one of the most beautiful and colorful Disney/Pixar films ever made, with a resonance that goes far beyond what the plot suggests.

LIVE-ACTION WESTERNS

WESTWARD HO THE WAGONS! (1956) directed by William Beaudine

Walt Disney's first live-action western, featuring Fess Parker (TV's Davy Crockett) and some of the Mouseketeers as part of a group of pioneers crossing the dangerous Oregon Trail in 1844.

TONKA (1958) directed by Lewis R. Foster

The tale of a wild stallion, Tonka, who is tamed by a young Native American boy, taken by the U.S. Cavalry to ride for them in the Battle of the Little Bighorn, and then reunited with his master.

THE ADVENTURES OF BULLWHIP GRIFFIN (1967) directed by James Neilson

A stuffy British butler (Roddy McDowall) is mistaken for a rowdy boxer in this western comedy.

SCANDALOUS JOHN (1971) directed by Robert Butler

A modern rancher who fancies himself a cowboy hero goes on one last cattle drive with his portly Mexican companion to stop a greedy land tycoon. Loosely based on *Don Quixote*.

THE APPLE DUMPLING GANG (1975) directed by Norman Tokar

The most famous Disney western, a comedy about a card sharp (Bill Bixby) in 1879 California who wins three young orphans in a poker game. He tries desperately to pawn them off on others, until the kids discover gold and he has to protect them from everyone in town who has taken a sudden interest in adopting them. Two bumbling crooks and an evil gunslinger and his gang round out the story. It was so popular that a sequel and a TV series followed.

HOT LEAD & COLD FEET (1978) directed by Robert Butler

Twin brothers battle in a madcap romp for ownership of an Old West town their father built.

TOMBSTONE (1993) directed by George P. Cosmatos (a Hollywood Pictures Film)

Kurt Russell as Wyatt Earp and Val Kilmer as Doc Holliday bring this classic western tale, chronicling the events leading up to the infamous gunfight at the OK Corral, to new life.

TALL TALE (1995) directed by Jeremiah Chechik

A young twentieth-century boy trying to save his family's frontier farm calls to life three legendary Old West characters to help him—Pecos Bill, John Henry, and Paul Bunyan.

SHANGHAI NOON (2000) directed by Tom Dey (a Touchstone Film)

A "fish out of water" tale of a Chinese visitor (Jackie Chan) on a rescue mission in 1890s Nevada to save a princess, partnering with a local cowboy (Owen Wilson) to battle gunslingers.

THE LONE RANGER (2013) directed by Gore Verbinski

A big-budget retelling of the classic western pulp series about a lawman with a secret identity, as seen through the perspective of Johnny Depp's Tonto. In honor of Walt, it had some of the most amazing railroad chase scenes ever put on-screen.

HONORABLE MENTION

THE ALAMO (2004) directed by John Lee Hancock (a Touchstone Film)

One of the most expensive movies ever made. A gigantic fifty-one-acre set was built in Austin, Texas, to re-create San Antonio's doomed Alamo mission as it looked in 1836, when men like Davy Crockett, Jim Bowie, and William Travis fought valiantly to defend it against Mexican general Santa Anna's overwhelming forces. With this beautifully made and well-acted and well-directed film, Disney had hopes for a blockbuster like *Titanic*, but *The Alamo* made back less than a quarter of its monstrous budget.

LIVE-ACTION SCI-FI/FANTASY FILMS

MOON PILOT (1962) directed by James Neilson

An alien girl falls in love with a U.S. astronaut in Disney's first outer space feature film.

ESCAPE TO WITCH MOUNTAIN (1975) directed by John Hough

Two alien orphans with incredible psychic powers flee the clutches of an evil tycoon.

THE CAT FROM OUTER SPACE (1978) directed by Norman Tokar

An extraterrestrial feline has to repair his spacecraft before the military captures him.

THE BLACK HOLE (1979) directed by Gary Nelson

Disney's ambitious answer to *Star Wars*. This story of a stranded spaceship crew tangling with a madman bent on taking them through a black hole earned the first PG rating for the studio.

TRON (1982) directed by Steven Lisberger

With its revolutionary use of computer animation in a live-action film, *TRON* was ahead of its time. It didn't do as well as Disney had hoped in theaters, but the video games that were produced based on the plot—where a programmer gets trapped inside his own game—and the home video release, helped it find a dedicated fan base that demanded, and got, a sequel decades later. It revitalized the franchise, with a TV show and theme park attractions.

FLIGHT OF THE NAVIGATOR (1986) directed by Randal Kleiser

A young Florida boy disappears for eight years and returns to find that everyone but him has aged. He then discovers that he was chosen to help an alien navigate his spacecraft.

THE CHRONICLES OF NARNIA: THE LION, THE WITCH AND THE WARDROBE (2005) directed by Andrew Adamson

Based on the beloved novel by C. S. Lewis, this film about four children who enter a portal from their closet to another realm was once Disney's biggest live-action box office hit.

THE SORCERER'S APPRENTICE (2010) directed by Jon Turteltaub

Nicolas Cage stars as a benevolent and reclusive wizard who has to save New York City—and the world—from an evil sorcerer. He recruits a young apprentice to help him. Based very loosely on the famous Mickey Mouse short from *Fantasia*.

TOMORROWLAND (2015) directed by Brad Bird

One of the best parts of this film—about a young girl who happens upon a pin that transports her to a different world built by optimistic futurists—is the faithful re-creation of the 1964 World's Fair and, especially, the It's a Small World ride.

STAR WARS: THE FORCE AWAKENS (2015) directed by J. J. Abrams

Fans were skeptical when, shortly after its purchase of Lucasfilm, Disney announced plans to move ahead with episodes 7, 8, and 9 of the Skywalker saga. Those doubts were quelled when the movie premiered and was a critical and commercial darling. The story of the next generation of a galaxy far, far away—with appearances by favorites like Luke, Leia, and Han—helped turn *The Force Awakens* into the highest-grossing film in Hollywood history.

HONORABLE MENTION

SIGNS (2002) directed by M. Night Shyamalan (a Touchstone Film)
Crop circles and mysterious alien figures made this creepy thriller another hit for Shyamalan.

LIVE-ACTION ADVENTURE/ SUPERHERO FILMS

CONDORMAN (1981) directed by Charles Jarrott

A worthy entry into the comic book genre, this mostly forgotten Disney film stars Michael Crawford as the title character, a comic book artist and inventor who gets mixed up with spies and has to pretend to be a superhero. Filmed all over Europe, with beautiful cinematography, cool cars, and incredible gadgets.

DICK TRACY (1990) directed by Warren Beatty (a Touchstone Film)

Winner of three Academy Awards (for makeup, set design, and best song), this adaptation of Chester Gould's classic Depression-era comic strip about a straitlaced detective in a world full of colorful goons is one of the most dazzling films you'll ever see. Director and star Warren Beatty used a bright primary color scheme to evoke the look of comic books.

THE ROCKETEER (1991) directed by Joe Johnston

Set in 1938, this film follows the adventures of a young pilot in Hollywood who stumbles upon an experimental rocket pack and helmet, giving him the look of a superhero as he fights off Nazis and saboteurs. A cult classic; there's been talk of a remake and/or TV show.

ARMAGEDDON (1998) directed by Michael Bay (a Touchstone Film)

A ragtag crew of drillers are trained as astronauts and tasked with saving Earth from the approach of a rogue asteroid in this mega-blockbuster made with the cooperation of NASA.

UNBREAKABLE (2000) directed by M. Night Shyamalan (a Touchstone Film)

Bruce Willis, who starred in two of the biggest Disney hits of all time (*Armageddon* and *The Sixth Sense*), returns for this film, about an ordinary man who discovers he has superpowers.

NATIONAL TREASURE (2004) directed by Jon Turteltaub

Billed as "Indiana Jones meets the Smithsonian," this film stars Nicolas Cage as an American historian on the trail of a treasure map hidden on the back of the Declaration of Independence. It was filmed at many real-life American historical sites, like Independence Hall and Trinity Church.

SKY HIGH (2005) directed by Mike Mitchell (a Touchstone Film)

What would happen if there was a high school just for superheroes? This film answers that question, mixing comedy and action. Lynda Carter (TV's Wonder Woman) plays the principal.

UNDERDOG (2007) directed by Frederik Du Chau

A live-action version of the classic 1960s cartoon about a dog with superpowers battling a mad scientist. Jason Lee provides the voice of Underdog.

G-FORCE (2009) directed by Hoyt Yeatman

The government breeds and trains lab animals as an elite force of spies, and mayhem ensues.

THE AVENGERS (2012) directed by Joss Whedon

The biggest comic book franchise of all time, with iconic characters like Iron Man, Captain America, the Hulk, Black Widow, Hawkeye, and Thor teaming up to battle extraterrestrial forces and save Earth. Released shortly after Disney acquired Marvel, it's just one part of a universe of connected films released over a decade, culminating in the two-part "Infinity Wars" films of 2018 and 2019.

HONORABLE MENTION

GUARDIANS OF THE GALAXY (2014) directed by James Gunn

Another Marvel film that could just as easily have been placed on the list of sci-fi films. This comic romp has a more refreshing, freewheeling feel than most epic superhero films. It introduced audiences to a diverse and interesting band of characters: a trash-talking raccoon with lots of firepower, a scavenger orphan from Earth who fancies himself a hero, a hulking alien criminal, a green-skinned bounty hunter, and a sentient tree who knows only three words. Though they appeared in comics long before Disney took over Marvel, their prior obscurity to most moviegoers makes the Guardians feel like all-new characters.

LIVE-ACTION SPORTS FILMS

THE WORLD'S GREATEST ATHLETE (1973) directed by Robert Scheerer

Disney's first pure sports movie, a "fish out of water" slapstick comedy about a missionary's kid from Africa being recruited to compete in NCAA decathlon events in Los Angeles.

GUS (1976) directed by Vincent McEveety

A Yugoslavian mule with incredible place-kicking ability is hired and brought to the United States with his owner to play pro football for the hapless California Atoms.

THE MIGHTY DUCKS (1992) directed by Stephen Herek

Minnesota is the icy location for this film about a former hockey-playing star who is roped into coaching a diverse team of raw young players. He turns them into champions, and they learn a few lessons about life along the way. It was such a big hit that it inspired several sequels, a TV series, and Disney's 1993 entry into the NHL with a real-life pro team called the Mighty Ducks.

COOL RUNNINGS (1993) directed by Jon Turteltaub

Inspired by the actual Jamaican bobsled team that competed in the 1988 Winter Olympics, this film is both comical and inspirational.

ANGELS IN THE OUTFIELD (1994) directed by William Dear

A remake of a 1951 film about a last-place pro baseball team that receives help from an unlikely heavenly source. Like *The Mighty Ducks*, this movie also started Disney's association with a real-life team, Major League Baseball's California Angels. Disney purchased 25 percent of the team, its neighbor in Anaheim, one year after this film's release.

REMEMBER THE TITANS (2000) directed by Boaz Yakin

High school football is the focus of this film, dealing with the integration of a team in Alexandria, Virginia, in the 1970s. It's a film that transcends sports, with its strong messages of tolerance, perseverance, and inclusion.

THE ROOKIE (2002) directed by John Lee Hancock

Based on the true story of a former minor league baseball pitcher turned teacher in Texas, who is convinced by his students to try out for the majors a second time.

MIRACLE (2004) directed by Gavin O'Connor

One of the most famous moments in American sports was the upset win of the United States Olympic hockey team over the Soviet Union in the 1980 Winter Olympics in Lake Placid, New York. This film captures all of the spirit and exuberance of that night, and the events and training leading up to it. Kurt Russell turns in a phenomenal performance as coach Herb Brooks.

THE GREATEST GAME EVER PLAYED (2005) directed by Bill Paxton (a Touchstone Film)

Set in 1913, this movie relives the true story of twenty-year-old Francis Ouimet (Shia LaBeouf)—a former golf caddy who shocked the world by winning the U.S. Open.

SECRETARIAT (2010) directed by Randall Wallace

Legendary 1973 Triple Crown–winning horse Secretariat gets his own biopic, which focuses mostly on his owner, Penny Chenery (Diane Lane), who didn't have much racing experience.

HONORABLE MENTION

AIR BUD (1997) directed by Charles Martin Smith
The first entry into a highly successful series of sports-themed films and spin-offs for Disney, it's the story of a golden retriever dog with remarkable basketball shooting abilities who inspires a small-town school's team to reach the state finals.

LIVE-ACTION NATURE FILMS

In 1948, Walt took a calculated risk by releasing the first of his *True-Life Adventures* films, featuring footage shot in the wild. It paid off, with Oscar-winning results and big box office receipts. Disney has been making nature films ever since. Here are some of the best.

SEAL ISLAND (1948) directed by James Algar

The first in the *True-Life Adventures* series, a fascinating short film about the daily habits of Alaskan seals. It won the Academy Award for Best Documentary.

THE LIVING DESERT (1953) directed by James Algar

The first feature-length *True-Life Adventures* film, chronicling the day-to-day life of the many creatures who reside in the arid desert climates of the world. An Oscar winner.

Disney's nature documentary *The Living Desert* (1953) won the Academy Award for Best Documentary Feature. (Buena Vista Pictures/Photofest)

BEAR COUNTRY (1953) directed by James Algar

Yet another Academy Award winner, this short film chronicles the life cycles of American bears.

PERRI (1957) directed by N. Paul Kenworthy Jr. and Ralph Wright

Walt's weirdest live-action nature film, based on a story by Felix Salten, the author of *Bambi*. While it uses scenes shot in the wild, the footage was edited and manipulated to tell a scripted story about a brave squirrel who protects his home from predators and falls in love.

THE VANISHING PRAIRIE (1954) directed by James Algar

A conservation film about the animals who once populated America's Great Plains in large numbers but whose populations were quickly dwindling. An Oscar winner.

THE AFRICAN LION (1955) directed by James Algar

Three years of filming on location in Africa went into making this feature-length documentary about the "King of the Beasts." It was such an influential film that the animators and creators of *The Lion King* often cite it as one they turned to when looking for ideas.

WHITE WILDERNESS (1958) directed by James Algar

Earth's most frigid arctic climates were endured for three years by the filmmakers for this feature-length, Oscar-winning chronicle of natural life among the frozen oceans and snowcaps.

THE INCREDIBLE JOURNEY (1963) directed by Fletcher Markle

Not a pure nature film like the others, this movie actually has human actors in it. It's the story of two dogs and a cat who travel 200 miles across Canada together looking for their owners. Remade by Disney in the 1990s.

NEVER CRY WOLF (1983) directed by Carol Ballard

Charles Martin Smith plays an intrepid scientist sent into the frozen tundra by the Canadian government to study a pack of wolves that seem to be killing off the caribou there. During the course of his work, he bonds with the innocent wolves and becomes part of their pack.

EARTH (2009) directed by Alastair Fothergill and Mark Linfield

Disney returned to making nature documentaries in a big way, with this first in its new series of Disneynature films. This was the most expensive documentary of all time, costing more than forty million dollars and taking more than four thousand days to shoot. Unlike in all of Walt's earlier documentaries, most of the footage was captured remotely from the air so as not to disturb the wildlife while filming.

LIVE-ACTION MUSICALS (CLASSIC)

SONG OF THE SOUTH (1946) directed by Wilfred Jackson and Harve Foster

A true Disney classic that has been taken out of circulation, *Song of the South* was Walt's first major attempt at a live-action film. He did rely on some animated sequences to bridge the story of Uncle Remus, who delights children with the fables of Br'er Rabbit, Br'er Bear, and Br'er Fox. The score was nominated for an Oscar, with "Zip-a-Dee-Doo-Dah" winning for Best Song. This film inspired one of Disney's most beloved theme park attractions, Splash Mountain.

SO DEAR TO MY HEART (1948) directed by Ham Luske and Harold Schuster

Another mix of live action and animation, it's the story of a young boy who adopts a little black lamb and trains it to win a prize at the county fair. Said to be one of Walt's favorite films, it evokes the era he loved best. Burl Ives sings the song "Lavender Blue (Dilly Dilly)," which became a popular radio hit and was nominated for an Oscar.

BABES IN TOYLAND (1961) directed by Jack Donohue

Annette Funicello stars in Walt's first attempt at a big-budget live-action fairy tale musical, an adaptation of Victor Herbert's classic operetta about Mother Goose and her Story Book Village characters facing off against the evil Barnaby (played by a cast-against-type Ray Bolger). The oversized toy soldiers from this film are still featured in Disney's Christmas parades.

SUMMER MAGIC (1963) directed by James Neilson

The Sherman Brothers wrote the songs for this intimate musical, featuring Hayley Mills and Dorothy McGuire, about a family struggling to live in small-town New England in the early years of the twentieth century. Burl Ives has the distinction in this film of having both *the* most unusual Disney character name (Osh Popham) and featured song ("The Ugly Bug Ball").

MARY POPPINS (1964) directed by Robert Stevenson

Walt's ultimate triumph, utilizing everything he and his studio staff had learned in forty years of filmmaking, both animated and live action. It was nominated for an astonishing thirteen Oscars, winning five of them, two for the catchy music composed by the Sherman Brothers. It remains one of the most memorable musicals ever produced by any studio in Hollywood.

Considered to be Disney's greatest live-action film, *Mary Poppins* (1964) won five Academy Awards, including Best Actress for Julie Andrews. (Walt Disney Pictures/Photofest)

THE HAPPIEST MILLIONAIRE (1967) directed by Norman Tokar

It's hard to follow an instant classic like Mary Poppins, but this was the job given to star Fred Mac-Murray with this film about an eccentric, wealthy Philadelphia family and their Irish immigrant butler. Almost three hours long, it featured twelve Sherman Brothers songs, but it didn't capture the public's imagination like *Poppins* did and was a box office dud.

THE ONE AND ONLY, GENUINE, ORIGINAL FAMILY BAND (1968) directed by Michael O'Herlihy

An all-star cast (Walter Brennan, Buddy Ebsen, Lesley Ann Warren, John Davidson, Wally Cox, Kurt Russell, and Goldie Hawn, in her first feature film) was the main draw of this Sherman Brothers musical about the 1888 U.S. presidential election, and a family divided by it.

BEDKNOBS AND BROOMSTICKS (1971) directed by Robert Stevenson

A return to the award-winning mix of live action and animation. This film, about children seeking refuge in the British countryside during the Nazi air raids of London who meet a witch and an eccentric professor and go with them on an adventure to a fantasy world, reunited much of the crew from *Mary Poppins*, including the Sherman Brothers, co-star David Tomlinson, and director Stevenson. An Oscar winner for special effects, it's since become a Disney fan favorite, but didn't do well in theaters when first released.

PETE'S DRAGON (1977) directed by Don Chaffey

An orphan with a mysterious, sometimes invisible dragon as his best friend has adventures in a small Maine seaport village in this fun, slapstick romp, whose musical score by Al Kasha and Joel Hirschhorn was nominated for two Academy Awards. Singer Helen Reddy made her movie debut in this film, which was another box office disappointment for Disney.

BEACHES (1988) directed by Garry Marshall (a Touchstone Film)

Two girls meet on an Atlantic City beach and continue a friendship that sees them through all life's joys and disappointments. A true tearjerker, it is a showcase for the talents of its star, Bette Midler, who sings most of the songs in the film. The song "Wind beneath My Wings" became a number one hit all over the world and is still a sentimental favorite.

LIVE-ACTION MUSICALS (MODERN)

NEWSIES (1992) directed by Kenny Ortega

Alan Menken, along with Jack Feldman, provided the songs for this tale of New York City newsboys in the early twentieth century who stage a strike. A young Christian Bale starred. It later became a hit Broadway show.

THE MUPPET CHRISTMAS CAROL (1992) directed by Brian Henson

Another version of the holiday classic, with Sir Michael Caine (playing it straight) as Scrooge, Kermit as Bob Cratchit, and Gonzo as Charles Dickens. Music and lyrics by Paul Williams.

SISTER ACT (1992) directed by Emile Ardolino (a Touchstone Film)

Whoopi Goldberg stars as a lounge singer who disguises herself as a nun to escape a band of criminals. It used secular pop music mixed with traditional church hymns to great effect. A sequel and a Broadway show came from this box office hit.

EVITA (1996) directed by Alan Parker (a Hollywood Pictures Film)

Sir Andrew Lloyd Weber and Tim Rice's theatrical hit took decades to make it to the big screen. This version, starring Madonna in the title role of an Argentinian pauper who became a political powerhouse, won the Oscar for Best Song, "You Must Love Me."

O BROTHER, WHERE ART THOU? (2000) directed by Joel and Ethan Coen (a Touchstone Film)

A Cajun-flavored, bluegrass-tinged version of Homer's *Odyssey* set in the Depression-era Deep South. The fictional protagonists of this film—the Soggy Bottom Boys—had an album taken from the soundtrack that won five Grammys, including Album of the Year.

STEP UP (2006) directed by Anne Fletcher (a Buena Vista Release)

A troublemaker is sent to a school for the arts and discovers that he has a talent for dance.

ENCHANTED (2007) directed by Kevin Lima

A traditional animated Disney princess enters the very real world of New York City and charms everyone she meets, often getting them to break into song. Alan Menken and Stephen Schwartz were responsible for the score.

THE MUPPETS (2011) directed by James Bobin

The tune "Man or Muppet" from this film, a throwback to the classic madcap Muppet style of the 1970s and '80s movies, won the Oscar for Best Song.

INTO THE WOODS (2014) directed by Rob Marshall

The deeper, darker, and more mature thematic elements of Broadway legend Stephen Sondheim's work seem like an odd choice for Disney. Since this musical is about classic fairy tale characters interacting with each other in the woods, with a cast including Meryl Streep and Johnny Depp, it was indeed produced by Disney. The reception was split, with diehard Disney fans either loving or loathing it.

BEAUTY AND THE BEAST (2017) directed by Bill Condon

The 1991 animated version of this story is perfect from beginning to end, so remaking it in live action meant risking negative reaction from devoted fans. They definitely passed the test, with a film that seems original, even though we already know the plot and outcome. Emma Watson and Dan Stevens are outstanding in the title roles, while Luke Evans and Josh Gad steal every scene they are in as the vain villain Gaston and his conflicted companion LeFou.

SONGS FROM DISNEY FILMS (CLASSIC)

"WHO'S AFRAID OF THE BIG BAD WOLF?" (1933)— The Three Little Pigs

Music and lyrics by Frank Churchill.

"HEIGH-HO" (1937)—Snow White and the Seven Dwarfs

Music and lyrics by Frank Churchill and Larry Morey.

"WHEN YOU WISH UPON A STAR" (1940)—Pinocchio

Music and lyrics by Leigh Harline and Ned Washington.

"ZIP-A-DEE-DOO-DAH" (1946)—Song of the South
Music and lyrics by Allie Wrubel and Ray Gilbert.

"BIBBIDI-BOBBIDI-BOO" (1950)—Cinderella
Music and lyrics by Jerry Livingston, Mack David, and Al Hoffman.

"YOU CAN FLY! YOU CAN FLY! YOU CAN FLY!" (1953)—Peter Pan
Music and lyrics by Sammy Fain and Sammy Cahn.

"CRUELLA DE VIL" (1961)—101 Dalmatians
Music and lyrics by Mel Leven.

"CHIM CHIM CHER-EE" (1964)—Mary Poppins
Music and lyrics by Richard and Robert Sherman.

"WINNIE THE POOH" (1966)—Winnie the Pooh and the Honey Tree
Music and lyrics by Richard and Robert Sherman.

"THE BARE NECESSITIES" (1967)—The Jungle Book
Music and lyrics by Terry Gilkyson.

HONORABLE MENTION

"THE LORD IS GOOD TO ME" (1948)—Melody Time
Music and lyrics by Kim Gannon and Walter Kent.
The rare secular song from a movie that became a Sunday standard in many churches.

SPECIAL MENTION

"FEED THE BIRDS" (1964)—Mary Poppins
Music and lyrics by Richard and Robert Sherman.
According to Richard Sherman, this was Walt's sentimental favorite among all the Disney songs.

SONGS FROM DISNEY FILMS (MODERN)

"UNDER THE SEA" (1989)—The Little Mermaid
Music and lyrics by Alan Menken and Howard Ashman.

"BE OUR GUEST" (1991)—Beauty and the Beast
Music and lyrics by Alan Menken and Howard Ashman.

"A FRIEND LIKE ME" (1992)—Aladdin
Music and lyrics by Alan Menken and Howard Ashman.

"WHAT'S THIS?" (1993)—The Nightmare before Christmas
Music and lyrics by Danny Elfman.

"THE CIRCLE OF LIFE" (1994)—The Lion King
Music and lyrics by Elton John.

"YOU'VE GOT A FRIEND IN ME" (1995)—Toy Story
Music and lyrics by Randy Newman.

"COLORS OF THE WIND" (1995)—Pocahontas
Music and lyrics by Stephen Schwartz and Alan Menken.

"IF I DIDN'T HAVE YOU" (2001)—Monsters, Inc.
Music and lyrics by Randy Newman.

"LET IT GO" (2013)—Frozen
Music and lyrics by Robert and Kristen Lopez.

"YOU'RE WELCOME" (2016)—Moana
Music and lyrics by Lin-Manuel Miranda.

HONORABLE MENTION

"REFLECTION" (1998)—Mulan
Music and lyrics by Matthew Wilder and David Zippel.
The version on the soundtrack sung by former Mouseketeer Christina Aguilera, who was seventeen at the time, became an international hit and led to her successful recording career.

LOVE SONGS FROM DISNEY FILMS (CLASSIC)

"I'M WISHING" (1937)—Snow White and the Seven Dwarfs
Music and lyrics by Frank Churchill and Larry Morey.

"BABY MINE" (1941)—Dumbo
Music and lyrics by Frank Churchill and Ned Washington.

"LOVE IS A SONG" (1942)—Bambi
Music and lyrics by Frank Churchill and Larry Morey.

"YOU BELONG TO MY HEART" (1944)—The Three Caballeros
Music and lyrics by Ray Gilbert and Agustin Lara.

"TOO GOOD TO BE TRUE" (1947)—Fun and Fancy Free
Music and lyrics by Buddy Kaye and Eliot Daniel.

"SO THIS IS LOVE" (1950)—Cinderella
Music and lyrics by Jerry Livingston, Mack David, and Al Hoffman.

"BELLA NOTTE" (1955)—Lady and the Tramp
Music and lyrics by Peggy Lee and Sonny Burke.

"ONCE UPON A DREAM" (1959)—Sleeping Beauty
Music and lyrics by Sammy Fain (based on Tchaikovsky's theme) and Jack Lawrence.

"LOVE" (1973)—Robin Hood
Music and lyrics by George Edward Bruns and Floyd Huddleston.

"CANDLE ON THE WATER" (1977)—Pete's Dragon
Music and lyrics by Joel Hirschhorn and Al Kasha.

HONORABLE MENTION

"(LOVE IS) a Most Befuddling Thing" (1963)—The Sword in the Stone
Music and lyrics by Richard and Robert Sherman.
    Not your typical love song, as Merlin tries to explain all of the mysterious qualities of love.

LOVE SONGS FROM DISNEY FILMS (MODERN)

"KISS THE GIRL" (1989)—The Little Mermaid
Music and lyrics by Howard Ashman and Alan Menken.

"BEAUTY AND THE BEAST" (1991)—Beauty and the Beast
Music and lyrics by Howard Ashman and Alan Menken.

"A WHOLE NEW WORLD" (1992)—Aladdin
Music and lyrics by Howard Ashman and Alan Menken.

"CAN YOU FEEL THE LOVE TONIGHT?" (1994)—The Lion King
Music and lyrics by Elton John.

"I WON'T SAY I'M IN LOVE" (1997)—Hercules
Music and lyrics by David Zippel and Alan Menken.

"YOU'LL BE IN MY HEART" (1999)—Tarzan
Music and lyrics by Phil Collins.

"MA BELLE EVANGELINE" (2009)—The Princess and the Frog
Music and lyrics by Randy Newman.

"I SEE THE LIGHT" (2010)—Tangled
Music and lyrics by Glen Slater and Alan Menken.

"LOVE IS AN OPEN DOOR" (2013)—Frozen
Music and lyrics by Robert and Kristen Lopez.

"REMEMBER ME" (2017)—Coco
Music and lyrics by Robert and Kristen Lopez.

HONORABLE MENTION

"THAT'S HOW YOU KNOW" (2007)—Enchanted
Music and lyrics by Stephen Schwartz.
A live-action musical romp through Central Park, with Amy Adams and friends blending classical, calypso, jazz, Broadway show tunes, and other styles.

GREATEST SOUNDTRACKS

SNOW WHITE AND THE SEVEN DWARFS (1937)
This was the first time that songs from a movie were released together on a record album. Every single one of these tunes, by Frank Churchill and Larry Morey, written in the style of operetta popular at the time, went to number one on radio's Your Hit Parade.

PINOCCHIO (1940)
In another winner for Disney, Leigh Harline and Ned Washington mixed classical style with pop sounds to enduring effect. This was also the first time that the word "soundtrack" was officially used to describe an album full of songs from a movie.

CINDERELLA (1950)
For his postwar return to the princess films that made Disney great, Walt hired outside help. It was the team of Tin Pan Alley songwriters Mack David, Jerry Livingston, and Al Hoffman who gave Cinderella a more modern and less operatic feel.

ALICE IN WONDERLAND (1951)
With thirty songs, *Alice in Wonderland* still holds the record for most tunes in a Disney animated film. The majority of them, written by Bob Hillard, Sammy Fain, Mack David, Jerry Livingston, and Al Hoffman, are included on this jazzy and psychedelic soundtrack.

MARY POPPINS (1964)
This masterpiece by the Sherman Brothers successfully mixes a variety of song styles, from British music hall to nonsense patter. There's not a clunker in there. The song "Let's Go Fly a Kite" provides the best musical conclusion to any Disney film. In addition to winning two Oscars and a Grammy, the soundtrack spent fourteen weeks at number one on the *Billboard* charts.

THE LITTLE MERMAID (1989)
One of the biggest-selling soundtrack albums of all time, this Oscar- and Grammy-winning collaboration between Alan Menken and Howard Ashman gave each character a unique orchestral sound and several hit songs. It has gone platinum seven times.

BEAUTY AND THE BEAST (1991)
Ashman and Menken did it again, with this Oscar-winning score where every single song serves a purpose. There's no filler. A single from this album, a version of the title song by Peabo Bryson and Celine Dion, was a huge hit and won a Grammy. In addition, *Beauty and the Beast* remains the only animated movie soundtrack to be nominated for Best Album at the Grammys.

THE LION KING (1994)

Still the best-selling soundtrack to an animated film (ten times platinum) ever, this Oscar- and Grammy-winning score by Elton John, Tim Rice, and Hans Zimmer brought pop music together with African rhythms and created a sound that's unforgettable.

TARZAN (1999)

Pop star Phil Collins had been out of the spotlight for a few years. This soundtrack album put him back on top. It's one of the few Disney films where most of the songs are sung not by the characters in the film, but about them by a narrator (Collins). "You'll Be in My Heart" won the Oscar for Best Song. The album itself—with an appearance by NSYNC—won a Grammy.

FROZEN (2014)

This Kristen and Robert Lopez score—featuring the monster hit "Let It Go"—was an Oscar and Grammy winner, but also accomplished something that no Disney soundtrack album since *Mary Poppins* had done. It was named *Billboard*'s number one album of the year.

HONORABLE MENTION

GUARDIANS OF THE GALAXY (2014)

The second-best-selling album of 2014, behind only *Frozen*. *Guardians* isn't filled with songs sung by the characters. Rather, it's a re-creation of a compilation mixtape of 1970s and '80s classics. In the movie, Peter Quill's mother makes the mixtape for him just before her death. This album topped the *Billboard* charts for eleven weeks. It also reached number one, the first time that had happened for a soundtrack album filled with previously released songs.

UNDERRATED DISNEY FILMS

THE STORY OF ROBIN HOOD AND HIS MERRIE MEN (1952) directed by Ken Annakin

Overshadowed by the 1973 animated version, this film—with Richard Todd in the title role of the legendary British outlaw—was Walt's second live-action feature film.

JOHNNY TREMAIN (1957) directed by Robert Stevenson

A character who should be better known to young Disney fans, Johnny (Hal Stalmaster) is a silversmith's apprentice, teenager, and patriot in Boston who gets caught up in the dramatic events that lead to the Revolutionary War.

TOBY TYLER, OR TEN WEEKS WITH A CIRCUS (1960) directed by Charles Barton

Kevin Corcoran is the star of this film about an orphan who runs away to join the circus. It's an excellent peek into the daily lives of circus performers as they traveled the country by rail, setting up their tents in small towns along the way.

FOLLOW ME, BOYS! (1966) directed by Norman Tokar

A love letter to the Boy Scouts of America. Fred MacMurray stars as a man with ambitions of being a traveling musician who winds up settling in a small town and becoming its beloved scoutmaster. Kurt Russell made his big-screen debut in this film.

THE GNOME-MOBILE (1967) directed by Robert Stevenson

Another attempt to capitalize on the success of *Mary Poppins*. The two children from that film (Matthew Garber and Karen Dotrice) co-star with Walter Brennan in a fanciful story about a wealthy lumber tycoon and his grandchildren who meet several gnomes in California's redwood forest. The Sherman Brothers wrote the title song.

MIDNIGHT MADNESS (1980) directed by David Wechter and Michael Nankin

An all-night scavenger hunt around Los Angeles drives the plot of this film, which was the second PG one released by Disney (though Disney didn't attach its name to it when it was first released). It features the first on-screen appearance of Michael J. Fox, who was just eighteen years old.

ONE MAGIC CHRISTMAS (1985) directed by Phillip Borsos

This bittersweet holiday film, in the style of *It's a Wonderful Life*, stars Mary Steenburgen as a harried mother at wits' end who is saved by a heavenly presence.

RETURN TO OZ (1985) directed by Walter Murch

Walt purchased the rights to L. Frank Baum's *Wizard of Oz* stories and fully intended to make a film based on them (a 1950s TV show with the Mouseketeers even previewed a musical number from it), but the increased popularity of the 1939 MGM film killed those plans. The company finally made an Oz film in the 1980s. It was a daring departure from the tone and style of the previous film. Unfortunately, audiences found it to be too dark, and it died at the box office. It's since become a cult classic.

CHICKEN LITTLE (2005) directed by Mark Dindal

The second fully computer-animated film made by Disney (after 2000's *Dinosaur*), it's a sweet take on the "sky is falling" fable of a nervous chicken who rings the alarm bell too many times. While often silly, it has its charms and also offers a bunch of memorable characters.

MEET THE ROBINSONS (2007) directed by Stephen Anderson

A time-traveling story about a young inventor and orphan who longs for a family, this animated film was overshadowed in theaters by *Ratatouille*, *Shrek the Third*, and *The Simpsons Movie*, all released

HONORABLE MENTION

HOME ON THE RANGE (2004) directed by Will Finn and John Sanford

One of the last of Disney's traditionally animated films, this one was a misfire in theaters but actually has a fun story. It's about three cows and a stallion who team up with other barnyard friends to fight an evil western outlaw with a seductive yodel (really!) named Alameda Slim, who has designs on their little Patch of Heaven farm. Alan Menken and Glenn Slater contributed the musical score, with lots of country inflection, including a song by k.d. lang.

the same year. It deserves to be seen by more people. It combines a tug-at-your-heart Disney story line with a wacky plot, clever gags, a dastardly villain, and a simple message—aligned with Walt's philosophy—that puts it in the company of all the great Disney classics.

MOST UNUSUAL DISNEY FILMS

During a meeting with his staff in the 1950s to discuss future projects, one of Walt's employees said about a script, "We can't make that, it's not a typical Disney film!" Walt immediately shot back that as Walt Disney even *he* didn't know what a "typical" Disney film was. We all grew up with Disney films, so we instinctively feel like we know what they should be. That's why it's so jarring when we come across one that just doesn't seem to fit the brand.

Here are ten that fall into this unusual category.

VICTORY THROUGH AIR POWER (1943) directed by James Algar

After America's entry into World War II, the Disney Studios facility in Burbank, California, was taken over by the military. Walt had to curtail or shut down his work on several planned feature films. He mostly made shorts for the military, but was also inspired after reading a book by a Russian military hero named Alexander de Seversky, called *Victory through Air Power*. The book advocated the formation of an Allied air force made up of long-range planes to bomb the Axis forces into submission. Disney pushed for a screen adaptation, which contained interesting bits of animation, including a short on the history of aviation. Most of the movie, however, consisted of de Seversky directly addressing the camera in his thick Russian accent. Released in theaters, it was not a box office hit. President Franklin D. Roosevelt and British prime minister Winston Churchill, however, were both enthusiastic supporters. De Seversky's ideas were adopted, and long-range bombers were indeed put into production. This unheralded Disney film actually helped contribute to the Allies' success in WWII.

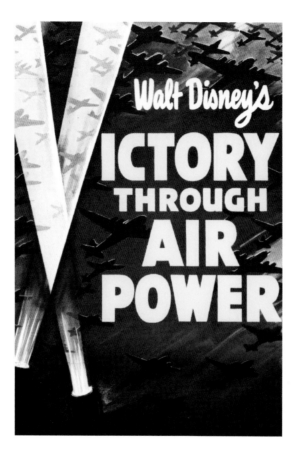

THE STORY OF MENSTRUATION (1946) directed by Jack Kinney

After the war ended, the Disney Studios was in severe financial distress. Walt and Roy were desperately looking for revenue streams. Corporate films were the easiest solution. The Kimberly Clark Company (then known as International Cello-Cotton), makers of feminine hygiene products, was one of the first to sign up for a custom-made Disney educational short.

It contracted Disney to make a ten-minute animated film about the female reproductive system, which was to be shown to girls during public school health classes. The film put great emphasis on biology and had a respected OB-GYN as script advisor, to help overcome any objections from the public or prudish school board members. The tastefully done short was so well made that it was awarded the Good Housekeeping Seal of Approval.

Disney mostly exited the corporate-sponsored educational film business a few years later, but films like *The Story of Menstruation* and *Advice on Lice* continue to be curious footnotes.

BON VOYAGE! (1962) directed by James Neilson

When described on paper, *Bon Voyage!* looks like a winner. A suburban American family travels overseas for the first time and has lots of wacky adventures. It even had a catchy Sherman Brothers title song, and two of Disney's biggest child stars, Tommy Kirk and Kevin Corcoran, to support its star, Disney legend Fred MacMurray. The problem was not in the plot, but in the themes, which proved to be too adult for family crowds. *Bon Voyage!* includes scenes of marital strife, hints at call girls propositioning minors, gigolos on the prowl, stereotypical "ugly American" behavior, and trips through the dark Paris sewers. Perhaps the biggest factor in its box office demise, however, was that *Bon Voyage!* runs over two hours long, while most family films are wise enough to realize that ninety minutes seems to be the breaking point for the attention spans and rear ends of smaller audience members. Sadly, *Bon Voyage!* remains one of Disney's least known live-action films.

MIRACLE OF THE WHITE STALLIONS (1963) directed by Arthur Hiller

Here's what you get in *Miracle of the White Stallions*: a war-torn Europe, power-hungry Nazis fighting among each other, starving villagers prone to looting and murder, bombed-out ruins, fancy show horses in peril, oh and General George S. Patton. Can this really be a Disney film? Yes, it is, and it's beautifully made. But you never quite get the sense that you are watching something produced by Disney. The closest tip-off comes when Eddie Albert, as a humane German officer, sings a lovely Sherman Brothers song written especially for the film. The plot is based upon the true story of a Nazi colonel, played by Robert Taylor, in charge of the famed Austrian school of Spanish Lipizzaner white stallions. As the war comes to an end, he desperately pleads with the Nazi high command to deliver the precious horses to safety. Hitler's minions are unsympathetic and unresponsive, so Taylor's character defies direct orders, risking his own life to save the stallions. He enlists the help of fellow horse lover Patton, who is marching the U.S. Army through the area, capturing Nazis on his way to Berlin. The conclusion of the film features performances by the actual Lipizzaner stallions, which are stunning. *White Stallions* has lots of pageantry and drama, but not much appeal for kids. With any other studio this would be a classic, but for Disney it is against type.

THE DEVIL AND MAX DEVLIN (1981) directed by Steven Hilliard Stern

By the dawn of the 1980s, Disney was trying desperately to appeal to younger crowds, who were eschewing G-rated films and growing used to edgier fare from other Hollywood studios.

Disney had already broken its live-action PG rating barrier with 1979's *The Black Hole*, so it went a step further and darker with *The Devil and Max Devlin*, which pushed the PG limits. This was the first Disney film to use swear words like "Damn!" and "son of a b*#ch!" Elliott Gould, one of Hollywood's top counterculture stars, was cast as Max. Devlin is a terrible person who is sent to Hell when hit by a bus. He's shown descending there, fire and brimstone and all. To save himself, he makes a deal with one of the Devil's top assistants, Barney Satin (Bill Cosby), to steal the souls of innocents. Max Devlin was definitely a strange addition to the roster of Disney's film heroes. Critics and audiences roasted this movie. The film did not, as intended, draw the younger crowds, who still thought of it as a Disney film, with no appeal to their generation. Disney began exploring options for a second film banner—Touchstone—that could release PG- and R-rated movies one step removed from the parent company and Disney brand.

SOMETHING WICKED THIS WAY COMES (1983) directed by Jack Clayton

Legendary author Ray Bradbury (*The Martian Chronicles*, *Fahrenheit 451*) was an unabashed Disney fan. He was also a personal friend of Walt's. It was no surprise, then, when Disney Studios finally got around to making one of his stories into a film. *Something Wicked* is Bradbury's semiautobiographical novel, written in 1962, about his childhood in Waukegan, Illinois, based on an encounter he had with a traveling carnival. The antagonist is the leader of this eerie carnival, Mr. Dark, played by Jonathan Pryce, in one of his earliest screen roles. He's a malevolent yet spellbinding stand-in for the Devil. The heroes are two preteen boys who sneak into the carnival one night and discover its evil secrets. Dark attempts to get the boys to join him. When that fails, he tries to have them killed. Eventually good wins out over evil, with an assist from the father of one of the boys (Jason Robards) who sees right through Mr. Dark. Bradbury and the critics were pleased with the film, but audiences were not, and it died at the box office. This movie, and another quasi-horror film, 1980's *Watcher in the Woods*, remain two of the most frightening ever produced by Disney.

TRENCHCOAT (1983) directed by Michael Tuchner

This is perhaps the most obscure Disney film ever made. Produced just before Touchstone Pictures came along, *Trenchcoat* was too mature for Disney's family audiences, but also deemed too tame for adult moviegoers. An unusual and unprecedented decision was made by Disney brass—to release it with absolutely no studio name attached to it. It appeared in cinemas all over the world as an "orphan" film. Disney's attempt at an Alfred Hitchcock–style suspense film, *Trenchcoat* stars Robert Hays, fresh off his starring role in the smash hit *Airplane*, and Margot Kidder, *Superman*'s Lois Lane, in a film about international spies in Malta. The title refers to the fabled outerwear of secret agents, detectives, and spies. There are mix-ups, terrorists, incompetent police, and nuclear secrets scattered throughout. It's a fun film hampered by a tangled plotline. *Trenchcoat* was released for home viewing once, on VHS, in 1983, then slipped through the cracks for decades. It's recently been made available for on-demand digital downloading.

THE BLACK CAULDRON (1985) directed by Ted Berman and Richard Rich

The twenty-fifth Disney animated classic, *The Black Cauldron* is one of its most misunderstood pictures, and also one of its biggest flops. It has the distinction of being the first Disney animated film to be rated PG. As most of the original Disney animation staff began to slow their output and/or retire in the 1980s, a new bunch of younger artists emerged. This was the first generation of animators weaned on the Disney style. They were eager to make their mark. Dungeons and Dragons and other role-playing games with medieval themes were popular then. These new animators wanted to work on something ambitious in scope, along the lines of J. R. R. Tolkien's classic *Lord of the Rings* trilogy, with characters going on a mythic quest. They couldn't secure the rights to Tolkien's stories, so Disney bought Lloyd Alexander's Chronicles of Prydain series instead. The main tale concerns a pig keeper named Taran who fancies himself a great warrior. He has a pig named Hen Wen who is stolen by the evil Horned King, who wants to use the pig to help forge a black cauldron, which will raise an army of the dead. Meanwhile, there is a princess named Eilonwy, who . . . well, audiences quickly tired of the cumbersome plot. When your movie has a sidekick with an unpronounceable name like Fflewddur Fflam, you know you're in trouble. *The Black Cauldron* cost a lot of money to make but brought in next to nothing at the box office. Disney took it out of circulation for years. It's gained a following and renewed respect in recent years, but is still a Disney misfire to some.

RUTHLESS PEOPLE (1986) directed by Jim Abrahams, David Zucker, and Jerry Zucker

Thanks to language and adult situations, 1986's *Down and Out in Beverly Hills* was the first R-rated feature to be released by Disney, under its Touchstone Pictures distribution arm. When *Ruthless People* was released by Touchstone a few months later, it made the prior film look tame. While *Down and Out* is a slightly raunchy, lighthearted fable with a happy ending, *Ruthless People* is a dark, dark comedy. Based loosely on the O. Henry classic tale "The Ransom of Red Chief," this film tells the story of Sam Stone (Danny DeVito), a self-made millionaire who hates his wife (Bette Midler) and is secretly delighted when she is kidnapped, hoping she will be killed. Judge Reinhold and Helen Slater play the sympathetic kidnappers. In this film, we are exposed to infidelity, nudity, hostility, premeditated murder, and allusions or references to animal cruelty and spousal abuse. The "F" word is used several times. Lest you forget this is a Disney movie, the kidnappers actually wear Donald Duck masks, and Sam whistles "Zip-a-Dee-Doo-Dah" when he thinks his wife has been murdered. At one point, Bette Midler's character says to the kidnappers, "Who are you supposed to be, Huey and Dewey?" (Poor Louie, no respect.) Midler and DeVito phoned each other after the film's premiere to commiserate about how they had just killed their careers by soiling Disney's name. The opposite was true. *Ruthless People* was a big hit. Both would go on to make several popular Disney films.

MARS NEEDS MOMS (2011) directed by Simon Wells

Walt was always exploring new innovations in animation, and was usually the first to bring them to the screen. No doubt he would have been pleased by the advancements made in the twenty-first century with performance capture digital animation, a unique method of placing computerized dots on an actor, which are then used by computers to draw an animated figure. It was as close to lifelike animation as anyone had ever gotten. Unfortunately, while audiences embraced this technology in live-action films, they never really warmed up to it in animated ones. It seemed to many to be creepy and fake, especially when depicting human characters. This hurt the chances of Disney's first two attempts at the process, 2009's *A Christmas Carol*, with Jim Carrey, and 2011's *Mars Needs Moms*. While the former film did okay in theaters because of its timeless Christmas theme and familiar tale, the latter was soundly rejected by critics and moviegoers alike. Set in a suburban neighborhood, *Mars Needs Moms* tells the story of nine-year-old Milo, whose mother is abducted by Martians. Made for more than $150 million, this film took in only a fraction of that, and remains one of the biggest box office bombs in history, and the biggest one ever for Disney. Two other Disney films with a Martian theme, 2000's *Mission to Mars* and 2012's *John Carter of Mars*, were also financial disappointments for the studio. Perhaps they should avoid visiting the Red Planet again.

LISTS ABOUT DISNEY CHARACTERS

ANIMATED DISNEY LEADING LADIES (CLASSIC)

SNOW WHITE (1937)—Snow White and the Seven Dwarfs
Voice of Adriana Caselotti.

    The first, and fairest, Disney princess of them all. Snow White set the standard.

Adriana Caselotti, the voice of Snow White. (RKO Radio Pictures/Photofest)

MRS. JUMBO (1941)—Dumbo

Voices of Verna Felton (speaking) and Betty Noyes (singing).

With a story line both tragic and tender, Dumbo's mom shines, and evokes tears.

BAMBI'S MOTHER (1942)—Bambi

Voice of Paula Winslowe.

Like Mrs. Jumbo, Bambi's mother also displays the power of the maternal instinct.

CINDERELLA (1950)—Cinderella

Voice of Ilene Woods.

A heroine everyone can relate to, Cinderella dreams of a life beyond her current station.

ALICE (1951)—Alice in Wonderland

Voice of Kathryn Beaumont.

Thrown into a confusing world, Alice manages to keep her wits about her the whole time.

WENDY (1953)—Peter Pan

Voice of Kathryn Beaumont.

Peter Pan might be the title character, but it's Wendy who is the real star of this film.

AURORA/BRIAR ROSE (1959)—Sleeping Beauty

Voice of Mary Costa.

Princess Aurora is only in her own movie for a short time, but she is the focal point.

MAID MARIAN (1973)—Robin Hood

Voice of Monica Evans.

Marian is in love with Robin, but is no damsel in distress. Her independence shines through.

PENNY (1977)—The Rescuers

Voice of Michelle Stacy.

Kidnapped by Madame Medusa, Penny stays resilient, even through her tough ordeal.

JESSICA RABBIT (1988)—Who Framed Roger Rabbit

Voice of Kathleen Turner.

Though resembling a classic Hollywood vamp, Jessica is a faithful and strong partner to Roger.

ANIMATED DISNEY LEADING LADIES (MODERN)

ARIEL (1989)—The Little Mermaid
Voice of Jodi Benson.

A strong-willed mermaid who yearns for life beyond her undersea world.

BELLE (1991)—Beauty and the Beast
Voice of Paige O'Hara.

Belle, a confident heroine, discovers that things are not always what they appear to be.

JASMINE (1992)—Aladdin
Voices of Linda Larkin (speaking) and Lea Salonga (singing).

Not willing to accept being told whom to marry, Jasmine asserts herself and then finds love.

POCAHONTAS (1995)—Pocahontas
Voices of Irene Bedard (speaking) and Judy Kuhn (singing).

A proud representative of her people, Pocahontas stands against invaders but also seeks peace.

LILO (2002)—Lilo & Stitch
Voice of Daveigh Chase.

Misunderstood by almost everyone around her, Lilo finds a best friend in Stitch, an unusual pet.

TIANA (2009)—The Princess and the Frog
Voice of Anika Noni Rose.

With dreams of being in charge of her own destiny, Tiana takes matters into her own hands.

RAPUNZEL (2010)—Tangled
Voice of Mandy Moore.

Locked in a tower most of her life, Rapunzel finds adventure, and her birthright, when set free.

MERIDA (2012)—Brave
Voice of Kelly Macdonald.

The first Disney princess not based on a preexisting character and without a love interest.

ELSA AND ANNA (2013)—Frozen
Voices of Idina Menzel and Kristen Bell.

Two royal sisters who, after misunderstandings and a separation, face the world together.

MOANA (2016)—Moana
Voice of Auli'i Cravalho.

Moana yearns for life beyond her shores, and seeks to right a wrong to save her people.

ANIMATED DISNEY LEADING MEN (CLASSIC)

PINOCCHIO (1940)—Pinocchio
Voice of Dickie Jones.

A mischievous little wooden puppet who dreams of being transformed into a real boy.

DUMBO (1941)—Dumbo
Voice of Mel Blanc (one uncredited hiccup in an otherwise silent role).

A challenge for Disney's animators—conveying simply by pantomime the emotions of this title character ostracized by his peers—was met and conquered.

BAMBI (1942)—Bambi
Voices of Bobby Stewart/Donnie Dunagan/Hardy Albright/John Sutherland.

The literal "babe in the woods," Bambi comes of age with help from his forest friends.

PETER PAN (1953)—Peter Pan
Voice of Bobby Driscoll.

You can hear the youthful exuberance in every line and action of this boy who never grows up.

PRINCE PHILLIP (1959)—Sleeping Beauty
Voice of Bill Shirley.

One of the few Disney princes with more screen time than his princess.

WART/ARTHUR (1963)—The Sword in the Stone
Voices of Richard Reitherman/Robert Reitherman/Rickie Sorensen.

An apprentice who finds himself, with the help of a wizard, and becomes the one true king.

MOWGLI (1967)—The Jungle Book
Voice of Bruce Reitherman.

This "man-cub," an adopted child of jungle creatures, learns his way as a human boy.

ROBIN HOOD (1973)—Robin Hood
Voice of Brian Bedford.

A dashing, charming take on the hero of Sherwood Forest, portrayed as a woodland fox.

BASIL OF BAKER STREET (1986)—The Great Mouse Detective
Voice of Barrie Ingham.

Inspired by Sherlock Holmes (and named for actor Basil Rathbone, who played Sherlock many times on-screen), the mouse Basil is one of Disney's smartest heroes.

ROGER RABBIT (1988)—Who Framed Roger Rabbit

Voice of Charles Fleischer.

> A daffy yet sweet-natured hero, ever loyal to his Toontown friends and to his wife, Jessica.

ANIMATED DISNEY LEADING MEN (MODERN)

BEAST (1991)—Beauty and the Beast

Voice of Robby Benson.

> Part lion, buffalo, bear, and gorilla, but all heart. The unlikeliest of all romantic heroes.

ALADDIN (1992)—Aladdin

Voices of Scott Weinger (speaking) and Brad Kane (singing).

> The actor Tom Cruise inspired the look and feel of this action hero "street rat."

HERCULES (1997)—Hercules

Voices of Tate Donovan (speaking) and Roger Bart (singing).

> The iconic Greek god translated into a classic Disney hero.

FLIK (1998)—A Bug's Life

Voice of Dave Foley.

> Another ordinary figure who's pressed into service fighting the bad guy and becomes the hero.

LIGHTNING McQUEEN (2006)—Cars

Voice of Owen Wilson.

> A cocky race car who is stranded in a small town and learns lessons in humility and teamwork.

FLYNN RIDER/EUGENE (2010)—Tangled

Voice of Zachary Levi.

> The outlaw who falls in love with a princess despite himself.

RALPH (2012)—Wreck-It Ralph

Voice of John C. Reilly.

> A bad guy who's not a bad guy, Ralph longs to be seen as the hero of his story.

KRISTOFF (2013)—Frozen

Voice of Jonathan Groff.

> The hero who doesn't know he's a hero, Kristoff is just an ice merchant trying to get by.

HIRO (2014)—Big Hero 6

Voice of Ryan Potter.

Devastated by the loss of his older brother, young inventor Hiro finds refuge and purpose with a group of eclectic friends and Baymax—a personal caretaker robot designed by his brother.

MAUI (2016)—Moana

Voice of Dwayne Johnson.

This Polynesian god is full of himself, but discovers that he does need the help of others.

ANIMATED FEMALE DISNEY VILLAINS

QUEEN GRIMHILDE/THE OLD HAG WITCH (1937)— Snow White and the Seven Dwarfs

Voice of Lucille La Verne.

The first classic Disney feature film villain. Still one of the scariest of them all.

THE QUEEN OF HEARTS (1951)—Alice in Wonderland

Voice of Verna Felton.

She is buffoonish at times; this queen's threats to decapitate others make her a comical villain.

AUNT SARAH (1955)—Lady and the Tramp

Voice of Verna Felton.

From her perspective, she's just a visiting relative looking out for her family. From Lady's perspective? Aunt Sarah is pure evil, out to destroy the family.

MALEFICENT (1959)—Sleeping Beauty

Voice of Eleanor Audley.

A sorceress who casts a spell on an innocent baby. Her name hints at the evil within.

CRUELLA DE VIL (1961)—101 Dalmatians

Voice of Betty Lou Gerson.

With two names that describe her character perfectly, Cruella is a menace to all creatures.

MADAM MIM (1965)—The Sword in the Stone

Voice of Martha Wentworth.

A daffy yet evil witch who tries to foil the good wizard Merlin at every turn with her spells.

MADAME MEDUSA (1977)—The Rescuers

Voice of Geraldine Page.

A kidnapper and coldhearted criminal; her best friends are two hungry alligators.

URSULA (1989)—The Little Mermaid
Voice of Pat Carroll.

A conniving, power-hungry sea witch who convinces Ariel to act against her best wishes.

YZMA (2000)—The Emperor's New Groove
Voice of Eartha Kitt.

An aged sorceress who longs to rule the kingdom. She is bent on murder, but her henchman foils her plans.

MOTHER GOTHEL (2010)—Tangled
Voice of Donna Murphy.

A mother who holds her daughter captive so that she can use her for her hair's magical powers.

ANIMATED MALE DISNEY VILLAINS

PEG-LEG PETE (1925, 1928)—The Alice Comedies, Steamboat Willie
Voice of Walt Disney.

The first Disney villain. He predates Mickey and still appears in TV shows and movies.

BIG BAD WOLF (1933)—The Three Little Pigs
Voice of Billy Bletcher.

A persistent threat to the three innocent pigs, the wolf was also viewed as a cartoon representation of the lingering dangers of poverty and hunger during the Great Depression.

CHERNABOG (1940)—Fantasia
No voice-over artist; a silent performance set to music.

The image of the Devil, this oversized, winged, red-eyed demon is the stuff of nightmares.

CAPTAIN HOOK (1953)—Peter Pan
Voice of Hans Conried.

A comically foppish villain, he constantly threatens to murder anyone who gets in his way and is bent on revenge against Peter, who caused his hand to be bitten off by a crocodile.

SHERE KHAN (1967)—The Jungle Book
Voice of George Sanders.

The performance of the ever-so-polite Sanders adds to the quiet charm of this fearsome tiger.

GASTON (1991)—Beauty and the Beast
Voice of Richard White.

Pompous, vain, and arrogant, Gaston is the type who would be the hero in many other stories (and is celebrated as such by the villagers with one of the best villain songs in Disney history) but who actually turns out to be the callous villain.

JAFAR (1992)—Aladdin

Voice of Jonathan Freeman.

Dripping with charm even when he's saying evil things; it's easy to see why the Sultan is so influenced by Jafar, his power-hungry advisor. Aladdin and Jasmine see right through him.

OOGIE BOOGIE (1993)—The Nightmare before Christmas

Voice of Ken Page.

The monster children have bad dreams about, made of a burlap sack body filled with maggots.

SCAR (1994)—The Lion King

Voice of Jeremy Irons.

Another in the line of power-hungry, honey-voiced Disney villains, Scar assists in the death of his own brother, traumatizes his nephew, and terrorizes the kingdom. For him, business as usual.

Jeremy Irons, the voice of Scar in *The Lion King* (1994). (Wikimedia Commons/ photo by Avda)

HADES (1997)—Hercules

Voice of James Woods.

The Devil as a smarmy, "Don't call me, I'll call you" Hollywood character makes what could have been a so-so villain even more memorable.

LIVE-ACTION DISNEY LEADING LADIES

KATIE COATES (1957)—Old Yeller
Played by Dorothy McGuire.

A frontier mom who holds her family together through hard times while her husband is away.

POLLYANNA (1960)—Pollyanna
Played by Hayley Mills.

An optimistic little girl whose infectious radiance changes the lives of those around her.

MARY POPPINS (1964)—Mary Poppins
Played by Julie Andrews.

Practically perfect in every way—that pretty much sums up everything about Mary Poppins.

Julie Andrews, Walt Disney, and P. L. Travers at the Los Angeles premiere of *Mary Poppins*, August 27, 1964. (Photofest)

ELEGANTINE PRICE (1971)—Bedknobs and Broomsticks
Played by Angela Lansbury.

A benevolent witch who journeys to find the elements of a spell to save Great Britain.

NORA (1979)—Pete's Dragon
Played by Helen Reddy.

A lighthouse caretaker who looks after young Pete while waiting for her sailor to return home.

MADISON (1984)—Splash
Played by Daryl Hannah.

A wide-eyed innocent newcomer to New York City who just happens to be a mermaid.

MIA THERMOPOLIS (2001)—The Princess Diaries
Played by Anne Hathaway.

A most reluctant princess, who wants to stay "normal" but eventually accepts her new role.

PRINCESS GISELLE (2007)—Enchanted
Played by Amy Adams.

A wide-eyed innocent newcomer to New York who just happens to be a fairy tale princess.

P. L. TRAVERS (2013)—Saving Mr. Banks
Played by Emma Thompson.

A somewhat chilly author, whose icy demeanor is slowly chipped away by Walt and his crew.

JYN ERSO (2016)—Rogue One
Played by Felicity Jones.

A brave young woman joins the rebellion against the Empire to steal plans for the Death Star.

LIVE-ACTION DISNEY LEADING MEN

JIM HAWKINS (1950)—Treasure Island
Played by Bobby Driscoll.

A young ship's mate who befriends a man who turns out to be a notorious pirate.

NED LAND (1954)—20,000 Leagues under the Sea
Played by Kirk Douglas.

A dashing harpooner who winds up as Captain Nemo's prisoner on the *Nautilus*, he sings a song called "Whale of a Tale" to amuse his shipmates on their perilous journey.

GEORGE BANKS (1964)—Mary Poppins
Played by David Tomlinson.

The proper, stuffy British banker father who learns to let loose and to be a fun dad.

DEXTER RILEY (1969)—The Computer Wore Tennis Shoes
Played by Kurt Russell.

The most popular guy on campus, he often gets himself into scrapes with shady characters.

JIM DOUGLAS (1969)—The Love Bug
Played by Dean Jones.

A down-on-his-luck race car driver whose fortunes change when he meets Herbie the Love Bug.

KEVIN FLYNN (1982)—TRON
Played by Jeff Bridges.

A laid-back video game designer zapped into his own creation, who has to play to survive.

EDDIE VALIANT (1988)—Who Framed Roger Rabbit

Played by Bob Hoskins.

A hard-boiled, toon-hating detective sent to investigate a murder in Toontown.

WAYNE SZALINSKI (1989)—Honey, I Shrunk the Kids

Played by Rick Moranis.

A typical suburban dad who also happens to be an inventor. His gadgets cause chaos.

MICHAEL CROMWELL (1997)—Jungle 2 Jungle

Played by Tim Allen.

A successful New York City businessman who brings the son he never knew from his home in the jungles of South America to the city. They bond and learn life lessons through each other.

BENJAMIN FRANKLIN GATES (2004)—National Treasure

Played by Nicolas Cage.

A fourth-generation American treasure hunter and historian, a man of action.

LIVE-ACTION FEMALE DISNEY VILLAINS

LETHA WEDGE (1978)—Return from Witch Mountain

Played by Bette Davis.

A greedy woman who conspires to control the telepathic hero and make him rob banks.

LENA GOGAN (1979)—Pete's Dragon

Played by Shelley Winters.

The head of a backwoods family who mistreats the hero and wants to destroy his dragon pal.

THE SANDERSON SISTERS (1993)—Hocus Pocus

Played by Bette Midler, Sarah Jessica Parker, and Kathy Najimy.

Winifred, Sarah, and Mary Sanderson are witches in 1600s Salem who are hanged but vow to return. They are accidentally resurrected in modern times, where they plot to kill the children of Salem and steal their souls to gain eternal youth. (Yes, this is a light Disney comedy.)

CRUELLA DE VIL (1996)—101 Dalmatians

Played by Glenn Close.

The animated British villain with a bloodlust for animal fur is brought to life. She's even crueler and scarier than her cartoon counterpart, but still left with comic touches.

Glenn Close as the villainous Cruella De Vil in the live-action version of *101 Dalmatians* (1996). (Walt Disney Pictures/Photofest)

LOUISE WALKER (2003)—Holes

Played by Sigourney Weaver.

The malicious warden of a juvenile detention camp, obsessed with digging holes in the desert.

QUEEN NARISSA (2003)—Enchanted

Played by Susan Sarandon.

A jealous and evil queen, she follows Princess Giselle to New York City to eliminate her.

CARLA SANTINI (2004)—Confessions of a Teenage Drama Queen

Played by Megan Fox.

The most popular girl at school, she feels superior and constantly tries to humiliate others.

JADIS, THE WHITE WITCH (2005)—The Chronicles of Narnia: The Lion, the Witch and the Wardrobe

Played by Tilda Swinton.

Deceptive and cunning, she aims to keep Narnia under the spell of an eternal winter.

IRACEBETH OF CRIMS, THE RED QUEEN (2010)— Alice in Wonderland

Played by Helena Bonham Carter.

Another animated character who is even more menacing as a live-action character. This queen is a true tyrant, determined to eliminate anyone, like Alice, who dares to oppose her.

HONORABLE MENTION

CAPTAIN PHASMA (2015)—Star Wars: The Force Awakens
Played by Gwendoline Christie.

Originally meant to be a male character, this "take no prisoners" head of an elite stormtrooper division—who wears one of the coolest Star Wars uniforms ever conceived—a shiny, polished silver-and-chrome suit with a cape—was changed to female when *Game of Thrones* star Christie impressed the filmmakers. Oddly, though her voice is heard, her face is never shown in the film.

MALEFICENT (2014)—Maleficent

Played by Angelina Jolie.

It was hard for me to put Maleficent on this list of villains, as the live-action version gives her character a sympathetic backstory and paints her as a hero who's been wronged.

LIVE-ACTION MALE DISNEY VILLAINS

LONG JOHN SILVER (1950)—Treasure Island

Played by Robert Newton.

Newton helped popularize the modern version of the pirate with his "Arrrrs" and "Shiver me timbers!" in this role, which was the template for buccaneers until Jack Sparrow came along.

CAPTAIN NEMO (1954)—20,000 Leagues under the Sea

Played by James Mason.

Not purely evil, Nemo is instead driven mad by the need to escape society and to keep his miraculous inventions safe. In the process, he destroys ships, killing and imprisoning sailors.

ALONZO HAWK (1961)—The Absent-Minded Professor

Played by Keenan Wynn.

A ruthless businessman with a cold heart, Hawk was played by Wynn in three separate films.

A. J. ARNO (1969)—The Computer Wore Tennis Shoes

Played by Cesar Romero.

A dapper criminal boss who controls all of the illegal activity near Medfield College, he's foiled by Dexter Riley on more than one occasion.

DR. TERMINUS (1979)—Pete's Dragon

Played by Jim Dale.

A slick con artist and snake oil salesman, intent on stealing Pete's magical dragon.

SARK/MCU (1982)—TRON

Played by David Warner.

This cutthroat businessman, and his digital alter ego, try to eliminate all competition.

JUDGE DOOM (1988)—Who Framed Roger Rabbit

Played by Christopher Lloyd.

The vindictive enemy of Toontown, he detests toons and wants to eliminate all of them.

KING STEFAN (2014)—Maleficent

Played by Sharlto Copley.

A king who wants no rivals, Stefan launches a murderous war against Maleficent's people.

KYLO REN (2015)—Star Wars: The Force Awakens

Played by Adam Driver.

The troubled grandson of Darth Vader who longs to rule the universe using the dark side.

BARBOSA AND DAVY JONES—Pirates of the Caribbean series

Played by Geoffrey Rush and Bill Nighy.

Two villains who turn out to be sometime allies to the heroes, when convenient to them.

DISNEY SIDEKICKS (CLASSIC)

THUMPER (1940)—Bambi

Voice of Peter Behn.

A young, mischievous rabbit who becomes the best friend and forest guide for Bambi.

TIMOTHY Q. MOUSE (1941)—Dumbo

Voice of Edward Brophy.

This little mouse helps Dumbo along on his journey to realize that he is someone special.

FAIRY GODMOTHER (1950)—Cinderella

Voice of Verna Felton.

Always there when Cinderella needs her, the Fairy Godmother is her protector and friend.

SMEE (1953)—Peter Pan

Voice of Bill Thompson.

Put upon and yet still loyal first mate of Captain Hook. His right-, er . . . left-hand man.

WHITE RABBIT (1955)—Alice in Wonderland

Voice of Bill Thompson.

Alice's harried guide through Wonderland, though she's constantly chasing him.

PIGLET AND EEYORE (1966)—Winnie the Pooh and the Honey Tree

Voices of John Fiedler and Ralph Wright.

Piglet is a timid little pink pig who is often the voice of reason for his best friend Pooh. They also pal around with Eeyore, a pessimistic donkey with a missing tail.

BALOO (1967)—The Jungle Book

Voice of Phil Harris.

A lovable, jazz scat-singing bear who acts as protector/best friend to the human Mowgli.

LITTLE JOHN (1973)—Robin Hood

Voice of Phil Harris.

Baloo in medieval England, this historical best friend to Robin Hood is more comical than most.

MR. SNOOPS (1977)—The Rescuers

Voice of Joe Flynn.

The softhearted and clumsy assistant to Madame Medusa. She treats him with disdain.

DODGER (1988)—Oliver & Company

Voice of Billy Joel.

This canine take on Dickens's Artful Dodger is a savvy New York City guide for little Oliver.

DISNEY SIDEKICKS (MODERN)

LEFOU (1991)—Beauty and the Beast

Voice of Jessi Corti.

The loyal and devoted, yet disrespected, follower of Gaston, whom he worships.

ABU AND IAGO (1992)—Aladdin

Voices of Frank Welker and Gilbert Gottfried.

The loyal companions to Aladdin and Jafar; both are there for their pals wherever needed.

PHILOCTETES (1997)—Hercules

Voice of Danny DeVito.

A rough-around-the-edges personal trainer to Hercules, whom he whips into shape for battle.

MUSHU (1998)—Mulan

Voice of Eddie Murphy.

Mulan's ancient, sass-talking, comedy-riffing dragon is one of Disney's funniest sidekicks ever.

TERK (1999)—Tarzan

Voice of Rosie O'Donnell.

Tarzan's gorilla best friend. The musical number where Terk trashes the camp is a highlight.

DORY (2003)—Finding Nemo

Voice of Ellen DeGeneres.

She might be forgetful, but Dory is the most helpful friend anyone can have, especially Marlin.

TOW MATER (2006)—Cars

Voice of Larry the Cable Guy.

Everybody's buddy, the eager tow truck helps Lightning McQueen out of some tight spots.

HONORABLE MENTION

GENIE (1992)—Aladdin

Voice of Robin Williams.

The ultimate Disney sidekick, and a star in his own right. As he puts it himself to Aladdin, "You ain't never had a friend like me!" He's absolutely right. We should all have someone as loyal as Genie at our side, magical powers or not.

Genie and Aladdin from *Aladdin* (1992). (Walt Disney Studios/ Photofest)

PASCAL (2010)—Tangled

Voice of Frank Welker.

Part protector, part conscience, part best friend, Pascal is Rapunzel's reptile companion.

OLAF (2013)—Frozen

Voice of Josh Gad.

Created by Queen Elsa, Olaf is a snowman with a child's innocence and also a devoted friend.

HECTOR RIVERA (2017)—Coco

Voice of Gael García Bernal.

A guide for Miguel through the spirit world, Hector longs to be reunited with his family.

DISNEY CANINES

DINAH AND BUTCH—PLUTO FILMS

Dinah, a dachshund, appeared in five shorts with Pluto and was his love interest (often unrequited). Butch, a bulldog, was Pluto's nemesis in eleven shorts.

NANA (1953)—Peter Pan

A Saint Bernard who acts as the caretaker and nanny for the Darling children.

LADY AND THE TRAMP (1955)

Voices of Barbara Luddy and Larry Roberts.

A young female cocker spaniel and the scruffy mutt she falls in love with.

PEG (1955)—Lady and the Tramp

Voice of Peggy Lee.

A stray dog who tries to woo Tramp with her feminine charms. Singer Peggy Lee's version of "He's a Tramp" for this character led to the dog being renamed Peg and modeled after her.

OLD YELLER (1957)

A mongrel with a yellow coat wanders onto a Texas ranch and proves a loyal and faithful companion to them, even to the point of tangling with a rabid animal.

PONGO AND PERDITA (1961)—101 Dalmatians

Voices of Rod Taylor and Cate Bauer.

Two dalmatians who meet in a park when their owners get tangled and then have a brood of fifteen puppies, which grows exponentially when they take in eighty-four more.

ZERO (1993)—The Nightmare before Christmas

The ghostly dog who is a faithful companion to Jack Skellington.

BOLT (2008)—Bolt

Voice of John Travolta.

A white American shepherd who was the heroic star of a TV show, unaware that he's just an actor. He has to make a dangerous cross-country trek to reunite with his owner.

DUG (2009)—Up

Voice of Bob Peterson.

An eager yellow Lab discovered at Paradise Falls who is—SQUIRREL!—equipped with a special device that translates his barks into English. He becomes a true, loyal friend to Carl and Russell.

DANTE (2017)—Coco

This Xoloitzcuintli dog, an almost hairless breed, is the national dog of Mexico. Dante accompanies Miguel on his journey through the spirit world and is his protector.

HONORABLE MENTION

SLINKY DOG—THE TOY STORY FILMS

Voice of Jim Varney.

Technically a toy, with the head and tail of a dachshund connected by a Slinky that enables him to stretch great distances, Slinky Dog is one of the most helpful members of the *Toy Story* gang.

DISNEY FELINES

JULIUS—The 1920s Alice Shorts

The very first cartoon character ever named by Walt Disney, Julius is an animated, silent cat who helps the live-action Alice on her adventures in the cartoon world.

FIGARO (1940)—Pinocchio

A minor silent co-star of Pinocchio, he proved so popular that he was spun off into his own series of seven shorts, and then became Minnie Mouse's pet cat.

LUCIFER (1950)—Cinderella

Voice of June Foray.

Lady Tremaine's house cat. He terrorizes Cinderella's mouse friends, who always outsmart him.

THE CHESHIRE CAT (1951)—Alice in Wonderland

Voice of Sterling Holloway.

A curious combination of purple and pink, this sometimes invisible cat—except for his famous grin—is unlike any other feline ever seen. He assists Alice on her trip through Wonderland.

SI AND AM (1955)—Lady and the Tramp

Voice of Peggy Lee.

These two pets of Aunt Sarah seem innocent, but they are deceptive, cunning, vindictive, and sneaky. Peggy Lee actually sang both harmony parts of their song "We Are Siamese."

THOMASINA (1963)—The Three Lives of Thomasina

A ginger cat in Scotland who comes back from near death to reunite a father and his daughter.

TIGGER (1968)—The Winnie the Pooh Films

Voice of Paul Winchell.

The most wonderful thing about Tigger is that he's the only one. That sums him up perfectly. Christopher Robin's adorable stuffed tiger is full of exuberance and optimism, making everyone around him smile at every opportunity. He's also just as popular as Pooh.

DUCHESS, O'MALLEY, BERLIOZ, TOULOUSE, AND MARIE (1970)—THE ARISTOCATS

Voices of Eva Gabor, Phil Harris, Dean Clark, Liz English, and Gary Dubin.

Duchess is a fancy, spoiled cat who lives in Paris with her alley cat love interest and her three kittens.

OLIVER (1988)—Oliver & Company

Voice of Joey Lawrence.

An orphaned kitten lost in New York who falls in with a group of kind and rascally criminal dogs.

MITTENS (2008)—Bolt

Voice of Susie Essman.

A sassy New York City house cat, abandoned by her family but doing okay on her own. She is dragged along and reluctantly helps Bolt on his quest to reunite with his owner.

DISNEY CRITTERS

FLOWER (1942)—Bambi

Voices of Stanley Alexander and Sterling Holloway.

A skunk Bambi mistakenly calls a flower. A good friend to Bambi, even naming his son after him.

SEBASTIAN (1989)—The Little Mermaid

Voice of Samuel E. Wright.

Tasked by King Triton to watch over Ariel, this calypso-loving crab finds that it's not an easy job.

MEEKO (1995)—Pocahontas

Voice of John Kassir.

A feisty, stubborn, and selfish raccoon, he's often at the side of Pocahontas.

HEIMLICH (1998)—A Bug's Life

Voice of Joe Ranft.

A portly and hungry caterpillar who bravely helps Flik and the ants battle the grasshoppers.

STITCH (2002)—Lilo & Stitch

Voice of Christopher Sanders.

AKA Experiment 626, this oddball alien creature lands in Hawaii and finds a family with Lilo.

CRUSH (2003)—Finding Nemo

Voice of Andrew Stanton.

A 150-year-old, laid-back turtle dude who, with his own son Squirt, helps Marlin find his son.

REMY (2007)—Ratatouille

Voice of Patton Oswalt.

A rat with dreams of being a chef. He partners with a young chef, Alfredo, to make it happen.

LOUIS (2009)—The Princess and the Frog

Voice of Michael-Leon Wooley.

A jazz-loving alligator from the bayou who plays a mean trumpet himself. A friend to Tiana.

BAYMAX (2014)—Big Hero 6

Voice of Scott Adsit.

An inflatable robot caretaker. Though not human, he shows more compassion than most.

HEIHEI (2016)—Moana

Voice of Alan Tudyk.

Moana's pet rooster, who loves to peck and isn't particularly bright. He sneaks onto her boat.

HONORABLE MENTION

ZAZU AND RAFIKI (1994)—The Lion King

Voices of Rowan Atkinson and Robert Guillaume.

Two of Mufasa's closest advisors, this hornbill bird and zen baboon come to Simba's aid, too.

DISNEY COUPLES

MICKEY & MINNIE (1928)
Various voices.

One of the most famous fictional couples in history. They've co-starred in more than one hundred movies and several television series. It's hard to think of one without the other.

HORACE & CLARABELLE (1929)
Various voices.

A horse and a cow who are sweethearts, they've been paired frequently since the 1930s. Horace started out as an anonymous barnyard animal but evolved into one of Mickey's pals. Clarabelle, a bit of a gossip and sometimes ditzy, is one of Minnie's best friends.

DONALD & DAISY (1937)
Various voices.

Right up there with Mickey and Minnie, this couple has been together for eighty years. Daisy came along after Donald, so she's listed just outside of "the Fab Five," but she's so close to all of them and appears in so many projects with them that Daisy's a de facto member of that group.

PECOS & SLUE FOOT SUE (1948)—Melody Time
Voice of Roy Rogers (narration).

Legendary Wild West sweethearts and Disney favorites. Pecos Bill and Slue Foot Sue's love story has been featured in both an animated and a live-action film, on stage in *The Golden Horse-shoe Revue*, and at a quick-service restaurant at Walt Disney World.

ROGER & JESSICA RABBIT (1988)—Who Framed Roger Rabbit
Voices of Charles Fleischer and Kathleen Turner.

The ultimate example of opposites attracting; their devotion for each other sees this married couple through thick and thin.

JACK & SALLY (1993)—The Nightmare before Christmas
Voices of Chris Sarandon and Catherine O'Hara.

The king of Halloween Town and the rag doll who pines for him. They each help the other to learn valuable lessons and then find contentment as a couple.

MUFASA & SARABI (1994)—The Lion King
Voices of James Earl Jones and Madge Sinclair.

The royal couple of the Pridelands, they provide a wonderful example to Prince Simba—both in death and in life—of how to conduct oneself as a leader.

MR. & MRS. POTATO HEAD (1995)—Toy Story

Voices of Don Rickles and Estelle Harris.

Two ordinary toys made extraordinary by the characterizations given to them as a bickering yet loving longtime married couple.

Mr. and Mrs. Potato Head were immortalized in the Toy Story trilogy. (Wikimedia Commons/photo by Geof Shepherd)

WALL-E & EVE (2007)—WALL-E

Voices of Ben Burtt and Elissa Knight.

Who would have thought that the gentle story of two robots falling in love in space would bring such genuine emotional reactions from human audiences? WALL-E and Eve did just that.

CARL & ELLIE FREDRICKSEN (2009)—Up

Voices of Jeremy Leary (young Carl)/Ed Asner and Elie Docter (young Ellie).

In the beginning, it's Ellie who does all the talking about their childhood dreams of a full life together. By the end, it's Carl who expresses those thoughts. One of the greatest love stories about a married couple that Disney has ever produced, told mostly through music and images.

DISNEY DUOS

HONEST JOHN (AKA J. WORTHINGTON FOULFELLOW) AND GIDEON (1940)—Pinocchio

Voices of Walter Catlett and Mel Blanc (one hiccup).

Two con men partners, a fast-talking fox and a mute cat, who get Pinocchio in trouble.

CHIP AND DALE (1943)

Various voices.

Mischievous chipmunks who just want to be left alone with their acorns in their treehouse but are often disturbed by the likes of Donald and Pluto. By the 1980s, this duo was so popular that they were given their own animated television series. You can tell them apart by their noses. Dale's nose is red, and Chip's is dark brown—like a chocolate chip.

Disney characters Chip and Dale greet children at Epcot. (Wikimedia Commons)

GUS AND JACQUES (1950)—Cinderella

Voice(s) of Jimmy MacDonald.

Two mice who keep Cinderella's spirits up and assist in her preparations for the ball. They speak their own unique language, which sometimes sounds like English.

TWEEDLEDUM AND TWEEDLEDEE (1951)—Alice in Wonderland

Voice(s) of J. Patrick O'Malley.

Playful twin brothers who love telling stories, reciting poems, and singing songs to Alice.

KANGA AND ROO (1966)—Winnie the Pooh and the Honey Tree

Voices of Barbara Luddy and Clint Howard.

A mother-son kangaroo combination, friends of Pooh, found in the Hundred Acre Wood.

TOD AND COPPER (1981)—The Fox and the Hound

Voices of Keith Coogan/Mickey Rooney and Corey Feldman/Kurt Russell.

Two young animals, best buddies, who don't realize that others see them as mortal enemies.

COGSWORTH AND LUMIÈRE (1991)—Beauty and the Beast

Voices of David Ogden Stiers and Jerry Orbach.

Two servants—the stuffy major domo and the ebullient maître d'—in the Beast's castle. They are transformed into a clock and a candelabrum by the spell cast on all of them. Together, they try to help the Beast find love, removing the curse so that they can become human again.

TIMON AND PUMBAA (1994)—The Lion King

Voices of Nathan Lane and Ernie Sabella.

Two buddies, a meerkat and a warthog, who happen upon a young Simba when he runs away to the savanna after Mufasa's death. Together, they teach him the laid-back lesson of "Hakuna Matata"—or "No worries for the rest of your days."

MIKE AND SULLEY (2001)—Monsters, Inc.

Voices of Billy Crystal and John Goodman.

Friends since college, Mike—an aspiring scare floor worker—and Sulley—one of the best scarers ever on that scare floor—team up on a wild adventure to save their hometown and their factory from forces that want to change them forever.

NICK WILDE AND JUDY HOPPS (2016)—Zootopia

Voices of Jason Bateman and Ginnifer Goodwin.

An unlikely duo. Judy Hopps—the first bunny ever admitted on the Zootopia police force—has to team up, against her better judgment, with the lazy and sly fox Nick Wilde to help solve a tough case. They learn to appreciate each other and become great partners.

DISNEY TRIOS

FIDDLER, FIFER, AND PRACTICAL PIG (1933)—The Three Little Pigs

Voices of Dorothy Compton, Mary Moder, and Pinto Colvig.

All three pigs have distinct personalities. Practical is the one with the most common sense.

HUEY, DEWEY, AND LOUIE (1937)

Various voices.

Donald's nephews are just like regular kids, well meaning but always getting into jams.

BR'ER RABBIT, BR'ER BEAR, AND BR'ER FOX (1946)—Song of the South

Voices of Johnny Lee, Nicodemus Stewart, and James Baskett.

Br'er Fox, a smart and sly creature, teams up with the dimwitted Br'er Bear, and the two are always trying to capture their adversary, Br'er Rabbit, usually with futile results.

ANASTASIA, DRIZELLA, AND LADY TREMAINE (1950)—Cinderella

Voices of Lucille Bliss, Rhoda Williams, and Eleanor Audley.

A mother and her two daughters who treat their new family member, Cinderella, with disdain.

MAD HATTER, MARCH HARE, AND DORMOUSE (1951)—Alice in Wonderland

Voices of Ed Wynn, Jerry Colonna, and James MacDonald.

A wacky trio, led by the Hatter, who host a wild "un-birthday" tea party for Alice.

WENDY, MICHAEL, AND JOHN (1953)—Peter Pan

Voices of Kathryn Beaumont, Tommy Luske, and Paul Collins.

The three Darling family children, who join Peter on an adventure to Neverland.

FLORA, FAUNA, AND MERRYWEATHER (1959)—Sleeping Beauty

Voices of Verna Felton, Barbara Jo Allen, and Barbara Luddy.

Benevolent fairies who hide Princess Aurora from Maleficent, changing her name to Briar Rose.

LOCK, SHOCK, AND BARREL (1993)—The Nightmare before Christmas

Voices of Paul Reubens, Catherine O'Hara, and Danny Elfman.

Three mischievous, trick-or-treating goblins who cause havoc in Halloween Town.

SHENZI, BANZAI, AND ED (1994)—The Lion King

Voices of Whoopi Goldberg, Cheech Marin, and Jim Cummings.

Scar's loyal hyena henchmen; they do his bidding with the hopes of ruling the Pridelands.

VICTOR, HUGO, AND LAVERNE (1996)—The Hunchback of Notre Dame

Voices of Charles Kimbrough, Jason Alexander, and Mary Wickes/Jane Withers.

Talking gargoyles at the Cathedral of Notre Dame in Paris who befriend Quasimodo.

DISNEY GROUPS

THE SEVEN DWARFS (1937)—Snow White and the Seven Dwarfs

These seven diminutive miners who live in the woods are the friends and protectors of Snow White, who helps to look after them. Their names can be remembered this way: two S's (Sleepy and Sneezy), two D's (Dopey and Doc), and three emotions (Bashful, Grumpy, and Happy).

THE BEAGLE BOYS (1951)

The bad guys of Duckburg, this family of villains is constantly trying to disrupt the lives (and steal the gold) of Scrooge McDuck and his grandnephews, Huey, Dewey, and Louie.

THE LOST BOYS (1953)—Peter Pan

Loyal followers of Peter, who live with him in perpetual youth in Neverland. Cubby, Slightly, Nibs, and Tootles love having adventures and fighting pirates, but also long for their real families and their real mothers, of whom Wendy reminds them.

SCAT CAT AND THE ALLEY CATS (1970)—The Aristocats

The trumpet-playing leader of a jazz band, Scat Cat befriends O'Malley and Duchess, helping them escape the bad guys. He's joined by four musicians, Shun Gon, Peppo, Billy Bass, and Hit Cat. Their song "Everybody Wants to Be a Cat" is a highlight of the film.

THE WEASELS (1988)—Who Framed Roger Rabbit

Judge Doom's henchmen, dressed in zoot suits; they help carry out his evil Toontown schemes.

THE LITTLE GREEN ALIENS (1995)—Toy Story

Worshippers of the claw machine from which they came, these many squeaky toy aliens have also proven to be good and helpful friends to Buzz, Woody, and the gang.

P. T. FLEA'S CIRCUS (1998)—A Bug's Life

A traveling troupe of performers (Manny, Gypsy, Dim, Tuck & Roll, Rosie, Francis, and Heimlich) who are mistakenly roped into defending the ant colony from Hopper and the grasshoppers.

THE PARR FAMILY (2004)—The Incredibles

Bob and Helen Parr are typical suburban parents who also just happen to have superpowers. When the villain Syndrome hits town, the Parrs, along with their three children—Violet, Dash, and Jack—suit up to become a super team.

THE STABBINGTON BROTHERS AND THE THUGS (2010)—Tangled

Denizens of the Snuggly Duckling, a notorious pub full of outlaws, the Stabbington Brothers (former partners of Flynn Rider)—Hook Hand (an aspiring concert pianist), Big Nose, and the mysterious Attila—are a group that seems intimidating but prove themselves to be softies.

JOY, SADNESS, FEAR, AND ANGER (2015)—Inside Out

This foursome of emotions who monitor eleven-year-old Riley's life from inside her brain learn that each one of them depends on the others as teammates to help Riley succeed in life.

UNDERRATED DISNEY CHARACTERS

OSWALD (1927)

The first breakout star of the Disney Studios, Oswald was the forerunner of Mickey, appearing in twenty-six shorts. When Walt lost him to Universal in 1928, Oswald disappeared from pop culture. In 2006, Oswald was reacquired from Universal in a straight-up trade for sportscaster Al Michaels, whom NBC wanted for their football games but was under contract to Disney/ABC.

THE BLUE FAIRY (1940)—Pinocchio

Voice of Evelyn Venable.

Cinderella's Fairy Godmother gets all the adulation from fans (maybe because she has a big musical number), but the Blue Fairy came first. Her appearances in *Pinocchio* are brief but meaningful. Without her, the little puppet never comes to life or becomes a real boy.

UNCLE REMUS (1946)—Song of the South

Played by James Baskett.

Song of the South has been in the Disney vault for years, so many modern fans aren't that aware of its protagonist, the kindly Uncle Remus, who always has a story or two to share. Based on the classic American character by Joel Chandler Harris, James Baskett played Remus to perfection, earning him the first Academy Award given to a male African American actor.

WILLIE THE GIANT (1947)—Fun and Fancy Free

Voice of Billy Gilbert.

One of the most popular Disney characters of the 1940s, this lovable giant from *Mickey and the Beanstalk* disappeared by the 1960s. He was brought back for *Mickey's Christmas Carol* and has made appearances on Disney TV shows, but he's still not as visible as a giant like him should be.

ALAN-A-DALE (1973)—Robin Hood

Voice of Roger Miller.

When audiences think of Disney's *Robin Hood*, it's not medieval melodies that come to mind, it's twangy, down-home country music. Roger Miller, who plays the troubadour Alan-a-Dale, was a Grammy-winning country music superstar. He wrote and sang most of the songs from the movie, including "Oo-De-Lally" and the catchy title theme, which he whistled (it was later sampled electronically as "The Hampsterdance Song"). Alan ties the movie's scenes together.

ELLIOTT (1977)—Pete's Dragon

Voice of Charlie Callas.

Poor Elliott; lots of people don't even know his proper name. They just call him "Pete," not quite seeing the possessive apostrophe in the film's title. This oversized animated green dragon with tiny pink wings steals every scene he's in. Elliott is also one of the last Disney characters to be supervised or animated by the old guard of Disney artists before they retired.

BOWLER HAT GUY (2007)—Meet the Robinsons

Voice of Stephen J. Anderson.

An underrated villain from an underrated movie, Bowler Hat Guy is someone whose ambition it is to be a bad guy. He even dresses the part, with a long black cape, the eponymous hat, and a mustache made for evil twirling. He also has a backstory that makes him sympathetic.

PRINCESS VANELLOPE VON SCHWEETZ (2012)— Wreck-It Ralph

Voice of Sarah Silverman.

The Disney princess club is pretty exclusive and has some rules (no live-action characters, must be actual royalty or married to royalty—sorry, Tinker Bell). For some odd reason, Vanellope, who meets all the qualifications, has been excluded. This former glitchy video game race car driver who discovers she's a royal is fiercely independent and is a great help to Ralph.

BING BONG (2015)—Inside Out

Voice of Richard Kind.

Riley's imaginary childhood playmate, Bing Bong never got proper credit when the film came out. He is a fun character, a stand-in for the imaginary friends most of us had in our youth, and touches several emotions, which is fitting for this film.

MAMA COCO (2017)—Coco

Voice of Ana Ofelia Murguía.

Another case of having your name in the tile of the movie but nobody really knowing your character. Mama Coco is the heart of her film, the link that ties the whole family—on Earth and in the spirit world—together. She deserves more recognition.

FORGOTTEN DISNEY CHARACTERS

CLARA CLUCK (1934)

This pretentious, opera-singing chicken appeared in nine Disney shorts in the 1930s and was a popular comic foil for Donald. Florence Gill provided her mellifluous voice.

TOBY TORTOISE AND MAX HARE (1935)

The co-stars of two popular *Silly Symphonies* shorts. The first was an Oscar-winning retelling of Aesop's "Tortoise and the Hare" fable. The sequel, *Toby Tortoise Returns*, saw the two competing in a boxing match, with other Disney stars at ringside. The animators at Warner Brothers used the look and personality of Max Hare as inspiration for their own superstar, Bugs Bunny.

ELMER ELEPHANT (1936)

A big-selling character on Disney merchandise of the late 1930s, the now obscure Elmer was the star of a *Silly Symphonies* short in which he saves a tiger from a fire.

FERDINAND (1938)

The star of his own Oscar-winning short (not part of the *Silly Symphonies* series), Ferdinand is a timid bull who loves smelling flowers and doesn't want to fight a matador.

BONGO (1947)—Fun and Fancy Free

Bongo is a young circus bear who falls in love with another performing bear but has to compete for her attention with a much larger bear.

LITTLE TOOT (1948)—Melody Time

The Andrews Sisters narrated the story of this small tugboat with heart, who is shunned by others but saves the day in the end.

LAMBERT (1952)

A baby lion who is mistakenly delivered to a mother sheep, Lambert grows up with many "sheepish" qualities, but by the end of his short cartoon shows true courage as a lion.

RANGER J. AUDUBON WOODLORE AND PROFESSOR OWL (1953)

Bill Thompson provided the voice for both of these narrator characters, who were seen in many of Disney's educational films and shorts in the 1950s and '60s.

KING LEONIDAS (1971)—Bedknobs and Broomsticks

The ruler of the Isle of Naboombu, who possesses a magical medallion everyone wants. Leonidas was a popular walk-around character in the parks until the late 1980s, but now causes folks to look at their autograph books and photos from that era and say, "Who's King Leo?"

B.O.B. AND V.I.N.CENT (1979)—The Black Hole

Disney's version of the Star Wars characters R2D2 and C3PO, V.I.N.Cent (an acronym for "Vital Information Necessary, Centralized") and B.O.B. ("BiOsanitation Battalion") help the crew of the *Palomino* as they square off against the Captain Nemo–like character Dr. Hans Reinhardt in *The Black Hole*. This comical robot pair never quite caught on like their Lucasfilm counterparts, though B.O.B.'s design was cited as inspiration for the droid BB-8 in *The Force Awakens*.

LISTS ABOUT DISNEY CAST MEMBERS

When most people think of Disney, they think of cartoon characters. That might have remained the case had Walt not branched out to live-action films in the 1950s. He was trying to increase the studio's revenue stream, but he inadvertently created his own star-making machine. Over the years, many actors have made Disney their home base for projects, while others have used Disney as the launchpad for successful Hollywood careers. Here are some of the most notable.

ACTORS WHO FOUND A HOME AT DISNEY

ED WYNN

A favorite of Walt's, Ed Wynn was an actor whose career stretched all the way back to the vaudeville era, where he perfected the art of the baggy pants clown. Wynn provided the totally unique voice of the Mad Hatter in *Alice in Wonderland* and then returned to Disney again and again in TV shows and films like *Babes in Toyland*, *The Golden Horseshoe Revue*, *Son of Flubber*, *That Darn Cat!*, and his career capper, in which he played the laugh-loving Uncle Albert in *Mary Poppins*.

FESS PARKER

While casting for Davy Crockett, Walt watched a science fiction film called *Them!*, advised that its star, James Arness, would be perfect for Crockett. It was another actor, Fess Parker, who instead drew Disney's attention. Walt offered Parker the role of Crockett, and it made his career. While Fess Parker will always be remembered as Davy Crockett, he also fulfilled several other roles under his Disney contract, including the valiant Union colonel Andrews in *The Great Locomotive Chase*, Jim Coates in *Old Yeller*, and Del Hardy in *The Light in the Forest*. In his later years, Parker owned and operated a successful vineyard in the Napa Valley, returning to Disney for reunion shows and specials, his iconic coonskin cap always at the ready.

FRED MacMURRAY

The very first person to be named a Disney Legend, Fred MacMurray was already an established Hollywood star (mostly playing the heavy) when Walt hired him to play against type as the befuddled dad in *The Shaggy Dog*, the studio's first live-action comedy. That began a string of appearances for MacMurray in Disney films, some of his most famous roles. It also led to a resurgence in his career on the big screen and on television in the 1960s and '70s.

Actor Fred MacMurray revived his career in *The Shaggy Dog* (1959) followed by *The Absent-Minded Professor* (1961) and *Son of Flubber* (1963). (Walt Disney Pictures/Photofest)

DICK VAN DYKE

A big TV star with an eponymous hit show, rubber-faced and lithe American comedian Dick Van Dyke was an interesting selection by Walt when he was casting the role of the cockney chimney sweep Bert in *Mary Poppins*. It turned out to be the perfect choice. Accent aside, Van Dyke brought just the right amount of charm and humor to Bert, the perfect complement to Julie Andrews's portrayal of Mary. He also did an uncredited turn in the film, with heavy age makeup applied, as the stuffy boss of George Banks. Van Dyke followed that with two other Disney movies, *Lt. Robin Crusoe, U.S.N.* (written for him by a certain "Retlaw Yensid," who looked similar to the studio boss and spent a lot of time in his office) and *Never a Dull Moment*. Named a Disney Legend in 1998, Van Dyke has appeared in almost every Disney TV special since the 1970s.

DON KNOTTS AND TIM CONWAY

Both men had separate and successful comedy careers outside of Disney, but Don Knotts and Tim Conway's numerous appearances—together and apart—in films and projects for the studio have linked them forever to the company. Conway, named a Disney Legend in 2004 (oddly, Knotts hasn't yet been given the distinction) is best known for his decades as a co-star on *The Carol Burnett Show*, but he excelled in playing slightly dim-witted characters in Disney films like *The World's Greatest Athlete*, *Gus*, and *The Shaggy D.A.* He teamed up with Knotts as bumbling crooks Amos and Theodore in *The Apple Dumpling Gang*, which was a box office hit, and they reprised the roles in the sequel. Knotts, an Emmy winner for his role as Andy Griffith's deputy Barney Fife, appeared in *Herbie Goes to Monte Carlo*, *No Deposit, No Return*, *Hot Lead & Cold Feet*, and as the voice of Mayor Turkey Lurkey in 2005's *Chicken Little*, his last big-screen role.

BETTE MIDLER

One of Michael Eisner and Jeffrey Katzenberg's goals when they took over the company was to revitalize its film division by signing big-name stars to development and production deals, with offices on the Disney lot in Burbank. Bette Midler was one of the first to do so. A major recording star who'd done some film work, Midler enjoyed a huge career boost from her Disney work, starting with the rated-R Touchstone twosome of *Down and Out in Beverly Hills* and *Ruthless People* in 1986. She followed those films with the madcap comedies *Outrageous Fortune* and *Big Business* and the tearjerkers *Stella* and *Beaches*. She also voiced Georgette in *Oliver & Company* and hosted a segment of *Fantasia 2000*. Midler's most famous Disney role, however, was as Winifred Sanderson in *Hocus Pocus*, now a Halloween classic.

STEVE MARTIN

An Orange County native, Steve Martin started working at Disneyland at the magic shop on Main Street while still in his teens. His idol was the Golden Horseshoe's Wally Boag, who taught him the basics of stagecraft and showmanship, which Martin later used to great effect in his groundbreaking stand-up comedy career. In the 1990s, Martin, by then a major movie star, returned to Disney to make a series of successful films, the most famous of which was the *Father of the Bride* series. He also hosted a segment of *Fantasia 2000* and made a cartoon with Donald Duck in honor of Disneyland's fiftieth anniversary.

ROBIN WILLIAMS

Another California native and stand-up comedian who was influenced heavily by the magic of Disney as a child, Robin Williams was like an animated character come to life. His casting as Genie in 1992's *Aladdin* seemed like destiny. Prior to that, he'd done several live-action Disney films, two of which, *Dead Poets Society* and *Good Morning, Vietnam*, earned him Oscar nominations and displayed the Juilliard-trained actor's dramatic chops to audiences only used to his comic riffs. Williams also appeared in attractions for the Disney parks. The film *Old Dogs*, released the same year he was named a Disney Legend, was one of Williams's last projects before his untimely death in 2014.

JOHNNY DEPP

An Academy Award–nominated actor with a strong résumé and an uncanny ability to disappear into his characters, Johnny Depp first worked for Disney as the star of *Ed Wood*. He returned a decade later to create the iconic Captain Jack Sparrow in the *Pirates of the Caribbean* films. After that, he put his talents to work in such diverse roles as the Mad Hatter, Tonto, and Red Riding Hood's Wolf. Depp works for other studios, too, but his films have made billions for Disney and he was named a Disney Legend in 2015.

LINDSAY LOHAN

Filling the shoes of an actress who has played a role before you in a beloved film is hard. Lindsay Lohan did it twice. She started her career at Disney by playing twins in the well-received 1998 remake of *The Parent Trap*, and then topped that in 2003 with a remake of *Freaky Friday*, all while still under eighteen. Her breakout role came in *Confessions of a Drama Queen*, and then she introduced Herbie the Love Bug to twenty-first-century audiences as his owner and driver in *Herbie Fully Loaded*. She's taken a hiatus from films, but Lohan was the face of Disney for years.

ACTORS WHOSE CAREERS BLOSSOMED AT DISNEY

JULIE ANDREWS

When Walt Disney saw Julie Andrews in a Broadway performance of *Camelot* in 1962, he realized that he had found the perfect actress to play his Mary Poppins. Filming began on her breakthrough role in 1963. Thanks to the efforts of Walt and his crew, and a classic Oscar-winning score by the Sherman Brothers, *Mary Poppins* was a smash hit. In her screen debut, Julie Andrews won the Academy Award for Best Actress, which is an extremely rare occurrence.

Andrews went on to a stellar Hollywood career after *Mary Poppins*. She starred in one of the biggest box office successes of all time, *The Sound of Music*, and was nominated for her third Academy Award with 1983's *Victor/Victoria*. In recent years, she has returned to the Disney fold, with roles in both *Princess Diaries* movies, the adaptations of the *Eloise* books, and as the narrator of *Enchanted*. She remains the grande dame of Disney and one of the biggest names in its galaxy of live-action film stars.

JAMES MacARTHUR

Best known for his role as Danno on the 1970s hit TV show *Hawaii Five-O*, James MacArthur started off as one of Disney's first on-screen heartthrobs. The son of acting legend Helen Hayes, herself the star of several Disney films, MacArthur took time off from college to appear in Disney's *Light in the Forest* and 1959's *Third Man on the Mountain*—the film that inspired Walt to build the Matterhorn ride at Disneyland. MacArthur was so well received in those films that he left college to do two more Disney movies. *Kidnapped* was a modest success, but *Swiss Family Robinson* was an enormous hit in 1960, making him a mainstream star.

DEAN JONES

From 1965 to 1977, there was no more dependable actor for Disney than Dean Jones. Though he had prior credits in other films and TV shows, Jones's career took off once he came to work for Disney. Walt used to stop by and chat with Jones, a favorite of his, on the sets of the hit films he starred in, like *That Darn Cat!*, *The Ugly Dachshund*, and *Blackbeard's Ghost*. Jones was one of the last few people at the studio to see Walt alive. Mr. Disney had a conversation with him as he made his rounds before checking himself into the hospital, where he died days later.

The biggest success in Jones's career came after Walt's death, with his role as Jim Douglas in 1969's *The Love Bug*. He starred in six more Disney films, did several other major motion pictures, starred on Broadway, and was honored as a Disney Legend.

KURT RUSSELL

Disney had a lock on discovering and minting child stars, but many of them faded from Hollywood after their teen years passed. Not so with Kurt Russell, who went from being just another Disney discovery to a bona fide A-list star. In 1966, Walt signed fifteen-year-old Kurt to a ten-year contract. He made his Disney debut in *Follow Me, Boys!* and soon became the studio's biggest star, surpassing Dean Jones. Russell helped Disney appeal to a younger generation thanks to his portrayal of the likeable college student Dexter Riley in a trilogy of popular films, as well as the laid-back surfer boyfriend matched against an overprotective father in *Superdad*. Shortly after the conclusion of his Disney contract, Russell took the role of Elvis Presley in a 1979 made-for-TV biographical movie that was a ratings bonanza for ABC. His move into superstar status was sealed with classic 1980s sci-fi/action-hero feature films like *Escape from New York* and *The Thing*. He's since starred in critically praised films like *Silkwood*, *The Mean Season*, *Backdraft*, and *Tombstone*. Russell speaks highly of his time at Disney and has occasionally returned to the studio, appearing in *The Fox and the Hound*, *Sky High*, *Miracle*, and *Guardians of the Galaxy Vol. 2*.

SEAN CONNERY

Most people assume that Sean Connery began his Academy Award–winning career in his most iconic role, James Bond. While 1962's *Dr. No* did make Connery a superstar, it was not his first leading role. That honor goes to a Disney film. *Darby O'Gill and the Little People*, released in 1959, saw Connery playing an Irishman named Michael McBride. It was a special effects-laden film about leprechauns in which he was the romantic suitor of leading lady Janet Munro. They even had a duet to sing in the film, "A Pretty Irish Girl." The song was recorded by Brendan O'Dowda and lip-synched by Connery. Albert Broccoli, who held the film rights to the James Bond novels, was so charmed by Connery's performance in this Disney film that he cast him instantly as his 007. Connery played James Bond in seven films and spent forty years crafting a legacy that would lead him to be knighted by Queen Elizabeth. He always thanks Disney for giving him his big break.

Before Sean Connery was agent 007 he was Irishman Michael McBride in *Darby O'Gill and the Little People* (1959). His co-star was Janet Munro as Katie O'Gill. (Buena Vista/Photofest)

JODIE FOSTER

One of the top child stars of the 1970s, Jodie Foster showed maturity and depth in her performances even at an early age. Foster was nominated for her first Academy Award at age fourteen for her role in the gritty picture *Taxi Driver*. That same year, she appeared in her most famous Disney film, 1976's *Freaky Friday*. Foster had actually been under contract with Disney for a while, beginning with *Napoleon and Samantha* four years earlier. She made four films for the studio. According to legend, Foster's Disney contract cost her a shot at a role in one of the biggest films of all time. Supposedly, George Lucas wanted to test her for Princess Leia in *Star Wars* but couldn't get permission from Disney to do so (she was contractually committed to making *Candleshoe*), so Foster had to pass. It didn't hurt Foster's career. After she left Disney in 1977, she went on to a successful career, winning two Academy Awards for Best Actress and acclaim as a director and producer.

TIM ALLEN

Can you name the only entertainer in American history to have the top-rated television series, highest-grossing movie, and number one best-selling book all in the same week? If you guessed Tim Allen, you are correct. The multitalented Allen accomplished this remarkable triple feat in December 1994 with three Disney properties: Disney/ABC's *Home Improvement*, Disney Studios' *The Santa Clause*, and the Disney/Hyperion book *Don't Stand Too Close to a Naked Man*. Allen's "Tool Man" persona on stage during his stand-up performances in the late 1980s attracted the attention of Disney executives. They signed him to a development deal, building a sitcom around the character that Allen created. *Home Improvement* was a smash hit when it debuted in 1991, and Tim Allen became a superstar. One year after his three number ones accomplishment, Allen starred as the voice of Buzz Lightyear in the first *Toy Story*. In addition to continuing his roles as Buzz and Santa Claus for the studio in subsequent films, Allen also starred in *Jungle 2 Jungle* and a remake of *The Shaggy Dog*. He has been at the forefront of other hit films from other studios and returned to television in 2013 with *Last Man Standing*, which aired on ABC. Allen was named a Disney Legend in 1999, less than a decade after he started working with the company. That, more than anything, is a testament to how much Tim Allen came to embody the face and spirit of Disney at the end of the twentieth century and into the new millennium.

ELLEN DeGENERES

Ellen DeGeneres had been performing stand-up comedy for more than ten years when she was approached by Touchstone/Disney to create a sitcom. The show (first titled *These Friends of Mine*, then changed simply to *Ellen*) debuted in 1994. While never a huge hit like *Home Improvement*, the show did well enough to be renewed by ABC, eventually lasting five seasons.

Ellen's biggest film success came at Disney with her role as the voice of Dory in *Finding Nemo* and its 2016 sequel, *Finding Dory*. She also is one of the few real people to star as themselves in a Disney attraction. Ellen's Energy Adventure in Epcot was a thirty-minute ride co-starring Bill Nye that actually featured an audio-animatronic version of Ellen guiding guests through a primordial jungle. DeGeneres is currently the host of a popular talk show. While it is not produced by Disney, she often uses the show as a forum to promote Disney films and products.

ANNE HATHAWAY

Like Jodie Foster, Anne Hathaway made a successful transition from family films to more adult fare and has earned praise as one of the leading actresses of her generation. A stage performer from Millburn, New Jersey, Hathaway was cast, after just one audition, in the role of Mia Thermopolis in 2001's *The Princess Diaries*. Directed by Garry Marshall, the film was a huge hit. Hathaway reprised the role in a 2004 sequel. Hathaway then took supporting parts in dramatic films like *Brokeback Mountain* and *The Devil Wears Prada*. The acclaim from those movies led her to 1998's *Rachel Getting Married*, which earned Hathaway her first Academy Award nomination. In 2010, she appeared as the White Queen in Disney's 3-D reboot of *Alice in Wonderland*, directed by Tim Burton. She later hosted the Oscars, and won her own Academy Award for 2012's *Les Misérables*. No matter how long her career is and no matter how many awards she earns, Anne Hathaway will forever be linked with Disney as one of its favorite princesses.

SHIA LaBEOUF

Not too many performers can say they began as stand-up comedians at the age of ten. Shia LaBeouf did just that. His family was struggling, so he went onstage to help make ends meet. His act got the attention of Disney executives, who cast him as Louis Stevens in the Disney Channel show *Even Stevens*, which ran from 2000 to 2003 and was spun off into a TV movie. LaBeouf won an Emmy for his work on the show. LaBeouf was so popular with audiences that Disney chose him to star in its adaptation of Louis Sachar's best-selling book *Holes*. The 2003 film did well at the box office. His follow-up Disney film was a biographical sports movie, 2005's *The Greatest Game Ever Played*. Since LaBeouf left Disney, he has gone on to star in some of the biggest blockbusters of the twenty-first century, including the *Transformers* movies and the fourth installment of the Indiana Jones series. In fact, Steven Spielberg said that he knew LaBeouf was the right person to play Indy's son after seeing him in all of those Disney projects.

HONORABLE MENTION

ZAC EFRON

As Troy Bolton, the Romeo of Disney Channel's *High School Musical* in 2006, Zac Efron won a generation of hearts. The role, which he reprised in two sequels, made him an international superstar. He capitalized on that with follow-up roles in hit films as diverse as *Hairspray*, *The Lucky One*, *Neighbors*, and *The Greatest Showman*. Efron's career is definitely on the rise.

CHILD STARS OF DISNEY

VIRGINIA DAVIS

In 1923, while still living in Kansas City, Walt hired five-year-old Virginia Davis to star in a short film based on *Alice in Wonderland*. The twist was that Alice would enter the cartoon world, instead of cartoons entering ours, which is what other animators were doing at the time. When he arrived in Hollywood, Disney encouraged Virginia's parents to bring her west to continue playing Alice. She made thirteen of the *Alice* films, then worked another twenty years in Hollywood, occasionally returning to do voice-over gigs for Disney.

BOBBY DRISCOLL AND LUANA PATTEN

Disney's first contract players, Driscoll and Patten were both younger than ten when they were signed to star in a series of films for Walt. They were usually paired together. Best known for *Song of the South* and *So Dear to My Heart*, they also appeared in Disney's package films. Though Patten had a longer Hollywood career, Driscoll—who passed away at age thirty-one—gained more fame at Disney, as the model and voice for Peter Pan and the star of *Treasure Island*.

THE MOUSEKETEERS

When Walt started his own daily children's television program in 1955, he knew that he needed children to populate the cast to appeal to younger viewers. He did not want seasoned child actors for his *Mickey Mouse Club*, so a search went out for "regular" kids. Dubbed "Mouseketeers," thirty-nine children ranging in age from eight to sixteen were cast. They became overnight stars. The original run of *The Mickey Mouse Club* ended in 1959, but the show was rebooted in 1977, and again in 1989.

The Mouseketeers in 1957. (Wikimedia Commons/attributed to McFadden Publications)

In all, there were more than eighty Mouseketeers cast from 1955 to 1995, some of whom—like Sharon Baird, Don Grady, Bobby Burgess, Johnny Crawford, Paul Petersen, Lisa Whelchel, Britney Spears, Justin Timberlake, Christina Aguilera, Keri Russell, and Ryan Gosling—went on to successful show business careers beyond Disney.

ANNETTE FUNICELLO

Discovered by Walt, Annette Funicello was one of the original Mouseketeers and quickly became the biggest star on the show. Her fame was such that she was the only Mouseketeer kept under contract by Disney after the original show ended. Walt created a spin-off series just for her, cast her in feature films, and released her hit albums on the Disney recording label. Annette was a dependable box office star and the female face of Disney for years. To many, she embodied the wholesome values that the Disney brand stood for. Even when she made films and commercials for other companies, Funicello consulted with Walt and was sure to stay true to the Disney image. In her later years, as she bravely battled multiple sclerosis, Funicello returned to Disney for TV shows and specials. She passed away in 2013, at the age of sixty-one.

TIM CONSIDINE

Mini serial films were included as part of *The Mickey Mouse Club* programming. Perhaps the best loved was *Spin and Marty*, which starred fifteen-year-old Tim Considine, alongside David Stollery. Considine was so popular with fans that he was also cast in another serial on the show, *The Hardy Boys*. He then appeared in *The Swamp Fox* and *The Shaggy Dog*. After Disney, Considine co-starred in *My Three Sons* on TV. He and Stollery were named Disney Legends.

KEVIN CORCORAN

Though he was technically never a Mouseketeer, Kevin Corcoran sure felt like one. As a boy, he appeared on *The Mickey Mouse Club* many times in serials, mostly playing a character called Moochie who desperately wants to hang out with the older kids. The character, and Corcoran, was so popular with viewers that Moochie was given his own TV specials. Corcoran was one of Walt's favorites, starring in several live-action hits like *Old Yeller*, *Swiss Family Robinson*, and *The Shaggy Dog*. In his later years, he retired from acting and became a production assistant.

TOMMY KIRK

A frequent co-star of Corcoran's (they played brothers in five different Disney films), Kirk had also co-starred with Tim Considine in *The Hardy Boys*. He came into his own, however, starting with 1964's *The Misadventures of Merlin Jones*—which was a big hit—and then its sequel, *The Monkey's Uncle*. After his second turn as Merlin Jones, the twenty-four-year-old Kirk left Disney.

HAYLEY MILLS

The daughter of British screen legend Sir John Mills, who played the father of Kevin Corcoran and Tommy Kirk in *Swiss Family Robinson*, Hayley Mills made only six films for Disney, from the age of fourteen to nineteen, yet she remains one of the brightest stars in its history. Her debut with Disney, 1960's *Pollyanna*, was a success, earning Mills the Oscar for best juvenile performance—the last time that award was given. Her second film with Disney, *The Parent Trap*, in which she played twin sisters, was a worldwide box office hit. Mills came back to Disney in the 1980s to make a series of TV sequels to *The Parent Trap*, and was named a Disney Legend in 1998.

JONATHAN TAYLOR THOMAS

Tim Allen was the star of the hit 1990s TV show *Home Improvement*, but ten-year-old Jonathan Taylor Thomas, who played his middle son, Randy, was the matinee idol among the younger crowd. His face graced the cover of every popular teen magazine of the time. Disney capitalized on that, casting Thomas in a series of films, like *Man of the House* and *Tom and Huck*. His biggest Disney contribution, though, is as the voice of young Simba in *The Lion King*.

RAVEN-SYMONÉ

Though she began her career as a child on such popular TV programs as *The Cosby Show* and *Hangin' with Mr. Cooper*, Symoné is best known for her work with Disney, where she played the title character in the Disney Channel show *That's So Raven* from 2003 to 2007. After it ended, she transitioned into a successful film and recording career. In recent years, Symoné has served as cohost of ABC's *The View* and returned to Disney with the spin-off show *Raven's Home*.

HONORABLE MENTION

HILARY DUFF AND CHRISTY CARLSON ROMANO
Two of the biggest Disney Channel stars in the early 2000s, Duff and Romano both had hit shows, *Lizzie McGuire* and *Even Stevens*, and then branched off into other areas of the company. Duff had some best-selling record albums for Disney, and Romano voiced an animated character (Kim Possible) and took a turn as Belle in Broadway's *Beauty and the Beast*. Both actresses appeared together in a popular Disney Channel film, *Cadet Kelly*, before departing for other ventures.

DISNEY VOICE-OVER ARTISTS (CLASSIC)

JIMMY MacDONALD

Business matters began to take up more and more of Walt's time, so in 1946 he turned the job of voicing Mickey Mouse over to Jimmy MacDonald, who was the sound-effects maestro for most of Disney's classic feature films and shorts. He began at Disney in 1934 and stayed on until 1976, doing double duty as both the head of the sound department and performing as Mickey.

CLARENCE "DUCKY" NASH

According to several Disney history books, Walt was listening to the radio one evening in 1934 when he heard a contestant on an amateur hour program reciting "Mary Had a Little Lamb" in an unusual squawking voice. He knew that he had to have the man, Clarence Nash, on staff at the studio. Nash was hired, and the animators soon found a use for his talents, giving voice to an irascible duck in 1934's *The Wise Little Hen*. Donald was an instant hit. Nash continued doing the world-famous duck's voice in more than two hundred Disney projects until his death in 1985.

PINTO COLVIG

As a former circus clown, Pinto Colvig had a hearty and boisterous stage laugh that was noticeable even to audience members way up in the rafters. That laugh came in handy when Colvig, a story man at Disney, was asked to voice a rowdy audience member in 1932's *Mickey's Revue*. This was supposed to be just a one-off background character, but Colvig's laugh distinguished him so much that filmgoers wanted more. He soon became the character known as Goofy. Colvig not only gave Goofy his distinctive sound (including the "Ya-hoo-hoo-hoo!" scream) but also voiced both Sleepy and Grumpy in *Snow White and the Seven Dwarfs*. He officially left Disney just after that, but was often brought back in to record Goofy's lines.

CLIFF EDWARDS

His voice is instantly recognizable, but his face and name aren't. Cliff Edwards was a popular crooner known as "Ukulele Ike" when Walt tapped him to play Jiminy Cricket in *Pinocchio*, a role he continued playing for decades. It's Edwards's version of "When You Wish upon a Star" that has become the anthem for Disney. He also voiced one of the crows in *Dumbo*.

BILLY GILBERT

His burly frame and blustery comic attitude made Billy Gilbert an in-demand actor in early Hollywood films, especially those of Hal Roach (his most notable appearance was as an unsatisfied customer in the 1932 Laurel and Hardy classic *The Music Box*). One of the things that Gilbert did well was an extended and exaggerated sneeze. This got Walt's attention, and he hired Gilbert to play—naturally—Sneezy. A few years later, the character Willie the Giant in *Mickey and the Beanstalk* had a scene that called for a sneeze, and Gilbert was cast again.

STERLING HOLLOWAY

A gentle Georgian with a shock of bright red hair and a distinctive drowsy tenor voice, Sterling Holloway was cast mostly in comedies after he arrived in Hollywood in the 1920s. Walt wanted Holloway to play Sleepy, but it didn't work out. His first role for Disney was Mr. Stork in *Dumbo*. He followed that with the narration of the "Peter and the Wolf" segment of *Make Mine Music*, the Cheshire Cat in *Alice in Wonderland*, and the hypnotic snake Kaa in *The Jungle Book*. The most perfect casting, however, came when Holloway originated the role of Winnie the Pooh. It was a match made in vocal heaven. It's hard to envision Pooh without the voice Holloway gave him. In 1991, one year before he died, Holloway was named a Disney Legend, the first voice-over artist to be given that honor.

BILL THOMPSON

Tex Avery was a noted animation rival of Walt Disney in the 1940s, producing several ambitious cartoons and characters. One of them who made an immediate impact on pop culture was Droopy Dog. The character—like Donald with "Ducky" Nash—was specifically created to fit an existing vocal performance. In this case it was Bill Thompson who gave Droopy his downcast, jowly tone. Disney hired Thompson to be the voice of the White Rabbit in *Alice in Wonderland* and then asked him to create Mr. Smee in *Peter Pan*. For that role, Thompson did a variation of his Droopy voice. He continued his association with Disney until his death in 1971, voicing Jock the Scotty Dog, King Hubert, Professor Owl, and Ranger J. Audubon Woodlore. To bring things full circle, Droopy—voiced by someone else in the style of Thompson—made a memorable appearance as an elevator operator in 1988's *Who Framed Roger Rabbit*.

PAUL FREES

Known as "the Man of a Thousand Voices," Paul Frees was already an accomplished radio performer when he was hired in 1961 by Disney to voice Professor Ludwig Von Drake. Around the same time, Frees was also working for Jay Ward Productions as the voice of the villain Boris Badenov in *Rocky and Bullwinkle*. When the Haunted Mansion opened in 1969, Frees used his own deep bass voice for the role of the unseen Ghost Host, who narrates your journey through the attraction. He can also be heard several times on Pirates of the Caribbean, most famously exclaiming "Dead Men Tell No Tales!"

PAUL WINCHELL

Ventriloquists were a favorite of Walt's. The most famous of them all, Edgar Bergen, appeared in a few Disney projects. The casting directors took note of this when it came time to find the voice of Tigger, Winnie the Pooh's energetic pal, in 1968. They gave the role to Paul Winchell, who'd already gained fame on television as the voice of the ventriloquist dummies Jerry Mahoney and Knuckle-head Smiff. Winchell's distinctive lisping and bubbly speech patterns for Tigger helped the character quickly become one of the most popular in Disney history. He continued to voice the role of Tigger for the next few decades while also working on Saturday morning Hanna-Barbera TV shows, creating villains like Dick Dastardly and Gargamel. Winchell's last performance as Tigger came in 1999, for Walt Disney World's Winnie the Pooh ride.

THURL RAVENSCROFT

With one of the deepest singing voices ever recorded, Thurl Ravenscroft was made famous by his bass. He was a member of the Mellomen barbershop quartet, a group who sang harmony on several Disney films starting in 1940. Ravenscroft stood out and was cast as the lead voice in other projects for the studio. His biggest claim to Disney fame was as the voice of Fritz in the Enchanted Tiki Room. He also voiced Buff the Buffalo for the Country Bear Jamboree attraction and is one of the four singing busts in the Haunted Mansion (often mistaken for Walt because they both had pencil-thin mustaches). Most of the world knows Ravenscroft's deep voice from two things. He was Tony the Tiger ("They're Grrrrrrreat!") for Kellogg's Frosted Flakes for decades and sang "You're a Mean One, Mr. Grinch" in the classic Christmas TV special.

DISNEY VOICE-OVER ARTISTS (MODERN)

WAYNE ALLWINE AND RUSSI TAYLOR

Mickey and Minnie were never married to each other on-screen, but in real life, their off-screen voices were. Wayne Allwine was a sound-effects staffer who mentored under Jimmy MacDonald. The senior man taught his protégé the art of voicing Mickey Mouse, which he himself had learned from Walt. When MacDonald retired, Allwine got the job of providing the sound for Disney's biggest star in films, on TV, and in the parks. It was in the Disney recording studio that Allwine met Russi Taylor, who began voicing Minnie in 1986. The two fell in love and married in 1991. Sadly, Allwine passed away in 2009, at the age of sixty-two. Taylor, who also does voice work for *The Simpsons* on FOX, continued on as Minnie, the longest anyone has ever played that role.

TONY ANSELMO

When Clarence Nash was nearing his fiftieth anniversary of voicing Donald Duck, he knew that he needed to start grooming someone else for the role. Tony Anselmo became his apprentice. After three years of work with Nash, Anselmo had to take over on short notice when his mentor died in 1985. Anselmo's been playing Donald since.

BILL FARMER

Several actors have provided Goofy's voice since Pinto Colvig set the template. In 1986, Bill Farmer was given the role. He's been doing it ever since. Farmer has actually voiced Goofy more than anyone else, with the recent increase in movies, TV shows, video games, toys, and attractions that have Goofy as their star.

JIM CUMMINGS

In 1988, Jim Cummings did what many people thought was impossible. He was able to successfully and consistently replicate Sterling Holloway's unique voice while taking over the role of Winnie the Pooh. A veteran of more than four hundred voice-over projects, Cummings also provides the voices of Ed the Hyena, Ray from *The Princess and the Frog*, and Peg-Leg Pete. In 2005, after Paul Winchell's death, Cummings was officially given the role of Tigger, making him the rare actor who gets to play two roles in a project, whenever Pooh and Tigger have scenes together.

DAVID OGDEN STIERS

A classically trained actor who is probably best known for his portrayal of Dr. Charles Emerson Winchester on the hit TV show *M*A*S*H*, David Ogden Stiers began doing voice-overs for Disney with 1991's *Beauty and the Beast*, where he gave Cogsworth just the right blend of pomposity and charm. He reprised the role many times and went on to voice roles in eight more Disney films, including the villain Governor Ratcliffe in *Pocahontas*. In addition, Stiers appeared in several live-action films for the studio and was one of the featured presenters in the Candlelight Processional, an annual Christmas favorite at the parks.

JOHN RATZENBERGER

Typecast as Cliff the lovable, know-it-all mailman after a long run on the hit NBC show *Cheers*, John Ratzenberger found steady work behind the microphone at Pixar, voicing a character in every single one of its films, starting with his role as Hamm in *Toy Story*. He is Pixar's good-luck charm. It's apparently worked, since Ratzenberger's films have earned billions for Disney.

John Ratzenberger, the voice of Hamm in the Toy Story trilogy. (Wikimedia Commons/photo by David Shankbone)

JOHN GOODMAN

An Emmy-winning actor, well known by his voice and appearance, John Goodman started working with Disney in 1980s live-action films like *Stella*, *Arachnophobia*, and *O Brother, Where Art Thou?* His first role in one of its animated features was as Pacha in *The Emperor's New Groove*. A year later, he created the character of James P. Sullivan in *Monsters, Inc.*, a role that was tailored to his strengths and to his ability to play off of his friend Billy Crystal, who voices Mike Wazowski. Goodman also took over for Phil Harris as Baloo in the animated sequel to *The Jungle Book* and played "Big Daddy" La Bouff in *The Princess and the Frog*.

BONNIE HUNT

A stand-up comedian, talk show host, writer, director, and producer, the versatile Bonnie Hunt was cast in Pixar's second film, *A Bug's Life*, which led to a long association with the studio. She also did voices in *Monsters, Inc.* and its sequel, and the third *Toy Story*. Her most famous Pixar role is as Sally in the *Cars* films. She also played Bonnie Hopps in Disney's *Zootopia*.

ALAN TUDYK

In recent years, like Ratzenberger with Pixar, Alan Tudyk has become a good-luck charm for Walt Disney Animation Studios. He has been in every single one of its films since his debut as the King of Candy in *Wreck-It Ralph*. As an inside joke, Tudyk's role of the Duke of Weselton in *Frozen* was given a twist when he played a character named Duke Weaselton in *Zootopia*. He also voiced the droid K-2SO in *Rogue One: A Star Wars Story*.

PATRICK WARBURTON

Nobody plays lovable, lucky doofuses better than Patrick Warburton. He is best known for his on-camera television roles as Elaine's dim-witted boyfriend David Puddy in *Seinfeld* and as Jeff in *Rules of Engagement*. It was on the latter show that he was paired with David Spade. The duo co-starred in *The Emperor's New Groove*, with Warburton as the voice of Kronk being a highlight of the film. Kronk was then spun off into his own video sequel and TV series. In the Disney parks, Warburton provides a voice for Star Tours and is beloved as the deadpan preboarding video host of Soarin' around the World.

HONORABLE MENTION

NATHAN LANE AND ERNIE SABELLA

Broadway often provides great voice actors for Disney, especially when it comes to its musicals. That was the case in the early 1990s when two standouts from the Great White Way, Nathan Lane and Ernie Sabella, were hired to play the meerkat Timon and warthog Pumbaa in *The Lion King*. With little alteration to their own speaking voices, these frequent Broadway co-stars brought their chemistry and New York attitude to the characters and made them fan favorites. Both Lane and Sabella have reprised the roles several times for films, videos, games, toys, and theme park attractions. Lane also won an Emmy for his voicing of Spot/Scott in the TV show *Teacher's Pet*.

DISNEY CHARACTER ACTORS

J. PATRICK O'MALLEY

With a broad smile, a cheery British accent, and a frame and a name that stood out, J. Patrick O'Malley was one of Hollywood's most in-demand character actors of the 1930s and '40s. Walt recognized his talents and had O'Malley dub the voice of Br'er Fox in *Song of the South* when James Baskett couldn't complete it. O'Malley followed that with roles in *Ichabod and Mr. Toad*, and then one of the most remarkable feats in Disney history: O'Malley played every single role—except for Alice—in the "Walrus and the Carpenter" sequence of *Alice in Wonderland*. His versatility with characters continued as he played several different roles in films like *Mary Poppins* and *The Jungle Book*. He appeared on camera in more than a hundred films and TV shows, including *Son of Flubber*, *The Adventures of Spin and Marty*, and *The Swamp Fox*, before his death in 1985.

HANS CONRIED

One of the busiest character actors in Hollywood, Hans Conried often played blustery authority figures, which made him ideal for the dual roles of Mr. Darling and Captain Hook in *Peter Pan*. When he wasn't busy with one of the hundreds of television, radio, and movie roles he played in his prolific fifty-year career, Conried would return to Disney, where he voiced Thomas Jefferson in the short *Ben and Me*, assumed the role of the Evil Queen's Magic Mirror on TV specials, and played a riverboat con man who assists Davy Crockett at the Alamo.

WALLY BOAG, FULTON BURLEY, AND BETTY TAYLOR

Three of the hardest-working performers ever, this trio of Disney Legends appeared in more than ten thousand performances of Disneyland's *Golden Horseshoe Revue* between 1955 and 1987. Boag is probably the best known of them for his comedy stylings, magic, and off-beat portrayal of Pecos Bill. He was also a mentor to a young Steve Martin. Burley, often the straight man to Boag, played an Irish tenor with a voice that captivated audiences. Taylor, the Slue Foot Sue to Boag's Pecos Bill, was the modern-day incarnation of a Wild West music hall character.

GENE SHELDON AND HENRY CALVIN

Walt was friends with Stan Laurel and Oliver Hardy and always admired their work as one of the great early film comedy duos. He would have loved to use them in a Disney project, but it never worked out. Luckily, he had two other actors under contract, Gene Sheldon and Henry Calvin, who were substitutes for the real thing. Calvin, the portlier of the two, played the role of the bumbling Sergeant Garcia in *Zorro*. The slender Sheldon played Zorro's mute assistant Bernardo. Sheldon and Calvin had great comic chemistry in their few scenes together, so they were paired in the circus-themed film *Toby Tyler*. For *Babes in Toyland*, Walt assigned them the roles of two hapless henchmen to the evil Barnaby. This was the film where they were basically doing a straight-up imitation of Laurel and Hardy, which was unmistakable since Laurel and Hardy had themselves made a film version of *Babes in Toyland* in 1934.

SEBASTIAN CABOT

The epitome of the proper British gentleman, Sebastian Cabot first appeared in the Disney live-action films *Westward Ho the Wagons!* and *Johnny Tremain* before being cast as the narrator and Sir Ector in *The Sword and the Stone*. His voice work in that film was so well received that he was cast as Bagheera in *The Jungle Book*, which also earned him great acclaim. Though he was busy with a role on TV as the butler Mr. French in *Family Affair*, Cabot still played the role of narrator in every single Winnie the Pooh film until his death in 1977.

RICHARD "DICK" BAKALYAN

Dick Bakalyan was another character actor with a face that gave him great appeal to casting directors. His cauliflower ears and flattened nose gave him the look of a boxer or thug, roles that he usually played. His voice was distinct, with a comical tough guy Brooklyn inflection that allowed him to break from type and portray nonthreatening criminals. That's what he did for Disney, appearing on-screen as a cartoony gangster in *Never a Dull Moment*, *The Computer Wore Tennis Shoes*, *The*

Strongest Man in the World, and *Escape to Witch Mountain*. Those vocal qualities made him perfect for animation, which he proved in the title role of M. C. Bird in the Oscar-winning short *It's Tough to Be a Bird* and as Dinky in *The Fox and the Hound*.

JOE FLYNN

The master of playing comically put-upon authority figures, Joe Flynn appeared in more than forty movies and TV shows like *McHale's Navy*, but his greatest work came with Disney. His Dean Higgins in the three Dexter Riley films made him the perfect foil for Kurt Russell and his Medfield College buddies. Flynn did variations on the Dean Higgins character (but with different names) in *The Barefoot Executive*, *The Million Dollar Duck*, and *Superdad*. His last role, before his untimely death at the age of forty-nine, was as the voice of Mr. Snoops in *The Rescuers*.

MICHAEL McGREEVEY

Every hero needs a best friend. Michael McGreevey played that role for Kurt Russell's Dexter Riley. His helpful redhead, Richard Schuyler, was a clumsy, affable buddy to Dexter, appearing in all three films of the Riley trilogy. McGreevey had done work for Disney before, in the TV movie *Sammy the Way-Out Seal*, and he continued playing roles in other Disney films, such as *Snowball Express* and *The Shaggy D.A.*

DICK VAN PATTEN

For a while there in the 1970s, it seemed like Dick Van Patten was in every single live-action Disney film. He often played a variation of the conniving corporate stooge or officious boss, doing so in movies like *Snowball Express*, *The Strongest Man in the World*, *Superdad*, *The Shaggy D.A.*, and *Freaky Friday*. His work at Disney led him to be cast in the role that defined him, lovable dad Tom Bradford on TV's *Eight Is Enough*.

MARTIN SHORT

A comedy superstar, Martin Short began lending his incredible talents for creating characters to Disney as the inept bank robber Perry in 1989's *Three Fugitives*. He topped that a few years later

The cast of *Father of the Bride Part II* (1995): Martin Short, Diane Keaton, Steve Martin, and Kimberly Williams (Buena Vista Pictures/Photofest)

with his role of Franck, the oddball wedding planner in *Father of the Bride*, a role he repeated in the sequel. He co-starred with Kurt Russell in *Captain Ron* and Tim Allen in *Jungle 2 Jungle* and *The Santa Clause 3* (as Jack Frost), each with a unique spin. Vocally, he portrayed the shipwrecked robot B.E.N. in *Treasure Planet*. A proud Canadian, Short appears in the film highlighting Canadian landmarks in the pavilion for that country in Epcot's World Showcase.

DISNEY SONGWRITERS/COMPOSERS

THE SHERMAN BROTHERS

Unquestionably the greatest songwriting team in Hollywood history. These two brothers, the sons of a Tin Pan Alley genius with a string of hits of his own, started working for Walt in 1961. He soon realized that they had the gifts to bring whatever emotions or message he wanted to convey to an audience to life with a song. Their incredible Disney legacy includes the scores of *The Parent Trap*, *Mary Poppins*, *Winnie the Pooh*, *The Jungle Book*, *The Aristocats*, and *Bedknobs and Broomsticks*. In all, they contributed songs to more than twenty-seven films. They have also done work for the Disney parks, with songs for—among others—the Carousel of Progress, the Enchanted Tiki Room, and the one that produced *the* most played song in history, It's a Small World.

OLIVER WALLACE AND FRANK CHURCHILL

Two of the most important employees in the early days of Disney animation. Wallace and Churchill scored almost every single short and feature from the *Silly Symphonies* to *Lady and the Tramp*. Before the Sherman Brothers, Wallace and Churchill's songs were the Disney sound.

JIMMIE DODD

A devout Christian minister, Jimmie Dodd is best known as the squeaky-clean leader of the Mouseketeers. He was also an accomplished songwriter, providing thirty tunes for the show, including the opening and closing themes. His songs often contained subtle moral lessons.

GEORGE BRUNS AND BUDDY BAKER

Hired in 1953 by Walt, George Bruns composed many of the title songs for Disney TV shows, and then for the live-action films of the 1960s and '70s. Before his retirement in 1975, he cowrote songs for several Disney parks attractions. Baker began at Disney two years after Bruns and was his frequent collaborator. After Bruns retired, Baker took over as the studio's staff composer. He was also musical director for Epcot's attractions. When he retired in 1983, the job title of Hollywood studio staff composer went with him. Most of that work is contracted out now.

ALAN MENKEN AND HOWARD ASHMAN

Without these two, there would have been no Disney renaissance in the 1990s. Their Broadway background made them the perfect pair to pen the popular and musically diverse scores for *The Little Mermaid, Beauty and the Beast*, and *Aladdin*. Ashman died at the age of forty, but Menken has continued writing songs for Disney with several different collaborators.

ELTON JOHN AND TIM RICE

These two British pop music titans collaborated on *The Lion King* in 1994 and later on the Broadway version of *Aida*. Rice also worked on *Aladdin* after Howard Ashman's death.

DANNY ELFMAN

A frequent collaborator of Tim Burton, Elfman provided the score and the singing voice of Jack Skellington in *The Nightmare before Christmas*. His unique style can also be heard in the films *Dick Tracy, Alice in Wonderland*, and *Frankenweenie*, and at Hong Kong Disneyland's Mystic Manor.

RANDY NEWMAN

Nominated for twenty Oscars, prolific songwriter Randy Newman has only won twice. Both times it was for a Disney song. The first was "If I Didn't Have You" from *Monsters, Inc.* His second was for "We Belong Together" from *Toy Story 3*. In addition to those films and their sequels, Newman, a multiple Grammy and Emmy winner, scored *James and the Giant Peach, A Bug's Life, Cars*, and *The Princess and the Frog* for Disney.

STEPHEN SCHWARTZ

A Broadway lyricist with hits like *Godspell, Pippin*, and *Wicked*, Schwartz worked for Disney on the scores of the films *Pocahontas, The Hunchback of Notre Dame*, and *Enchanted*.

ROBERT AND KRISTEN LOPEZ

This Emmy-, Grammy-, Oscar-, and Tony-winning couple first worked for Disney in 2007, writing the musical version of *Finding Nemo* for Disney's Animal Kingdom. In 2013, they wrote the score for *Frozen*, and then penned the Oscar-winning song "Remember Me" for 2017's Coco.

LISTS ABOUT DISNEY TELEVISION/ OTHER MEDIA

MILESTONES IN DISNEY MEDIA HISTORY

1930—PUBLISHING

The first Mickey Mouse books for children appeared in stores in 1930. In 1933, Whitman Publishing of Wisconsin got the license to produce Disney-branded titles. One of its imprints, Little Golden Books, remains the best-known and most beloved way that most children were first introduced to Disney characters and stories. Whitman also had the Dell and Gold Key Comics lines, which released the popular Disney comic books of the 1950s and '60s. Random House had a similar contract with Disney in the 1970s to produce educational books. In 1991, Disney started an in-house publishing company and took back all licenses. Hyperion—the address of the second Disney studio—was the name chosen for the main book imprints. Disney Publishing was also used. Many best sellers and movie tie-ins were released by them in the 1990s and 2000s. Young adult franchises were launched, too, with the Kingdom Keepers and Starcatcher series.

1938—RADIO

During the 1930s, radio was king. The movies were popular, but most people got their entertainment and news from Mr. Marconi's magical wireless device in their living rooms. It was only natural, then, that Mickey Mouse would make the move into radio after conquering the big screen. NBC was the home for *The Mickey Mouse Theater of the Air*, starting in 1938. Walt Disney did the voice of Mickey on each show. It didn't last long, but it led to appearances on popular radio shows by Disney voice-over artists to promote upcoming films. In 1955, in conjunction with his *Disneyland* TV show, Walt hosted a short-lived daily radio show called *The Magic Kingdom*. Radio went out of style for a while, and so did Disney's presence there. In 1996, it returned in a big way with the debut of Radio Disney, a twenty-four-hour station heard across the country. Aimed at preteens, it featured a number of musical genres. After the success of *Hannah Montana* and *High School Musical*, Radio Disney grew even more popular. In 2017, Radio Disney started syndicating its shows to terrestrial stations, focusing more on digital streaming.

1947—RECORD ALBUMS

In its early days, Disney used to license and sell its music and popular songs like "Who's Afraid of the Big Bad Wolf?" to other companies. The music rights to some of its early films like *Snow White* and *Dumbo* are still owned by other companies. In 1947, the Walt Disney Music Company was formed to prevent this from happening again. It took a few years, but by 1955, when it became officially known as Disneyland Records, things took off—thanks to sales of the "Ballad of Davy Crockett" record, which was a number one hit. Since Disneyland records were often classed as children's albums, even when they weren't, a new label—Buena Vista, named after the street in Burbank the studio stood on—was added, in 1959. Hits from the likes of Annette Funicello and Hayley Mills, as well as live-action soundtracks, were released by Buena Vista, while animated movie soundtracks and story albums got the Disneyland label. In 1989, Michael Eisner created the Hollywood Records label to release soundtracks from Touchstone and Hollywood Pictures films. By 2007, all three labels had been merged into one big company called Disney Music Group, or DMG.

1950—TELEVISION

Walt was the first Hollywood studio chief to embrace television. He not only endorsed the new medium, he appeared on it. The initial test was a Christmas Day special in 1950 called *One Hour in Wonderland.* Sponsored by Coca-Cola, with no commercial interruptions, just a few carefully placed Coke bottles, it had Walt celebrating Christmas at the studio with a bunch of kids—including his own—and the Magic Mirror from *Snow White* introducing scenes from the upcoming film *Alice in Wonderland.* It was basically a one-hour commercial for Disney, but the enormous ratings for it proved that Walt and Roy were right about TV. Walt did another successful Christmas special in 1951. The three networks were clamoring for a weekly show. Walt insisted that any network that wanted a show would also help him finance Disneyland. ABC agreed, so in 1954 Walt launched *Disneyland*—an anthology show hosted by him that also served as a commercial for his park. He also

Disney's anthology TV series went by various names over the years (1954–1990), but it remains the second-longest running primetime program in television history. (Walt Disney Productions/ Photofest)

gave ABC *The Mickey Mouse Club* and *Zorro*. In 1961, the anthology show moved to NBC and was broadcast in color. Once again, Walt was at the forefront of technology. He'd filmed almost all his shows for the black-and-white ABC series in color, at extra expense. He was able to use this backlog of material for the new show. Sales of color TVs skyrocketed. After Walt's death, his anthology series continued on for another seventeen years, eventually moving to CBS in 1981, making it one of the few shows to run on all three networks. Touchstone TV was formed in the 1980s, producing even more shows for all three networks.

1980—HOME VIDEO

Walt created a successful marketing strategy in the 1940s of rereleasing his classic films every seven years or so into theaters. He surmised that a new generation of children who hadn't seen these films yet would join the past generations in going to see them, which was almost pure profit for the studio. Television put a small dent in that strategy (which is what the other studios had feared), but Walt was smart enough to create original films for TV, keeping his classics away from broadcast. By the time home video players became a big thing in the late 1970s, Walt was long gone. Ron Miller had to make the choice whether or not to release some of the classic Disney films for sale to the public. Disney started with live-action films in 1980, releasing *The Apple Dumpling Gang*, *The Black Hole* (just one year after it was in theaters), *The Love Bug*, and *Escape to Witch Mountain*. Sales and rentals were brisk. In 1981, the first animated classic—*Dumbo*—was released on VHS. *Alice in Wonderland* followed a year later. The floodgates opened, and Disney wound up putting all its classics out for sale. It did figure out a way to mimic Walt's careful seven-year release strategy, which had been rendered obsolete by 1988. Disney creates a limited number of copies when it puts something out on VHS (and later DVD or Blu-ray), then keeps the title in stores for a limited time, creating demand for it. The home video and on-demand video markets now make up a big part of Disney's revenue stream.

1983—CABLE TV

Ron Miller saw the rise of pay cable television and knew that Disney needed to be part of it. He founded the Disney Channel, which began broadcasting in April 1983. In its first ten years, almost forty million people subscribed to this new network, which showed Disney programs twenty-four hours a day. Original shows and movies supplemented the treasures from the Disney vaults as programming. It switched to a basic cable channel in 1993, expanding the audience exponentially. By the 2000s, the Disney Channel had grown to include more than 150 international versions and several spin-off stations, like Disney XD and Disney Junior.

1987—COMMERCIALS

Disney is such a powerful brand name that it never really had to do much advertising. Media outlets all wanted to run stories about Walt and his amazing creations. This was free publicity. By the late 1980s, that magic had begun to wear off, as other entertainment and theme park companies began to create their own media buzz. Michael Eisner knew the power of television commercials, especially ones with a memorable tag line, to boost sales and brand recognition. He found his one in 1986, and it happened by chance at a dinner meeting. Eisner and his wife, Jane, were dining with a friend who had just climbed Mount Everest. Jane asked him what he was going to do next. His answer was casual: "I'm going to Disney World." That sparked Eisner's imagination. He came up with the idea of asking the winning quarterback of that year's Super Bowl in Pasadena to say the same line as he was walking off the field. The contest was between the New York Giants and the Denver Broncos. The Giants won, and their quarterback, Phil Simms, was the MVP. He was paid to say the line, which he did to perfection. The next day, the ad—backed by a recording of "When You Wish upon a Star" and featuring highlights from the game—aired on every network. It was a sensation, becoming one of the most famous ad campaigns in history. For the next thirty years, the "What's Next?" commercials aired after major sporting events, awards shows, and other big occasions. "I'm going to Disney World!" became a catchphrase, as Eisner had hoped, and ticket sales boomed at the Disney parks.

1995—BROADWAY

Disney had dipped its toes into the Broadway waters with a few shows in the 1980s and '90s, but it committed itself to becoming a power player on the Great White Way by signing a forty-nine-year lease in 1995 for the historic New Amsterdam Theater on 42nd Street. Built by impresario Florenz Ziegfeld in 1902, this grand palace had fallen into disrepair by the early 1990s, with holes in the roof and an infestation of rats. Disney spent two years and millions of dollars renovating the place, restoring it to its former glory. It opened with a concert in 1997, and then the theatrical phenomenon *The Lion King*, which was a good omen for a theater that is just as much a part of the experience as what's on stage.

1995—DIGITAL

Home computers and the internet had started to blossom in 1994 when Disney established Disney Interactive Media Group, an umbrella division that handled anything related to online media or video games. Within a year, an online portal, Go.com, was created to allow fans their own email addresses and other incentives to do all their surfing and searching through Disney. Those types of sites were obsolete by the early 2000s. The division then moved into software, producing console games like *Epic Mickey* and *Disney Infinity*. They also had popular apps like *Where's My Water?* and *Club Penguin*, which used unique characters, not Disney icons. The rise of mobile phones allowed Disney to expand its app and streaming offerings, bringing in even more revenue. In 2017, CEO Bob Iger announced that Disney would soon be launching its own Netflix-style streaming service, keeping it relevant as twenty-first-century viewing habits progress.

1996—NETWORK OWNERSHIP

The American Broadcasting Company (ABC) staked Walt five million dollars to fund the building of Disneyland in 1954, and became part owners of the park. Walt eventually bought the shares back for eight million dollars and moved his TV shows to other networks, but ABC was a big part of Disney history. That came full circle in 1996, when Disney merged with ABC (then owned by Capital Cities) for nineteen billion dollars. This included not only the ABC network but associated cable channels like ESPN, A&E, Lifetime, and the History Channel. This, combined with the Disney Channel, turned Disney into a media powerhouse overnight. It was then able to use these various outlets for corporate synergy and promotion of its parks, merchandise, and films.

LIVE-ACTION DISNEY TV SERIES

ZORRO (1957 TO 1959)
Guy Williams stars as the swashbuckling defender of powerless villagers in early California. It still ranks as one of the best action-adventure series to appear on television.

THE MICKEY MOUSE CLUB/MMC (1955 TO 1995)
Walt's wildly popular daily children's television series, featuring the Mouseketeers. It was revived in the 1970s, and then again in the 1980s and '90s, renamed *MMC*.

THE GOLDEN GIRLS (1985 TO 1992)
A multiple Emmy Award-winning sitcom about four friends (Blanche, Rose, Dorothy, and her mother Sophia) in the twilight of their years, yet still active and full of life, who share a modest house in southern Florida. There were laughs and tears in almost every episode.

DINOSAURS (1991 TO 1994)
Characters created by the Henson Company populated this Emmy Award-winning prehistoric comedy about a suburban family of dinosaurs. The Baby dinosaur was a breakout star.

HOME IMPROVEMENT (1991 TO 1999)
Not just one of the top ten live-action Disney shows, *Home Improvement* ranks up there as one of the greatest situation comedies in history. The Taylor family, their neighbor Wilson, and the co-stars of *Tool Time*—the show within the show hosted by Tim—made each episode a delight.

BOY MEETS WORLD (1993 TO 2000)
Life as a teenager isn't easy for Cory Matthews, balancing home, school, and his girlfriend Topanga, in this hit comedy. A sequel, *Girl Meets World*, aired almost twenty years later.

WHO WANTS TO BE A MILLIONAIRE (1999 TO 2002)
This game show phenomenon, hosted by Regis Philbin, topped the ratings for weeks at a time and even spawned an attraction at Walt Disney World.

LOST (2004 TO 2010)
A mysterious island holds many riddles for the survivors of a plane crash as they work together to survive in this Emmy-winning drama.

ONCE UPON A TIME (2011 TO 2018)
Many classic Disney and fairy tale characters come to life—with a new twist—in this series set in the mysterious New England village of Storybrooke.

AGENTS OF S.H.I.E.L.D. (2013 TO PRESENT)

The small-screen companion to the Marvel Universe. The agency so prominent in *The Avengers* gets its time to shine in this weekly series, which often references the events in the films.

ANIMATED DISNEY SERIES

D-TV (1984 TO 1989)

The Disney Channel's answer to MTV, using Disney characters in videos for popular songs.

DUCK TALES (1987 TO 1990)

Huey, Dewey, and Louie are led on adventures by their super-rich granduncle Scrooge McDuck. Disney made an animated feature film based on it, and it was also revived as a TV series in 2017.

CHIP 'N' DALE: RESCUE RANGERS (1988 TO 1990)

Disney's two favorite chipmunks lead a group investigating and solving international mysteries.

GARGOYLES (1994 TO 1996)

A dark show, about New York City gargoyles who come to life at night to battle evil.

THE DISNEY AFTERNOON (1990 TO 1997)

With the syndicated success of *Duck Tales*, *Chip 'n' Dale*, and *Gargoyles*, Disney created this two-hour package of original animated series for local stations, intended to be aired in the afternoons, when kids came home from school. In addition to the previously mentioned shows, others that were part of this unique programming block were *Tale Spin*, *The Adventures of the Gummi Bears*, *Darkwing Duck*, *Goof Troop*, *Bonkers*, *Quack Pack*, and *The Mighty Ducks*.

HOUSE OF MOUSE/THE MICKEY MOUSE CLUBHOUSE (2001 TO 2009)/(2006 to 2016)

Mickey returned to regular television with the premiere of *House of Mouse*, where the premise is that he owns a nightclub frequented by Disney characters. Shorts, musical numbers, and sketches were interspersed with the main action, all traditionally animated. In 2006, a CGI version of Mickey and friends debuted in *The Mickey Mouse Clubhouse*, a show made primarily for younger children. It brought Mickey up to date for the twenty-first century.

KIM POSSIBLE (2002 TO 2007)

An average teenage girl doubles as a super spy, heading on missions around the world.

PHINEAS AND FERB (2007 TO 2015)

Two inventive brothers set out to enjoy their 104 days of summer vacation, despite the interruptions of their older sister and their pet platypus, who is also a secret agent.

JAKE AND THE NEVER LAND PIRATES (2011 TO 2016)

A show for toddlers, inspired by *Peter Pan*, about a young pirate and his friends who have adventures looking for buried treasure in Never Land, while avoiding Captain Hook.

ELENA OF AVALOR (2016 TO PRESENT)

The first Latina Disney princess, Elena rules her kingdom wisely while thwarting a sorceress.

EPISODES OF DISNEY'S ANTHOLOGY SERIES

"THE DISNEYLAND STORY" (OCTOBER 27, 1954)

The very first *Disneyland* TV show, a preview of Walt's dream park, and a history of Mickey.

"OPERATION UNDERSEA" (DECEMBER 8, 1954)

Walt previews *20,000 Leagues under the Sea*. This show won the Emmy for best program.

"MAN IN SPACE" (MARCH 9, 1955)

Using innovative animation, theories of space travel are explained. It helped inspire NASA.

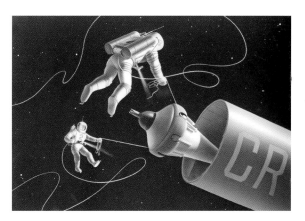

Man in Space (1955). (Walt Disney/ Photofest)

"THE STORY OF ANIMATION" (NOVEMBER 30, 1955)

Walt goes all the way back to 1906 to explain the history of animation in film.

"WHERE DO STORIES COME FROM?" (APRIL 4, 1956)

Walt answers the many questions about how Disney comes up with its cartoon ideas.

"TRICKS OF OUR TRADE" (FEBRUARY 13, 1957)

Walt helps explain the science behind animation, using scenes from Disney films.

"I CAPTURED THE KING OF THE LEPRECHAUNS" (MAY 29, 1959)

Walt and actor Pat O'Brien visit Ireland in search of leprechauns (to help promote *Darby O'Gill*).

"DISNEYLAND AFTER DARK" (APRIL 15, 1962)

Walt tours Disneyland at night, with appearances by the Osmonds and Louis Armstrong.

"DISNEYLAND GOES TO THE WORLD'S FAIR" (MAY 17, 1964)

Walt gives a history of World's Fairs and a glimpse of Disney's attractions at the 1964 NYC Fair.

"DISNEYLAND'S 10TH ANNIVERSARY" (JANUARY 3, 1965)

Walt looks back on the first decade of his park and previews some new rides and attractions.

HONORABLE MENTION

"DISNEYLAND AROUND THE SEASONS" (DECEMBER 18, 1966)
Walt hosts the celebration of the opening of It's a Small World at Disneyland. This pretaped airing was a bit somber, as it came just three days after Walt's unexpected death.

MADE-FOR-TV DISNEY MOVIES

SAMMY, THE WAY-OUT SEAL (OCTOBER 28, 1962) directed by Norman Tokar

Originally aired as two episodes of the *Disneyland* show, this tale of two boys (Michael McGreevey and Billy Mumy) who adopt an injured seal and hide him from their family was so popular that Disney ran it in several TV seasons and released it as a theatrical film overseas.

ATTA GIRL, KELLY! (MARCH 5 TO 19, 1967) directed by James Sheldon

This three-part movie tells the story of Kelly, a Seeing Eye dog, from the viewpoint of her puppy raiser, her trainer, and the blind man (Beau Bridges) who is eventually partnered with her. Shot on location at the Seeing Eye's campus in Morristown, New Jersey, which rarely gave access for this sort of thing. Almost twenty years later, Disney would produce another TV movie about the history of the Seeing Eye, called *Love Leads the Way*.

THE WHIZ KID AND THE MYSTERY AT RIVERTON (JANUARY 6 TO 13, 1974) directed by Tom Leetch

Based on the book *Alvin Fernandez: Mayor for a Day*, this two-part film follows the exploits of a young inventor (Eric Shea) and his friends as they use their wits to foil a bunch of crooks. It was so popular that Disney made a sequel in 1977, *The Whiz Kid and the Carnival Caper*.

THE GHOST OF CYPRESS SWAMP (MARCH 13, 1977) directed by Vince McEveety

Rather than a film broken up into installments as had previously been done, this was billed as the "very first feature length Disney movie made exclusively for television." It's an adventure tale about a boy hunting for a rogue panther who's terrorizing Delaware's Cypress Swamp.

POLLY! (NOVEMBER 12, 1989) directed by Debbie Allen

A musical retelling of *Pollyanna*, set in the Deep South with an African American cast.

TOOTHLESS (OCTOBER 5, 1997) directed by Melanie Mayron

Kirstie Alley stars as a dentist who passes away and comes back to earth as the Tooth Fairy.

TOWER OF TERROR (OCTOBER 26, 1997) directed by D. J. MacHale

Based on the attraction at Disney/MGM Studios in Florida, and partly filmed there, this movie, starring Steve Guttenberg and Kirsten Dunst, provides an eerie backstory for the thrill ride.

RUBY BRIDGES (JANUARY 18, 1998) directed by Euzhan Palcy

A civil rights story about the integration of the New Orleans school system in the 1960s. President Bill Clinton and Disney CEO Michael Eisner introduced the film together.

DINOTOPIA (MAY 12 TO 14, 2002) directed by Marco Brambilla

A six-hour fantasy movie, aired over three nights, about man and dinosaurs living together.

THE MUPPETS' WIZARD OF OZ (MAY 20, 2005) directed by Kirk R. Thatcher

A new version of Baum's story, starring pop singer Ashanti as Dorothy, Kermit as the Scarecrow, Gonzo as the Tin "Thing," Fozzie as the Cowardly Lion, and Miss Piggy as all of the witches.

DISNEY CHANNEL SERIES

THE DISNEY FAMILY ALBUM (1984 TO 1986)

Twenty episodes were made of this series, which profiled some of the greatest Disney Legends.

MOUSERCISE (1983 TO 1986)

At the height of the home video aerobics craze, Disney produced this version aimed at kids.

AVONLEA (1990 TO 1996)

Based on the *Anne of Green Gables* stories, this Emmy-winning show follows Anne as she moves to the island town of Avonlea to live with relatives.

DUMBO'S CIRCUS (1985 TO 1987)

This innovative musical children's show utilized "puppetronics" to show Dumbo (who was now able to talk) and his traveling circus pals as they go around performing.

BEAR IN THE BIG BLUE HOUSE (1997 TO 2006)

The Henson Company created this oversized, friendly bear who teaches life lessons to preschoolers during playtime visits from his woodland friends.

EVEN STEVENS (2000 TO 2003)

A teenage class clown tries to live up to the reputation of his overachieving older sister.

LIZZIE McGUIRE (2001 TO 2004)

A high school girl deals with life in her own unique way. Lizzie's inner monologues are delivered straight to the audience by an animated version of herself.

WIZARDS OF WAVERLY PLACE (2007 TO 2012)

Three average teenage siblings are also wizards who help run their family's New York deli.

THE SUITE LIFE OF ZACK AND CODY (2005 TO 2008)

Twin teenage brothers live with their mother in a Boston hotel and get into wacky adventures.

LAB RATS (2012 TO 2016)

The teenage stepson of a billionaire inventor teams up with his three bionic creations.

DISNEY CHANNEL MOVIES

TIGER TOWN (1983)

This was the first Disney Channel movie. It follows a young boy who wishes that his beloved Detroit Tigers will win the pennant. Thanks to his favorite player, an aging star played by Roy Scheider, they do. Coincidentally, the real-life Tigers won the pennant that year. Also released in theaters.

LOTS OF LUCK (1985)

Annette Funicello returned to Disney to star in this film about a family whose winning streak causes more headaches than happiness.

GREAT EXPECTATIONS (1989)

A six-hour, three-part adaptation of the Dickens classic, with an all-star cast including Sir Anthony Hopkins, Jean Simmons, and John Rhys-Davies.

DANNY, THE CHAMPION OF THE WORLD (1989)

Jeremy Irons and his son star as father and son in this film about a poverty-stricken family standing up to a greedy land baron. Based on a Roald Dahl book.

HALLOWEENTOWN (1998)

A witch (Debbie Reynolds) enlists her mortal family to help her save benevolent Halloweentown from the forces of evil. Two sequels came from this highly rated hit.

LUCK OF THE IRISH (2001)

A junior high basketball player discovers that he's actually descended from Irish leprechauns and has to face off against an evil leprechaun to save his family.

THE CHEETAH GIRLS (2003)

The one that started the Disney Channel's shift to big-budget musical extravaganzas, with an eye on pop culture crossover. The four diverse girls in this "Cheetah-licious" (their words, not mine) singing group launched two sequels, a concert tour, a hit album, and a line of clothing.

CAMP ROCK (2008)

The Jonas Brothers and Demi Lovato were the featured stars of this film about a summer camp for musicians. A hit album and a sequel came from it.

HIGH SCHOOL MUSICAL (2006)

The Cheetah Girls paved the way, but *High School Musical* became the international phenomenon that put the Disney Channel on the map. This modern-day take on *Romeo and Juliet* spawned sequel after sequel, chart-topping albums, theatrical releases, concert tours, school productions, and billions in merchandise sales; made stars of its cast; and influenced a generation of filmmakers and musicians. It's the franchise that keeps on giving for Disney.

DESCENDANTS (2015)

As close as Disney has come to recapturing the *High School Musical* magic. Directed and choreographed by Kenny Ortega, who was responsible for the look and feel of *HSM*, *Descendants* is set in a magical world where the children of legendary Disney heroes and princesses live separately from the kids of the Disney villains. Four of those "evil" kids, Mal (daughter of Maleficent), Evie (daughter of the Evil Queen), Carlos (son of Cruella de Vil), and Jay (son of Jafar), wind up in the same school as the "good" kids, and complications ensue. Merchandise sales connected to this franchise and its sequels skyrocketed. Halloween costumes of the colorful characters were especially popular.

LIVE-ACTION DISNEY TV CHARACTERS

Since top ten TV characters like Davy Crockett, Zorro, Tim Taylor, and the Golden Girls have been represented on other lists, here are ten standouts who also deserve mention in this book.

ELFEGO BACA (1958)—Walt Disney Presents, Ten Episodes

Played by Robert Loggia.

A retired gunslinger in 1880s New Mexico who becomes a lawyer and sheriff and has to tangle with corrupt ranchers and murderous gangs of raiders.

TEXAS JOHN SLAUGHTER (1958)—Walt Disney Presents, Seventeen Episodes

Played by Tom Tryon.

A reluctant gunslinging hero who joins the Texas Rangers in 1870 to fight rogues and outlaws.

THE SWAMP FOX (1959)—Walt Disney Presents, Eight Episodes

Played by Leslie Nielsen.

The second-most-popular character from Walt's Frontierland episodes, this hero—loosely based on Revolutionary War patriot Francis Marion of South Carolina—uses his knowledge of the local geography and terrain to help his band of American rebels stay one step ahead of the British.

Known in later years as the "Olivier of spoofs" for such films as *Airplane* and *Naked Gun*, Leslie Nielson played the Revolutionary War hero Francis Marion in Disney's TV series *The Swamp Fox*. (American Broadcasting Company [ABC]/ Photofest)

DR. SYN (1964)—Walt Disney's Wonderful World of Color, Three Episodes

Played by Patrick McGoohan.

An eighteenth-century British vicar who disguises himself as a terrifying scarecrow to fight for justice.

MR. FEENY (1993)—Boy Meets World

Played by William Daniels.

Cory's teacher, who also happens to be his next-door neighbor. In later seasons, the wisdom-dispensing Feeny became Cory's principal and—incredibly—one of his professors at college.

AL BORLAND AND WILSON (1991)—Home Improvement

Played by Richard Karn and Earl Hindman.

Tim's cohost on *Tool Time* and his next-door neighbor, Al and Wilson are two who provide sound advice for the Tool Man, even if he doesn't always follow through. The bearded, flannel-wearing Al is loyal to Tim, though he doesn't get as much credit as he should on the fictional show within the show. Wilson is a helpful and sage neighbor who is heard but never fully seen (producers were very clever about masking his face in every episode).

PAT (1999)—Smart House

Played by Katey Sagal.

A sentient home computer reprogrammed by a teenage whiz kid to act as mother and protector of his house, PAT (an acronym for "Personal Applied Technology") takes her job too seriously and locks the boy's family inside to keep them safe from danger.

SHARPAY EVANS (2006)—High School Musical

Played by Ashley Tisdale.

The wealthy main antagonist at East High School, Sharpay schemes with her twin brother Ryan to control all aspects of the school's drama department. After repeatedly being humbled by her fellow students, Sharpay moves from New Mexico to New York to become a Broadway star.

JESSIE PRESCOTT (2011)—Jessie

Played by Debby Ryan.

A Texas girl who takes a job as a nanny to four New York City kids in a luxury high-rise.

MR. GOLD (2011)—Once upon a Time

Played by Robert Carlyle.

The pseudonym for Rumpelstiltskin, a wealthy sorcerer and antihero who warns those who deal with him at his enchanted pawn shop that "all magic comes at a price."

ANIMATED DISNEY TV CHARACTERS

PROFESSOR LUDWIG VON DRAKE (1961)—
Walt Disney's Wonderful World of Color

Voice of Paul Frees.

This eccentric uncle of Donald Duck, a lecturer and scientist from Austria, was created specifically for the *Wonderful World of Color*. He hosted eighteen episodes of that show, was the narrator of several records, and was on other Disney TV programs, like *House of Mouse*.

Paul Frees, voice of Professor Ludwig Von Drake, and so many others. (Photofest)

DARKWING DUCK (1991)—Darkwing Duck

Voice of Jim Cummings.

Drake Mallard is an unassuming suburban dad with a secret identity, the superhero Darkwing Duck, who keeps the town of St. Canard free from danger.

BONKERS D. BOBCAT (1993)—Bonkers

Voice of Jim Cummings.

A buffoonish former cartoon superstar who becomes a police officer patrolling Hollywood.

PEPPER ANN PEARSON (1997)—Pepper Ann

Voice of Kathleen Wilhoite.

An imaginative twelve-year-old girl at Hazelnut Middle School faces daily life with her friends Nicky and Milo. Each episode opened with Pepper Ann discovering something different in her desk.

STANLEY GRIFF (2001)—Stanley

Voice of Jessica D. Stone.

The magical *Great Big Book of Everything* provides preschooler Stanley and his pet goldfish Dennis with the answers they need to solve the daily situations they face.

MANUEL GARCIA III (2006)—Handy Manny

A repairman in Sheet Rock Hills, Manny is also a problem solver, often assisted by his anthropomorphic tools.

DR. HEINZ DOOFENSHMIRTZ (2009)—Phineas and Ferb

Voice of Dan Povenmire.

A bumbling scientist who aspires to join the ranks of evil geniuses by creating various machines with the suffix "-inator." His ultimate goal—until being hampered by Agent P, which almost always happens—is to take over the "tri-state area."

WAYNE AND LANNY (2009)—Prep & Landing

Voices of Dave Foley and Derek Richardson.

Two elves who work on Santa's elite advance team, Prep & Landing. Wayne is the more experienced and has to train the newbie, Lanny. They stumble a bit, but fix their mess.

DOTTIE McSTUFFINS (2012)—Doc McStuffins

Voices of Laya DeLeon Hays and Kiara Muhammad.

An eight-year-old girl with a magical stethoscope that brings toys to life, she dreams of being a doctor like her pediatrician mother.

SOFIA (2013)—Sofia the First

Voice of Ariel Winter.

A young girl whose mom marries into royalty, Sofia has a magical amulet allowing her to talk to animals and summon Disney princesses for advice. The villain, Sir Cedric, covets the amulet.

HONORABLE MENTION

SCROOGE McDUCK (1947)

Created for the comic books, not specifically for television, this wealthy uncle to Donald Duck rocketed to pop culture fame forty years later as the star of the 1987 TV series *Duck Tales*.

DISNEY TV THEME SONGS

"THE MICKEY MOUSE CLUB MARCH" (1955)
Music and lyrics by Jimmie Dodd.

"THE BALLAD OF DAVY CROCKETT" (1955)
Music and lyrics by George Bruns and Tom Blackburn.

"ZORRO" (1957)
Music and lyrics by George Bruns and Norman Foster.

"THE SWAMP FOX" (1959)
Music and lyrics by Buddy Baker and Lew Foster.

"THE WONDERFUL WORLD OF COLOR" (1961)
Music and lyrics by Richard and Robert Sherman.

"THANK YOU FOR BEING A FRIEND" (1985)—The Golden Girls
Music and lyrics by Andrew Gold.

"DUCK TALES" (1987)
Music and lyrics by Mark Mueller.

"CALL ME, BEEP ME" (2002)—Kim Possible
Music and lyrics by George Gabriel, Corey Charles Lerios, and Tony Phillips.

"IT'S THE MICKEY MOUSE CLUBHOUSE" (2006)
Music and lyrics by John Flansburgh and John Linnell (They Might Be Giants).

"THE BEST OF BOTH WORLDS" (2006)—Hannah Montana
Music and lyrics by Donald Black and Mark London.

"TODAY'S GOING TO BE A GREAT DAY" (2009)—Phineas and Ferb
Music and lyrics by Bowling for Soup and Dan Povenmire and Jeff Swampy Marsh.

DISNEY THEATRICAL/ TOURING PRODUCTIONS

SNOW WHITE LIVE: THE STAGE MUSICAL (1979)

A theatrical version of *Snow White* that played at Radio City Music Hall, where the film version of *Snow White* debuted on the East Coast in 1937. The sold-out audiences for this new live, on-stage *Snow White* helped save Radio City, which was in danger of being torn down.

DISNEY ON ICE (1981)

A partnership with the Feld Organization (which operated the Ringling Brothers and Barnum & Bailey Circus). This show, with Disney characters performing on an indoor skating rink, debuted at the Brendan Byrne Arena in New Jersey's Meadowlands in 1981 and still travels the world.

TOTAL ABANDON (1983)

Ron Miller's early attempt to move Disney into Broadway partnerships, it starred Richard Dreyfuss as a father accused of abusing his child, and ran for just a few performances.

BEAUTY AND THE BEAST (1994)

The composing duo of Ashman and Menken's background was in Broadway shows, so it seemed a natural to bring their *Beauty and the Beast* to Broadway, where it ran for more than ten years. The success of this show led to other Broadway adaptations, some successful (*Aladdin, Frozen*), some not so much (*The Little Mermaid, Tarzan*).

THE LION KING (1997)

A show that deepens the themes found in the source material. Director Julie Taymor won a Tony for her innovative designs, using a mix of puppetry and pageantry to tell a familiar story. The biggest theatrical success in the history of the world, it's made more than a billion dollars.

The Lion King theatrical version opened on Broadway in October 1997. (Wikimedia Commons/photo by Diego Torres Silvester)

AIDA (2000)

Sir Tim Rice partnered with Alan Menken for a live theatrical concert version of the story of King David. It had a critically acclaimed, limited three-night run on Broadway in 1997. Three years later, Rice teamed with Elton John to bring their version of Verdi's classic love story, about the love triangle between a soldier and two rival princesses, to Broadway. It ran for four years.

ON THE RECORD (2004)

It never made it to Broadway, but this "jukebox"-style musical, with a story set in a recording studio and featuring more than fifty classic Disney songs, is quite popular as a touring show.

MARY POPPINS (2006)

The Sherman Brothers worked with theatrical impresario Cameron Mackintosh and two new songwriters—George Styles and Anthony Drewe—to bring the world's most beloved nanny to Broadway, with six new songs added to the score. It played to sold-out houses for seven years.

NEWSIES (2012)

Based on the 1992 film, this live version of the story of newsboys who inspire a general strike in 1900s New York City started out at New Jersey's Paper Mill Playhouse but quickly moved across the Hudson River to Broadway. It was only supposed to run for a few months, but the show lasted for two years. Alan Menken and partner Jack Feldman won a Tony for their musical score.

PETER AND THE STARCATCHER (2012)

An experimental nonmusical show, based on the *Peter Pan* prequel novels by Ridley Pearson and Dave Barry, it opened on Broadway in 2012 and closed in 2013, but not before winning five Tony Awards. Christian Borle took home the Best Actor Tony for his scenery-chewing role as the villain Black Stache, aka a young Captain Hook.

MOST INFORMATIVE WEBSITES ABOUT DISNEY

www.Disney.com and https://d23.com (the official company sites)

www.WaltDisney.org

https://micechat.com

www.facebook.com (Note: This social media site is filled with informative Disney groups that have hundreds of thousands of members. Often they report breaking Disney news faster than most media outlets. Some of the best are Disney World Junkies, Disney by the Numb3rs, Stay Disney, Mousejunkies,

Disney Pirate and Princess Pals, Disney Fans and Bloggers Unite, I'm So Disney, Crazy for Disney, Die-hard Disney Nuts, Disney Fans and Annual Passholders, Disney Nerds, and Disney History 101.)

www.DisneyHistoryInstitute.com

https://ChipandCo.com

www.ImagiNerding.com

www.LaughingPlace.com

https://TheDisneyBlog.com

www.DisneyHistory101.com

PODCASTS ABOUT DISNEY

Connecting with Walt

The Disney History Institute Podcast

The Disney Dish with Jim Hill

WEDWay Radio

Creating Disney Magic

The Disney Story Origins Podcast

Animation Addicts

Magic Our Way

Disney DNA

Disney Nerds

HONORABLE MENTION

Jiminy Crickets! Podcast

LISTS ABOUT DISNEY PARKS AND ATTRACTIONS

MILESTONES IN DISNEY THEME PARK/ ATTRACTIONS HISTORY

1954—THE SELECTION OF ANAHEIM

The original idea for Walt's "Mickey Mouse Park" was a small themed area near his studio's property in Burbank, with a train ride and some miniature sets. He soon realized that this was impossible. The dream grew bigger. Harrison "Buzz" Price of the Stanford Research Institute was hired, at Walt's own expense, to survey land in southern California looking for the ideal location for this new Disney Land. Price concluded that the sleepy Orange County suburb of Anaheim was the place, so Walt— putting all his own personal assets on the line—closed on 160 acres of property near Harbor Boulevard and the Santa Ana Freeway. Shovels went into the ground with a time line of twelve months to opening day.

1955—DISNEYLAND OPENS

Walt committed to his dream and was promoting it on his weekly TV series, so it *had* to open on time, by July 1955. He got nervous as the day got closer. Walt was frustrated that 75 percent of the funds he'd scraped together went into clearing land and pouring cement for foundations, with no visible signs of the castle, island, or Main Street he'd envisioned. Eventually things fell into place, but the park still wasn't completely ready for the July 17, 1955, opening, broadcast live on national television. Walt, and his cohosts Art Linkletter, Ronald Reagan, and Bob Cummings, suffered through a series of snafus and technical malfunctions. It didn't matter. Disneyland was a success, with its millionth guest entering barely two months after opening.

Disneyland first opened on July 17, 1955. (Newspapers.com)

1956—DISNEYLAND PROMOTIONS BEGIN

One of Walt's mantras was that he would never cease updating and improving Disneyland, no matter the costs. This extended to promotion. Even though attendance was booming, he wanted to "plus" the experience for his guests. Disney added promotions like nighttime fireworks, parades, date nights, school graduation nights, and concerts by big names, all with minimal or no extra cost to visitors. They've since become standard at his parks. Other amusement park owners thought Walt was crazy, but—as usual—his ideas proved popular, and the rest followed suit.

1965—DISNEY WORLD IS ANNOUNCED

In November 1965, a press conference was hastily called at the Egyptian Room at the Cherry Plaza Hotel in Orlando. Walt, Roy, and the governor of Florida, Haydon Burns, were there to officially confirm that Disney was the mystery buyer of twenty-seven thousand acres of land in central Florida. He was going to build a new residential and business complex, with a theme park, in the Sunshine State. This was Walt's only public appearance in Orlando. He passed away one year later without ever seeing the project completed.

ge County Archives

Aerial view of Disneyland in 1962. (Orange County Archives)

1966—DISNEYLAND EXPANDS

Millions of dollars in profits poured into Disney's pockets during Disneyland's first decade. Walt could have kept them there, enlarging his personal bank account. Instead, he lived modestly and poured that cash right back in to the park. The result, in 1966, was a major expansion of Disneyland, just months before his death. The first addition was New Orleans Square. A little replica of the Louisiana city's French Quarter was tucked into the tight confines between Frontierland and Adventureland. Rather than being inconvenienced by the construction, guests were thrilled to see

View of Epcot and monorail. (Newspapers.com; Epcot: Wikimedia Commons/photo by Eric Marshall)

that Disney cared enough to constantly improve, update, and maintain the park—a standard that is expected of Walt's company to this day.

1971—WALT DISNEY WORLD OPENS

Roy saw his late brother's dream to completion. He pushed to have the Florida Project, now named Walt Disney World and changed from the original concept of a residential and commercial community, done in a five-year time frame. On opening day, he welcomed thousands. Within a few years, millions had visited. EPCOT Center, a modified version of Walt's vision, opened a little more than a decade later, thanks to Roy's successor, Card Walker. By 1983, Walt Disney World had become the most popular vacation destination on the planet, with hotels, restaurants, and recreational activities to keep folks occupied, even when they weren't at the Magic Kingdom or Epcot.

1983—TOKYO DISNEYLAND OPENS

Walt could hardly have imagined on those daddy/daughter days, when he dreamed of building a modest family theme park close to home, that one day his vision would be realized on the other side of the Pacific Ocean. Tokyo, Japan, was the location selected for the first international Disney park. Tokyo Disneyland opened on Tokyo Bay in April 1983 and quickly became the second-busiest theme park in the world, with more than seventeen million guests per year. It's also the only Disney theme park not wholly or partly owned by Disney. The owner—Oriental Land Company—licenses the use of the name, characters, attractions, and other Disney-related material. It chose not to make it a Japanese version of a Disney park, but a carbon copy of Disneyland and the Magic Kingdom. The Tokyo resort expanded in 2001 with Tokyo DisneySea.

Tokyo Disneyland. (Wikimedia Commons/ photo by J. Miers)

1985—AMERICAN HISTORY IS MADE AT WALT DISNEY WORLD

From the day it became America's capital city, Washington, D.C., has always hosted the presidential inauguration and the subsequent inaugural parade. That tradition was broken in 1985, and Disney played a big part. President Reagan was planning on having a big outdoor parade in Washington for his second inauguration, on January 20, 1985. Mother Nature had other plans, with snow and subzero temperatures making it too dangerous for marchers, including the president. Several high school bands had flown in—at their own expense—especially for the event. They were disappointed by the parade's cancellation until they heard happier news. Disney CEO Michael Eisner made an offer to the White House to host the inauguration at Walt Disney World at a later date. The president accepted the invitation. On Memorial Day 1985, President Reagan and First Lady Nancy Reagan stood outside the American Adventure pavilion at Epcot as thousands of high school kids marched by, for the only presidential inauguration parade ever held outside of Washington, D.C. It was a banner day for the president, and for Disney. Epcot—which had been subject to fan apathy—was given the presidential "thumbs-up" by Reagan, a personal friend of Walt's, who was there with him on Disneyland's opening day.

1990s—THE DISNEY DECADE

Michael Eisner was pleased with the attendance figures in Anaheim, Orlando, and Tokyo, but dreamed that the company could do even more. He boldly announced in the late 1980s that the 1990s would be "the Disney Decade." He put into motion a series of ambitious and synergetic projects—some successful, some not—related to the parks for the next ten years and beyond. The results of this plan included Disney-MGM Studios; the expansion of themed resort hotels, restaurants, clubs, and attractions at Walt Disney World to keep guests on-property; Euro Disney in Paris; Disney Cruise Line; Disney Vacation Club timeshares; professional sports franchises with facilities at or near the parks; the Disney Institute; Animal Kingdom; California Adventure; DisneyQuest; the Adventures by Disney travel company; and Disney retail stores in hundreds of malls and big cities, which would also sell park merchandise and tickets. This spreading of the magic on Eisner's part made Disney, once again, the leader in several fields.

2000s—TO INFINITY AND BEYOND

Bob Iger, while more mindful of the bottom line and shareholder concerns, chose to continue the Disney expansion after he took over from Eisner. This has included going back to correct some of the design flaws in projects like Euro Disney (now called Disneyland Paris) and California Adventure; expansion of resorts in Tokyo and Paris; brand-new resorts in Hong Kong and Shanghai; and billion-dollar projects to incorporate the Marvel, Pixar, Muppet, and Lucasfilm characters into existing parks. Thanks to Roy Disney, Ron Miller, Card Walker, Michael Eisner, Bob Iger, and the others who have continued to follow and expand upon Walt's original dream, Disney parks are in great position for the future.

IMAGINEERS

CLAUDE COATS

When he received his award for fifty years of service from Disney in 1985, Claude Coats could look back at one of the most remarkable and diverse careers in the company's history. He started as a background artist at the studio in the 1930s, then shifted over to WED in the 1960s. He was part of the design team of classic attractions like Pirates of the Caribbean, the Haunted Mansion, Horizons, Spaceship Earth, and the World Showcase at Epcot. Coats retired in 1989.

X ATENCIO

Francis Xavier Atencio was a multitalented artist and writer who always preferred to go by the nickname "X." That's how he's billed in Disney projects. He started as an assistant animator on *Fantasia* in 1938, did some stop-motion shorts in the 1950s, and then moved over to WED in 1965. He's best known as the man who penned the words to the Haunted Mansion's "Grim Grinning Ghosts" and "A Pirate's Life for Me!" for Pirates of the Caribbean.

ROLLY CRUMP

In the episode of Walt's TV show in which he previews the 1964 World's Fair, it's Rolly Crump who leads him on a tour of the fair's design models. Crump, who started as an employee at Disney in 1952, was a key man in the creation of several beloved Disney attractions. He branched out on his own in 1970, but consulted from time to time on projects like Epcot Center. He still posts on his website, http://RolandCrump.com.

BOB GURR

When you ride in a Disney vehicle at one of the parks, you can thank Bob Gurr, who was brought in by Walt specifically to consult on their designs. Gurr started with the Autopia vehicles in Tomorrowland at Disneyland, then worked on all the unique, turn-of-the-century transportation for Main Street, U.S.A. He also gave the sleek look to the bobsleds on the Matterhorn, the Disneyland submarines, and the monorail, as well as creating the Haunted Mansion's famed "Doom Buggies." His crowning achievement was not a vehicle, but the development of an audio-animatronic Abraham Lincoln for the 1964 World's Fair. Gurr often gives personal Disney history bus tours of Los Angeles and Burbank, which can be booked through his website, www.Waltland.com.

YALE GRACEY

Hired in 1939 as an artist on *Pinocchio* and *Fantasia*, Yale Gracey quickly moved over to special effects. All of his training in that area came into play when Walt wanted Disneyland to be just like a movie that guests could step into. Gracey designed many of the special effects that helped create that illusion. His work on the Haunted Mansion is especially renowned. In honor of that, the owner of the spooky home is always referred to as "Master Gracey."

HERB RYMAN AND HARPER GOFF

In 1954, Walt's revolutionary idea for a family theme park existed mostly in his head and the few rudimentary sketches he did to plan it out. To lure big investors to the project, something more substantial would be needed. Walt hired artist Herb Ryman to help him flesh out his vision. Ryman was so good at the job that not only were the investors impressed, so was Walt. He had such faith in Ryman's abilities that he gave him the honor designing Disneyland's centerpiece, Sleeping Beauty Castle. Ryman continued to do concept and design work for the Disney parks that followed and was working on Euro Disney when he passed away in 1989. Harper Goff joined Disney around the same time as Ryman, first as a set designer for movies (the look of the *Nautilus* submarine in *20,000 Leagues under the Sea* was his creation), and then went to work for WED. A native of Fort Collins, Colorado, Goff brought some of the style of his hometown's Main Street to Disneyland, blended with Walt's memories of Marceline. Goff, who died in 1993, also designed the Jungle Cruise and most of Epcot's original World Showcase.

ROGER BROGGIE

An avid interest in trains brought Roger Broggie to the attention of his boss, Walt Disney. Broggie, who started as a camera repairman at the studio in 1939, established Disney's machine shop operations. Walt—who was an amateur machinist himself—asked Broggie for his help in setting up a machine shop and railroad tracks in the Disney family's Holmby Hills backyard in the 1950s. Broggie later became the head of MAPO until his retirement in 1975. He was honored with the naming of a locomotive in Walt Disney World after him.

HARRIET BURNS AND ALICE DAVIS

Two of Walt's most trusted employees, Harriet Burns and Alice Davis, both joined WED around the same time in the late 1950s and played key roles in the development of many attractions. Burns was a set painter who helped to design the rides and buildings, as well as some of the interior parts. Davis was responsible for the costumes on the audio-animatronic characters. Between the two of them, they created the look of the Disney attractions as we know them.

TONY BAXTER

An employee of Disney since 1965, when he worked as a young man selling concessions at Disneyland, Tony Baxter kept submitting ideas to WED until he was finally transferred to that division. He eventually became the executive vice president in charge of design at all Disney parks. He is responsible for Big Thunder and Splash Mountains, as well as Epcot's Journey into Imagination and the Indiana Jones ride at Disneyland. He now works as an advisor for Imagineering and Disney parks development.

JOE ROHDE

The most recognizable Imagineer today, Joe Rohde has a personal style—with dangling earrings and a well-kept beard—that makes him stand out when he visits the parks. Rohde, who joined Disney in 1980 and worked on the Mexico and Norway pavilions in Epcot's World Showcase and Pleasure

BLAINE GIBSON

An artist who started at Disney Studios in 1939, Blaine Gibson moved over to WED in 1961. His prowess as a sculptor earned him the responsibility of heading WED's sculpture department, where they designed and brought forth the lifelike heads of most of the audio-animatronic characters used in the parks, including each of the U.S. presidents for the Hall of Presidents in Walt Disney World. His most lasting Disney legacy is the famous statue of Walt and Mickey (*Partners*) that graces the central hubs of Disney parks, as well as the one of Roy and Minnie in Walt Disney World's town square, two of the most photographed statues in the world.

Island at Downtown Disney, was chiefly responsible for the overall look and design of Disney's Animal Kingdom when it opened in 1998. He continues in that role as the lead designer of the recent *Avatar*-themed expansion at that park.

DISNEY RIDES / ATTRACTIONS (CLASSIC)

PETER PAN'S FLIGHT (1955)

One of Walt's favorites, it debuted at Disneyland on opening day. This flight takes guests—via a pirate ship—on a magical ride from the open window of the Darlings' nursery over London at night and then off to Neverland, all seen from Peter's point of view. The small vehicles mean that load times are lengthy. Lines build regularly, but it's still quite popular.

Darling bedroom set from Peter Pan's Flight ride at Disneyland. (Wikimedia Commons/ photo by Jeremy Thompson)

SNOW WHITE'S ADVENTURES (1955)

Like Peter Pan's Flight, this dark-ride attraction was there when Walt opened the gates to Disney-land on that first day. It's somewhat scary (mainly because the Old Hag Witch appears inside), so signs had to be posted outside warning families with young children about the scenes with the witch. The Florida version closed in 2012.

AUTOPIA (1955)

Sponsored by Richfield, this mini-freeway in Tomorrowland proved a big draw for younger guests from day one. It offers the opportunity for those not yet able to drive real cars to get behind the wheel of smaller versions. Major gasoline and automobile companies like Chevron and Honda have also been sponsors of the attraction over the years.

MR. TOAD'S WILD RIDE (1955)

An opening-day attraction in both Disneyland and Walt Disney World, this dark romp in an old-fashioned automobile, based on scenes from the film *Ichabod and Mr. Toad*, thrilled guests and became a beloved attraction, even if the source material was obscure. When the Florida version closed in 1998 to make way for a Winnie the Pooh ride, many fans protested.

DUMBO THE FLYING ELEPHANT (1955)

It took a month, but Walt's "spin" on the traditional lever-controlled flying ride joined Fantasyland in 1955 and soon became one of the most cherished. At Walt Disney World in Florida, Dumbo was given his own circus-themed area when Fantasyland was expanded in 2014.

THE ENCHANTED TIKI ROOM (1963)

A mechanical bird discovered in a New Orleans curio shop by Walt inspired this very first major audio-animatronics attraction in Disneyland. Hosted by four birds, Fritz, Michael, Pierre, and Jose, this is a fun musical revue, written by the Sherman Brothers. It co-stars other singing birds, flowers,

1964 World's Fair. Disney designed several attractions there, most notably It's a Small World. (Library of Congress)

and tiki gods. It lasts almost twenty minutes. It also plays in the Florida and Japan parks, though they've tinkered with the format and script a few times.

THE CAROUSEL OF PROGRESS (1964)

Originally built for the 1964 New York World's Fair, this innovative circular theater where the audience moves and the actors and sets stay in place (each of the four rooms that you cycle into has a different scene) was ahead of its time. Showing the evolution of electricity and technology from the turn of the century to the modern age, it features a regular American family going about their daily lives. The attraction was briefly moved to Disneyland in 1967 before relocating to Walt Disney World in 1973. The Sherman Brothers theme song, "There's a Great Big Beautiful Tomorrow," was replaced for a few years by a new song, "The Best Time of Your Life," until the demand of fans brought the original song back in 1993.

GREAT MOMENTS WITH MR. LINCOLN/ HALL OF PRESIDENTS (1964/1971)

Walt's love for Abraham Lincoln led him to push WED's Imagineers to one of their most difficult tasks, creating a lifelike audio-animatronic version of the sixteenth president for the 1964 World's Fair. They did an outstanding job. Mr. Lincoln amazed the packed audiences in New York who came to hear him speak in person (thanks to the actor Royal Dano) almost one hundred years after his death. In 1965, Great Moments with Mr. Lincoln was moved to the Disneyland Opera House, where he's remained since, with a few changes to the show here and there. When Walt Disney World opened in 1971, the decision was made to expand the idea to include all of the men who'd served as president of the United States, in an attraction called the Hall of Presidents.

SPACESHIP EARTH (1982)

The instantly identifiable symbol of Epcot, this sixteen-story geodesic globe known as Spaceship Earth houses an attraction inside. The ride up, around, and down the inside of the sphere tells the history of human communication and innovation from the caveman era to the twenty-first century. Since you're reading this now . . . you can thank the Phoenicians.

JOURNEY INTO IMAGINATION (1983)

This interesting pyramid-shaped glass pavilion with dancing fountains outside, sponsored by Eastman Kodak, was there on Epcot's opening day in 1982. The ride that debuted inside of it a year later, however, immediately made Journey into Imagination the most popular attraction in the whole park. Hosted by an original character named Dreamfinder, guests were taken on a voyage into what makes our imagination work. To help illustrate that vague notion, Disney created a small purple dragon, called Figment (as in "a figment of your . . ."), to assist Dreamfinder. In 1999, the ride was completely refurbished and shortened. Dreamfinder was replaced with comedian Eric Idle, playing the head of the Imagination Institute. Figment all but disappeared in favor of Idle. Fan outrage led Disney to bring Figment back (without Dreamfinder) in 2002, with a ride that evokes, but never comes close to, the classic version.

DISNEY RIDES / ATTRACTIONS (MODERN)

ALICE'S CURIOUS LABYRINTH (1992)

A fun, Disney-designed hedge maze in Disneyland Paris that looks deceptively simple but can take a while to get through to reach the ultimate destination—the Queen of Heart's castle.

ROGER RABBIT'S CAR TOON SPIN (1994)

It had been a while since Disney opened a classic dark ride, so in 1994, as part of the Mickey's Toontown area of Disneyland, Roger Rabbit's Car Toon Spin debuted. It's a manic trip with Roger in a yellow cab that guests can actually control themselves, making each ride unique.

BUZZ LIGHTYEAR'S SPACE RANGER SPIN/TOY STORY MANIA! (1998/2008)

The enormous popularity of *Toy Story* in 1995 meant that it wouldn't be long before park attractions were created around the characters. Space Ranger Spin was the first to open. It debuted at Walt Disney World's Tomorrowland in 1998. An interactive ride where the cars spin around while guests fire laser blasters at Buzz's evil counterparts, Emperor Zurg and his minions, racking up points on a digital scoreboard as they go, it was an immediate hit, with versions opening in Tokyo and Anaheim in 2004 and 2005. In 2008, a sequel to this ride was developed to simultaneously open at both the Disney World and Disneyland resorts—the first time that had ever happened. Toy Story Mania! (originally Toy Story Midway Mania!), a 3-D variation on the Buzz attraction, with guests competing in virtual carnival games, opened at Hollywood Studios in Florida and Disney's California Adventure within weeks of each other. It's just as popular.

KILIMANJARO SAFARIS (1998)

Walt's original idea for his Jungle Cruise in 1955 was to have his guests see real lions, hippos, zebras, giraffes, elephants, and other animals as they journeyed along the ride's route. He soon

Entrance to Disney's Animal Kingdom. (Wikimedia Commons/ photo by Jennifer Lynn)

realized that animals don't always behave exactly the way you want them to, so fake versions were installed. In 1998, the opening of Disney's Animal Kingdom, with a savanna larger than all of Disneyland and populated with animals from several continents, allowed Walt's dream to finally be realized. Kilimanjaro Safaris vehicles take visitors on a ride through the town of Harambe and then on to a hundred acres of open land where animals roam freely. With the searing Florida heat as a factor, there's no guarantee you'll see each of the animals outside on your trip, but there's a good chance you'll see most of them.

SINBAD'S SEVEN VOYAGES (2001)

A rare Disney attraction that isn't based on existing Disney characters, it opened at Tokyo Disney-Sea in 2001. Guests board a boat, like the ones found in Pirates of the Caribbean and It's a Small World, as they follow the adventures of Sinbad through fantastic realms and dangerous situations. Alan Menken and Glen Slater wrote a new song for this ride.

SOARIN' OVER CALIFORNIA (2001)

An innovative design by Imagineer Mark Summer sees riders lifted 40 feet in the air while they watch a movie projected all around them, giving the illusion of flight. Scents (pine trees, oranges, and salt air) are also pumped in to enhance the experience. In 2005, a version of the ride opened in Epcot's The Land, still featuring California. In 2016, both attractions were changed to Soarin' around the World in order to feature more of Earth's most famous locations.

MICKEY'S PHILHARMAGIC (2003)

A digital 3-D film, with live effects produced for the Magic Kingdom Theater previously occupied by animatronics and puppets. Donald gets hold of Mickey's sorcerer's hat and chaos ensues, with musical instruments and classic Disney characters involved.

TURTLE TALK WITH CRUSH (2004)

An attraction that impresses even the most jaded visitors, Turtle Talk with Crush—which opened at Epcot's Living Seas in 2004—features the laid-back turtle from Finding Nemo interacting with guests who watch him on a screen. It's astonishing to see Crush acknowledge questions in real time, comment on guests' clothes, and have a back-and-forth discussion, all thanks to the magic of instant digital voice animation. A version of this attraction opened at California Adventure in 2005. In 2007, the Magic Kingdom debuted Monsters, Inc. Laugh Floor, featuring Mike Wazowski and pals interacting with guests in a similar way.

MYSTIC MANOR (2013)

Instead of another copy of the Haunted Mansion, guests in Hong Kong Disneyland are treated to this entirely new, trackless attraction that shares similar themes, but is more about fantastic objects than haunted spirits. Henry Mystic and his pet monkey, Albert, have collected treasures from around the world and are showing them off inside his bizarre mansion. Albert opens a music box that brings the objects to life, accompanied by a Danny Elfman score.

RATATOUILLE: THE ADVENTURE (2014)

Disneyland Paris (of course) is the home to this dark ride. Guests are shrunk down to the size of Remy, the rat/chef from the Pixar film *Ratatouille*. It's a wild, trackless voyage through the wonders of France, with some Disney touches thrown in. A version is set to open in Epcot soon.

"E-TICKET" DISNEY RIDES (CLASSIC)

In 1955, Disneyland introduced special admission ticket books for its attractions. Each coupon in the book was given a letter designation, from A to C. As the park expanded, and some rides proved to be more popular than the others, two more letters—D in 1956 and E in 1959—were added. The classic E tickets were for the rides with the highest guest volume. While some, like the Matterhorn, were definitely thrill rides, others were a bit milder. The Disney parks ticket books were discontinued in 1982; nevertheless, the term "E-ticket ride" still means an exciting experience that gets the adrenaline pumping.

JUNGLE CRUISE (1955)

An opening-day attraction at Disneyland, this river voyage, with vehicles partly inspired by the Humphrey Bogart movie *The African Queen*, was one that Walt couldn't wait for guests to ride. He'd taken people through the cruise as it was being built. That progress was shown on his TV show, making Jungle Cruise a known commodity and hit from day one. As the years went by, more animals and scenery were added, with the cruise's "skippers" inventing a comical spiel to enhance the trip. It's in other Disney parks now, and is just as popular.

SUBMARINE VOYAGE (1959)

Walt was proud of his "fleet" of eight submarines when they made their debut at Disneyland in 1959. These innovative vehicles never actually submerge completely, but the Imagineers added enough tricks learned from moviemaking to fool guests into thinking they'd gone down to the very depths of the ocean. In 1971, a similar ride, themed to the movie *20,000 Leagues under the Sea*, opened in Walt Disney World. It ran for twenty-three years before closing. The Disneyland subs were re-themed to *Finding Nemo* in 2007.

MATTERHORN BOBSLEDS (1959)

At 174 feet, this southern California version of the famous Swiss mountain is much smaller than its double, but the real one doesn't have a roller coaster inside. The Matterhorn was the first roller coaster to use tubular rails and urethane wheels, which are now quite common. Other rides might be faster, but this one remains the original Disney mountain.

PIRATES OF THE CARIBBEAN (1967)

Though it was initially meant to be a walk-through wax figure attraction, the Imagineers convinced Walt to change Pirates to a boat ride featuring lifelike audio-animatronic pirates. It's the last park attraction that Walt personally oversaw. He passed away just a few months before it opened. The

View from the Pirates of the Caribbean ride at Disneyland. (Wikimedia Commons/photo by Picasa)

theme song written for the ride sets the tone, and the special effects (cannonballs landing in the water, fires raging) amaze. It's one of the most famous rides ever built for any theme park. Versions of it are also open in Orlando, Tokyo, and Paris. The Shanghai Disneyland Pirates ride—subtitled "Battle for the Sunken Treasure"—features vehicles that spin and go backward.

THE HAUNTED MANSION (1969)

Work on this silly and spooky exploration of a house filled with 999 ghosts (always room for one more!) began in 1962. It was intended to be a walk-through. When finally opened as a ride, on "Doom Buggies" with narration, it became a Disney classic. The Disneyland version is housed in a classic southern-style mansion in New Orleans Square; at Walt Disney World it's more of a Hudson River Gothic home, to better fit in with its Liberty Square surroundings.

Exterior of the Haunted Mansion in Florida. (Wikimedia Commons/photo by Benjamin D. Easham)

SPACE MOUNTAIN (1975)

Disney's second roller coaster, it debuted at Walt Disney World in 1975. Deceptively simple, it's a "wild mouse"-style coaster that the Imagineers placed in complete darkness. They added shooting stars and special effects to give the illusion that riders are traveling faster than they really are. The building that houses the ride is Disney's version of a futuristic mountain, with gleaming white spires, odd angles, and curves. The Disneyland version opened in 1977.

BIG THUNDER MOUNTAIN RAILROAD (1979)

Tony Baxter was largely responsible for bringing this "runaway train"–style coaster, set in an area meant to resemble the mountains and canyons of Utah, to Disneyland. The artwork and design are stunning, making it look like the weathered rocks (all fake) have been there for millennia. Baxter also added props and sets to evoke the Old West for guests as they zip around at great speed. The Walt Disney World version, which looks more like Arizona, opened in 1980.

SPLASH MOUNTAIN (1989)

When Disneyland's America Sings attraction closed in 1988, some other use had to be found for its more than one hundred audio-animatronic figures. Tony Baxter came up with the concept of taking a simple log flume ride and theming it around characters from the movie *Song of the South*. Br'er Fox and Br'er Bear are outwitted by Br'er Rabbit for most of the ride, until the finale, atop a 52-foot, 45-degree-angle drop. Riders get to see most of the America Sings cast bidding them farewell from aboard a steamboat. The Disney World version opened in 1992.

MAELSTROM (1988)

The Norway pavilion in the World Showcase was home to the very first thrill ride at Epcot. Scandinavian long boats took guests on a trip through Norwegian history, with trolls and a backward waterfall drop providing some mild, edge-of-your-seat excitement. A fan favorite, the ride track still exists at Norway, though it was re-themed to the movie *Frozen* in 2016.

STAR TOURS (1987)

Long before Disney acquired Lucasfilm, it partnered with George Lucas on this motion simulator in Disneyland's Tomorrowland, which brings guests into the world of Star Wars. Featuring familiar characters like C3PO and R2D2 mixed with new ones created for Disney, the attraction has been updated over the years as newer Star Wars movies were made. It also opened at Disney-MGM Studios and Tokyo Disneyland in 1989 and at Euro Disney in 1992.

"E-TICKET" DISNEY RIDES (MODERN)

THE TWILIGHT ZONE TOWER OF TERROR (1994)

A thirteen-story drop tower, themed to look like a decaying Hollywood hotel, this attraction instantly made attendance at Disney's Hollywood Studios rise to previously unseen levels. Rod Serling's *Twilight Zone* franchise was licensed to provide an eerie backdrop.

INDIANA JONES ADVENTURE (1995)

Another successful partnership between George Lucas and Disney, this rollicking ride at Disneyland takes guests on a trip with Indiana Jones through the Temple of the Forbidden Eye. The ride vehicles were quite innovative for their time and were duplicated, with slight modifications, for Animal Kingdom's Dinosaur: Countdown to Extinction attraction.

Indiana Jones Stunt Spectacular. (Wikimedia Commons)

ROCK 'N' ROLLER COASTER (1999)

An indoor roller coaster featuring inversions and a pulse-pounding soundtrack by Aerosmith, themed to a race to get to their concert, this ride—at Hollywood Studios in Florida—was the first at Disney to launch guests from 0 to 60 in less than three seconds.

TEST TRACK (1999)

This Epcot ride is designed to resemble an automobile testing facility. Test Track's cars reach speeds of up to 65 miles per hour as they bank around a track outside the show building for the grand finale after going through a series of experiments on the vehicles. The same basic ride design was copied for Disney's California Adventure's Cars Land, with a more fanciful theme, taking riders on a high-speed journey through Radiator Springs.

CALIFORNIA SCREAMIN' (2001)

An amazing roller coaster, in both design and look, California Screamin' dominates the waterfront at Disney's California Adventure. It features a style resembling classic wooden roller coasters found on turn-of-the-century boardwalks but is actually made of steel. The 360-degree loop in the middle of the ride originally made it look like the vehicles were careening through a silhouette of Mickey Mouse. It was re-themed to *The Incredibles* in 2018.

MISSION: SPACE (2003)

A ride so intimidating that Disney provides two versions in the same building, one mild and one intense. All the experiences that an astronaut would go through while launching into outer space are re-created here, using centrifugal force. It's the first Disney attraction to offer small disposable bags under the seats for guests, in case they suddenly become nauseous while riding.

RAGING SPIRITS (2005)

Tokyo DisneySea's looping roller-coaster ride around a perilous ceremonial mountain takes guests through all of the elements—fire, water, earth, and air—before plunging into the darkness.

EXPEDITION EVEREST (2006)

Disney's tallest "mountain" (and at just under 200 feet, the tallest "mountain" in the entire state of Florida), this ride at Disney's Animal Kingdom is one of the most elaborate and expensive roller coasters ever built. As guests speed around the outside and inside of the mountain, they traverse unique Nepalese-themed obstacles and come face-to-face with the legendary Yeti. When the ride first opened, the large Yeti animatronic would lunge at guests, but the hydraulics stopped working and now he just roars menacingly with strobes flashing as the trains go by.

TRON LIGHTCYCLE POWER RUN (2016)

When *TRON* was released in 1982, audiences everywhere wished that they, too, could jump into that digital space and take a ride on the speedy light cycles featured in the film. It took three and a half decades, but that dream was realized at Shanghai's Disneyland. On one of the fastest roller coasters ever built, light cycles take guests through the dazzling computer-generated world of *TRON*. A version of it will also be featured at Walt Disney World's Magic Kingdom.

AVATAR: FLIGHT OF PASSAGE (2017)

This fast-paced 3-D ride on the back of a banshee is the featured attraction at the new Pandora area of Disney's Animal Kingdom, based on the 2009 James Cameron film *Avatar*. Since its debut, Flight of Passage has been among the highest-rated experiences by Disney World visitors.

DISNEY HOTELS

DISNEYLAND HOTEL (1955)

Jack Wrather, a personal friend of Walt's, took charge in opening a hotel adjacent to the park in 1955. Though it was on Disney property, connected to the park by monorail and bearing the name Disneyland, this very first "Disney" hotel was independently owned and operated by the Wrather Corporation. In 1988, Disney purchased the corporation, and it now owns the hotel.

THE CONTEMPORARY/THE POLYNESIAN (1971)

Walt Disney World enjoyed the blessing of size that Disneyland didn't, and the company had more resources in 1971 than Walt did in 1955, so innovative resort hotels were part of the property's design from the very beginning. The first two to open were the Polynesian, a South Seas–themed resort directly across the Seven Seas Lagoon from the Magic Kingdom, and the Contemporary, an

A-frame hotel with the monorail line running right through the center. Forty-plus years later, they remain incredibly popular.

DISNEY'S BOARDWALK (1996)

In an effort to keep conventioneers on-property, Walt Disney World opened this gigantic resort area with a 1900s Atlantic City theme to house and entertain them. Located within walking distance to Epcot (there's a little-known back entrance to the park that connects to it), the Boardwalk has a regular hotel, villas, restaurants, nightclubs, shops, and convention facilities all situated around its replica of a New Jersey–style boardwalk.

ANIMAL KINGDOM LODGE (2001)

Hotel views don't get better than this. Rooms at this lodge have balconies overlooking Animal Kingdom's wide-open savanna, which means that glimpses of the animals are quite common.

THE GRAND CALIFORNIAN (2001)

Disney's California Adventure theme park was a tribute to the wonders of California when it first opened, so this hotel—which is also a valentine to the Golden State—was a natural to be located inside the park itself, the first time that had ever happened in Disney history.

ALL-STAR RESORTS (1994)

In the 1980s and early '90s, many visitors to Walt Disney World were choosing to stay off-property to save a bit of money, since the hotels at the resort were higher priced than some of the budget-rate ones found just outside the gates in Kissimmee and Orlando. Disney joined the competition by opening its own version of value hotels in 1994. Dubbed the All-Star Resorts, these modestly appointed rooms are split into three themed sections with their own pools and food courts. They are the All-Star Sports, All-Star Music, and All-Star Movies and are some of the most consistently booked hotels in the whole state of Florida.

HOTEL NEW YORK (1992)

A bit of the Big Apple in Paris, this New York City–themed hotel opened at Euro Disney in 1992. It features replicas of many iconic New York landmarks, including an outdoor version of the Rockefeller Center ice-skating rink during the winter months.

MIRA COSTA (2001)

Another hotel built right inside a Disney park, Mira Costa features three beautifully detailed, Italian-inspired sections that are blended seamlessly into three different themed areas of Tokyo DisneySea: Tuscany, Venice, and a typical Mediterranean harbor.

TOY STORY HOTEL (2016)

Buzz, Woody, and their friends are the featured stars of this hotel at the Shanghai Disney Resort. It's in the shape of a figure eight, since that number is a lucky one in Chinese culture.

AULANI (2011)

The only hotel on this list not part of a Disney parks resort. Located beachside on the island of Oahu, Aulani highlights the history and vibrancy of Hawaiian culture, with the Disney touch.

DISNEY RESTAURANTS

CASA DE FRITOS (1955)

An opening-year restaurant at Disneyland. Operated by the makers of Fritos, it served Mexican food and was famous for a fun coin-operated machine where the life-sized Frito Kid robot would send a bag of Fritos down a chute to you. This is also where Doritos were born, in 1964, when a worker had excess tortillas left over and coated them with a spicy Mexican powder. The restaurant is still at Disneyland, but it's now called Rancho del Zocalo.

The original Casa de Fritos in Disneyland. (National Museum of American History Archives)

CLUB 33/BLUE BAYOU (1967)

When Disneyland's Pirates of the Caribbean ride opened in 1967, it gave the Imagineers space to add two restaurants as part of New Orleans Square. The Blue Bayou, which is themed to perpetual nighttime in Louisiana, is one of the most beautiful eateries ever designed. Diners look up and can see twinkling stars and fireflies as they watch boats launching on their journey to the Caribbean. Sounds of the bayou add to the ambience. Above the entrance to Pirates is a more exclusive restaurant, Club 33, which was originally meant for VIPs who visited the park. It's now a members-only club, and extremely hard to get into. There have been many rumors as to the origin of the mysterious "33" in the club's name (Sideways Mickey ears? Mickey's initials turned sideways? Exactly 33 miles from the Disney Studios to that location?), but the official story is that it's the address inside Disneyland (33 Royal Street) for the restaurant.

VICTORIA & ALBERT'S (1988)

The first fine-dining restaurant at Walt Disney World, it's part of the Grand Floridian Resort and Spa. Individualized menus and gourmet dishes are served to guests by staff members, all of whom are named Victoria or Albert, while live classical music plays.

50'S PRIME TIME CAFÉ/SCI-FI DINE-IN THEATER RESTAURANT (1989/1991)

Two of the most fun restaurants Disney ever built, both located at Disney's Hollywood Studios in Florida. At the 50's Prime Time Café, guests are served by "Mom," a clone of the ever-so-perfect suburban mothers seen in sitcoms of the 1950s and '60s, in replica kitchens from those shows. Beware if you don't finish your veggies, or you won't get your dessert from Mom, and keep your elbows off the table or risk being sent to the corner. Classic convertibles are the seating choice over at the Sci-Fi Dine-In Theater, where you are made to feel like you're in a drive-in theater at night and watching B-movie trailers from the 1950s while eating your meal.

ANNETTE'S DINER (1992)

The most famous Mouseketeer of them all, Annette Funicello, provided the inspiration for this classic mid-century American roadside diner found at the Disneyland Paris Resort.

'OHANA (1995)

One of the most popular restaurants at Walt Disney World. Located in the Polynesian resort, it has a circular fire pit. Food is served to guests on long skewers for the whole table to enjoy.

JIKO/BOMA (2001)

Opened as part of the Animal Kingdom Lodge, these two restaurants evoke the spirit and flavors of Africa, with open kitchens, fire pits, wood-burning stoves, and a marketplace feel.

SKIPPER CANTEEN (2016)

Walt Disney World's Magic Kingdom has many great things to offer, but until recently themed restaurants weren't one of them. Most of the park was quick-service venues or copies of structures like the Crystal Palace in Disneyland. That changed in 2012 with the opening of Be Our Guest, themed to *Beauty and the Beast*, in Fantasyland. Another step forward was taken in 2016, when the old Adventureland Verandah was transformed into the Skipper Canteen. Themed as the home for off-duty Jungle Cruise skippers, with wild decorations to match, the Canteen has daring and eclectic food offerings unlike any other in the Magic Kingdom.

YAK & YETI (2007)

Located next to Mount Everest in Animal Kingdom, this restaurant has a Nepalese design and features gourmet food common to that region of Asia. It also offers a take-away window.

THE COZY CONE (2012)

Designed to fit in perfectly at Cars Land at California Adventure, the oversized traffic cones that house this restaurant are a throwback to the kitschy architecture that made Route 66 famous. Most of the food—like macaroni and cheese and chili—is served in edible cones made of bread.

SONGS FROM THE DISNEY PARKS

"THE TIKI, TIKI, TIKI ROOM" (1963)
Music and lyrics by Richard and Robert Sherman.

The original It's a Small World ride at the 1964 New York World's Fair. It was later moved to Disneyland. (Wikimedia Commons/photo by Paul Turner)

"IT'S A SMALL WORLD AFTER ALL" (1964)
Music and lyrics by Richard and Robert Sherman.

"THERE'S A GREAT BIG BEAUTIFUL TOMORROW" (1964)— The Carousel of Progress
Music and lyrics by Richard and Robert Sherman.

"YO HO (A PIRATE'S LIFE FOR ME)" (1967)—Pirates of the Caribbean
Music and lyrics by George Bruns and X Atencio.

"GRIM GRINNING GHOSTS" (1968)—The Haunted Mansion
Music and lyrics by Buddy Baker and X Atencio.

"IF YOU HAD WINGS" (1972)
Music and lyrics by Buddy Baker and X Atencio.

"BAROQUE HOEDOWN" (THE MAIN STREET ELECTRICAL PARADE THEME) (1979)
Music and lyrics by Jean Jacques Perry and Gershwin Kingsley.

"GOLDEN DREAM" (1982)—The American Adventure
Music and lyrics by Bob Moline and Randy Bright.

"LISTEN TO THE LAND" (1982)
Music and lyrics by Bob Moline and Randy Bright.

"REFLECTIONS OF EARTH/TAPESTRY OF DREAMS" (1999)— Illuminations
Music and lyrics by Gavin Greenaway and Don Dorsey.

HONORABLE MENTION

"ONE LITTLE SPARK" (1983)—Journey into Imagination
Music and lyrics by Richard and Robert Sherman.

Figment's popular theme song, which was taken away for a while, returned (in small samples) when the ride was refurbished for the second time in 2002.

DISNEY SHOWS AND PARADES

FANTASY IN THE SKY (1956)
The original Disney fireworks spectacular, approved by Walt himself. This musical pyrotechnics show over Sleeping Beauty Castle debuted in Disneyland one year after opening and ran until 2000. The Walt Disney World version of this same show lasted from 1971 to 2003, followed by the extremely popular *Wishes: A Magical Gathering of Disney Dreams.*

CANDLELIGHT PROCESSIONAL (1958)
A heartwarming holiday tradition that began at Disneyland, where a choir holding candles parades down Main Street, U.S.A., to be joined by a full orchestra and a celebrity narrator, telling the story of Christmas through words and song. The Florida version is held at Epcot's World Showcase, near the American Adventure.

FANTASY ON PARADE (1965)
An annual Christmas parade that began in Disneyland in 1965. Reindeer, toy soldiers, elves, and more than three hundred other performers all joined Disney characters in merrily celebrating the holiday season. In the 1980s it was replaced by Mickey's Very Merry Christmas Parade.

ELECTRICAL WATER PAGEANT (1971)

A parade often overlooked by visitors to Walt Disney World, it's been running since the resort opened. Every night at 9 p.m., a flotilla of barges cruises through Bay Lake and the Seven Seas Lagoon with colorful, electrically lighted designs that blink in time with synthesized music.

MAIN STREET ELECTRICAL PARADE (1972)

Arguably *the* best-loved Disney parade of them all. A synthesized score and five hundred thousand electric lights made this one of the most dazzling shows Disney's ever done, moving or otherwise. Lights in Disneyland and Walt Disney World had to be dimmed as it passed by, so as not to take away from its magic. It started in the United States but became so popular with fans that the international Disney parks ran it, too. It even had a first for a Disney parade, when it ran along New York City's famed Fifth Avenue, in honor of the opening of *Hercules*, in July 1997.

AMERICA ON PARADE (1976)

Created specifically to celebrate America's Bicentennial, running simultaneously at Disneyland and Walt Disney World, this patriotic parade included American tunes from the Revolutionary days until the 1970s; oversized figures of American heroes like Washington, Jefferson, Franklin, Ross, and Lincoln; and Disney characters all decked out in red, white, and blue.

FANTASMIC! (1992)

A nighttime, water-based pyro spectacular performed around Disneyland's Rivers of America, it features Sorcerer Mickey and characters from more than twenty Disney films. In 1998, a special amphitheater was built at Hollywood Studios in Florida to house a similar version of it.

WORLD OF COLOR (2010)

This nighttime water show, with projected images, fire, dancing fountains, and other special effects, boosted attendance at Disney's California Adventure from the moment it made its debut on Paradise Bay. Its title is a tribute to Walt's television show of the 1960s.

PAINT THE NIGHT (2014)

Hong Kong Disneyland was the first to have this innovative parade featuring LED technology to light up the floats and Disney characters instead of the traditional electric bulbs.

IGNITE THE DREAM (2017)

The newest Disney fireworks show, this spectacle over the Enchanted Storybook Castle in Shanghai Disneyland mixes the classic fireworks with twenty-first-century digital mapping technology, laser effects, water images, and other magical touches to tell the story of Mickey's journey through ninety-five years of Disney history.

DISNEY CHARACTERS UNIQUE TO THE PARKS

THE DAPPER DANS (1955)

A traditional barbershop quartet, the Dapper Dans are dressed in colorful, striped outfits like their 1900s counterparts. Since the opening of both Disneyland and Walt Disney World, this group, made up of rotating members, has performed nine shows daily on Main Street, U.S.A., and at the barbershop. They're often joined on Main Street by Disney's "Streetmosphere" characters such as the Mayor, the Fire Chief, the head of the Ladies Auxiliary, and Scoop, a roving reporter.

FRITZ, MICHAEL, PIERRE, AND JOSE (1963)—The Enchanted Tiki Room

These four avian hosts of the Tiki Room show were the first major audio-animatronic figures to appear in a Disney park. Their accents are similar to German, Irish, French, and South American.

THE CAROUSEL OF PROGRESS FAMILY (1964)

No last name is given for this animatronic American family who take guests through changes in technology from the 1900s to the 2000s. Each one of the family members has a distinct personality—including the dog(s). The father character drives the show, with its catchy song.

MADAME LEOTA/THE HITCHHIKING GHOSTS/THE GHOST HOST (1969)—The Haunted Mansion

Part of what makes the Haunted Mansion so much fun is the creepy characters featured inside. They include the Ghost Host narrator, who sets the tone from the beginning; Madame Leota, who speaks to guests from her floating crystal ball; and the three ghosts who try to hitch a ride home with departing visitors. (Unofficially, cast members and fans have given this trio of hitchhiking specters the names Gus, Ezra, and Phineas.) In 2015, Disneyland brought back the popular Hatbox Ghost, who had briefly appeared when the attraction first opened there in 1969.

THE COUNTRY BEARS (1971)—The Country Bear Jamboree

Originally designed to star at the never-built Disney ski resort of Mineral King in California, these eighteen animatronic bears perform a good old-fashioned hoedown for guests in their Country Bear Hall. This was the first major attraction to be unique to Walt Disney World. They've since been copied for other parks, adapted for holidays, and inspired a movie.

FIGMENT AND DREAMFINDER (1983)—Journey into Imagination

A mischievous imaginary purple dragon and his redheaded inventor pal. They were the original cohosts of Epcot's Imagination pavilion, and two of the most popular parks characters ever.

SONNY ECLIPSE (1995)—Cosmic Ray's Starlight Café

An animatronic alien lounge singer in Walt Disney World's Tomorrowland, he provides laughs as guests dine and cool off in this quick-service restaurant.

PUSH THE TALKING TRASH CAN (1995)

This fascinatingly simple robot is literally a garbage can on wheels, assisted by a nearby handler, who interacts with guests while roaming Tomorrowland. He was a fan favorite in Walt Disney World from 1995 to 2014, and has appeared in other Disney parks to similar acclaim.

LUCKY THE DINOSAUR (2003)

Not connected to any particular attraction, Lucky the Dinosaur represented a groundbreaking advancement in audio-animatronic technology. He was the first large robotic figure to move around independently greeting park guests. Lucky made appearances in California Adventure, Animal Kingdom, and Hong Kong Disneyland before being retired in 2006. This 9-foot-tall dinosaur now resides permanently at Walt Disney Imagineering headquarters in California.

DUFFY BEAR (2005)

A Japanese creation, this teddy bear was supposedly given to Minnie by Mickey and has become a popular character in the Tokyo Disneyland Resort, for both meet-and-greets and merchandise. He can also be found in Epcot and California Adventure.

DEARLY DEPARTED DISNEY RIDES/ATTRACTIONS

MICKEY MOUSE CLUB CIRCUS (1955 TO 1956)

One of the shortest-lived attractions ever at a Disney park, it lasted only two months. Walt had the idea to put a circus tent up in a corner of Disneyland and to feature some of his Mouseketeers performing on horseback and on trapezes under the big top. It didn't go over well with guests, who were dazzled by too many other things at Disneyland to spend time watching a circus.

THE SKYWAY (1956 TO 1999)

Disneyland, Walt Disney World, and Tokyo Disneyland all had these bucket-style vehicles that transported four passengers at a time high over the skies between Fantasyland and Tomorrowland. Safety, sight-line, and space issues saw them slowly phased out by 1999. A twenty-first-century gondola system will open in 2019 to transport guests around Walt Disney World.

FLYING SAUCERS (1961 TO 1966)

This one lasted only five years. A ride made up of vehicles floating on puffs of air—like an air hockey table—it was a nightmare to control and maintain. Nevertheless, fans and Imagineers longed for its return, so it was reimagined in 2012 as Luigi's Flying Tires at Cars Land in California Adventure. It faced similar problems and closed after three years.

IF YOU HAD WINGS (1972 TO 1987)

Guests on this ride were transported to areas around the world that Eastern Airlines—the official airline of Walt Disney World—serviced. It had a memorable title song playing on a loop.

RIVER COUNTRY/DISCOVERY ISLAND (1974 TO 2001)

Two curious footnotes in Walt Disney World history, River Country and Discovery Island were opened in the quieter times, before the big expansion of the 1990s. Both popular attractions were serene, with River Country's water park (one of the earliest in America) re-creating a typical summer in the country, as Walt, Tom Sawyer, or Huck Finn might have enjoyed. Discovery Island was a nature preserve and wildlife sanctuary where guests could explore while spotting some of the flora and fauna that were the only residents of the swampy land before Disney came along. Both were rendered obsolete by newer properties at Walt Disney World (Blizzard Beach and Typhoon Lagoon's water parks and Animal Kingdom's savanna). They remain the only Disney parks ever to be closed permanently.

KITCHEN KABARET (1982 TO 1994)

An audio-animatronic comedy and music show at Epcot's The Land, featuring dancing and singing food products extolling the value of nutrition. It was replaced by another show. Fans still ask cast members where to find Bonnie Appetite and Hamm & Eggz.

HORIZONS (1983 TO 1999)

If you took a poll asking Disney fans which departed attraction they'd like back more than any other, Epcot's Horizons would top that list every single time. This was the spiritual sequel to Walt's Carousel of Progress, taking visitors on an optimistic journey into the future. It was also the first Disney ride to allow guests to choose their own ending.

THE GREAT MOVIE RIDE (1989 TO 2017)

In this tribute to classic Hollywood films, from Busby Berkeley musicals, *Tarzan*, and *The Wizard of Oz* to *Raiders of the Lost Ark*, *Aliens*, *Mary Poppins*, and many other movies in between, guests were taken on large vehicles through scenes from these films. Along the way, the ride was taken over by either a cowboy or a gangster villain, before finishing in a room that showed a montage of the greatest movies ever. It was housed in a replica of Grauman's Chinese Theater. In 2017, it was removed to make way for a new Mickey Mouse-themed ride.

BACKSTAGE TOUR (1989 TO 2014)

When the Disney-MGM Studios theme park opened, the idea was that it would give guests a glimpse into a working motion picture and television production facility. This tour was part of that, a walking and driving (on a special tram) journey through the lot to see props, sets, and locations from a variety of Disney, Touchstone, and Hollywood Pictures productions. One of the highlights was when the tram drove through a canyon where special effects made it seem like guests were in danger. As the studio's soundstages began to shutter in the early 2000s, the ride shortened and was closed forever. The backstage area will soon be home to Star Wars: Galaxy's Edge.

PLEASURE ISLAND (1989 TO 2008)

An interesting experiment for Imagineers, this area at the formerly bucolic Disney Village was designed to host clubs and restaurants to give on-property guests something to do at night without leaving Walt Disney World. Part of it was conceived as its own themed land with a backstory given to its founder, shipbuilder and explorer Merriweather Pleasure. It was only open at night and had a separate cost to enter. New Year's Eve was celebrated every single night. In 1996, it became part of the Downtown Disney complex, with an east and west side. They stopped charging to enter in 2004, and the last nightclub closed in 2008. It's now part of the upscale, Florida-themed Disney Springs complex, which debuted in 2016.

HONORABLE MENTION

THE OSBORNE FAMILY SPECTACLE OF LIGHTS (1995 TO 2015)

An Arkansas family's home Christmas lights display was so elaborate and massive that it was moved to Hollywood Studios in Florida and placed along the backlot streets, where Disney guests could see them at night while fake snow fell around them. The changes to that theme park and the removal of its backlot streets ended the holiday favorite's run after a decade.

MOST UNDERRATED DISNEY RIDES/ATTRACTIONS

THE CASTLES (1955, 1971, 1983, 1992, 2003, 2017)

Marvels of architectural magic, the six Disney castles are some of the most-photographed landmarks in the world, yet many guests take them for granted. Next time you're near one, take a closer look. What appears from a distance to be a gigantic structure fashioned from stone is actually a smaller-sized building using forced perspective—a movie trick—to make it feel bigger. Each castle has its own unique qualities. Sleeping Beauty's castles in California and Hong Kong have a functional drawbridge, and in Paris there's a dragon. Cinderella's got a restaurant and secret suite inside her Florida castle and a walk-through attraction in her Tokyo one. Shanghai's Enchanted Storybook Castle is themed to several different Disney princesses.

THE DISNEYLAND RAILROAD (1955)

Walt's passion for trains is represented in several of his parks, including the California original, with steam-powered locomotives circling around the earthen berms that keep the outside world from being seen. They are often shunned in favor of more exciting rides by guests who feel they are not worth the time. A trip on these trains is a great way to step back into the past and to get a feel for the transportation method that inspired Walt as a boy.

THE CARROUSELS (1955, 1971, 1983, 1992, 2005, 2016)

Because the same type of rides can be found at many other amusement parks, zoos, and public areas, the Disney carousels (spelled with two r's by Disney) aren't as appreciated as they should be. Like the castles, they are all unique. The first, Disneyland's King Arthur Carrousel, was purchased by Walt from a Canadian park in 1954 and refurbished. It has sixty-eight leaping and prancing horses. The second, at Walt Disney World, was named Cinderella's Golden Carrousel and is a 1917 original that was housed in New Jersey for decades. Modified copies of it were opened in Tokyo and Hong Kong. The one in Paris is themed to the fictional French hero Sir Lancelot, and Shanghai's carousel features characters and music from the 1940 film *Fantasia*.

MAIN STREET CINEMA (1955)

Representing Walt's childhood memories of seeing silent black-and-white films in his local movie hall, this small cinema tucked along the right side of Disneyland's Main Street, U.S.A., shows Mickey shorts from the 1920s all day long on several screens arranged around a circular indoor bandstand. An old-fashioned ticket booth sits outside, adding to the ambience before you enter the darkened theater. Walt Disney World's Main Street Cinema is now a retail store.

THE MONORAIL (1959)

The supposed wave of the future when first introduced in his park by Walt, monorails never caught on with major cities as a daily mode of transportation for commuters, as he'd hoped. The one in Disneyland is more of a ride, while the monorails in Walt Disney World function as important connections to and from the ticket center, parks, and resorts. They've shown their age in recent years, and aren't as popular, but the monorails will always be part of the Disney parks and will forever be associated with Disney in most people's minds.

WEDWAY PEOPLEMOVER (1975)

A version of Walt's 1960s futuristic transportation method, these linear induction–powered cars take a slow ride around many of the Tomorrowland attractions at Walt Disney World. It moves so slowly that guests often skip it, but the WEDWay allows you to see the park at a leisurely pace while off your feet for a few minutes. The best part? It passes right through Space Mountain, and you get a peek at the roller-coaster cars as they whiz around in the darkness. If the lights happen to be on inside? Even better! The original PeopleMover in Disneyland was shut down in 1995, so the one in Florida is the only way to experience it in a Disney park.

THE AMERICAN ADVENTURE (1982)

Some people avoid this attraction in Epcot's World Showcase because they think of it as nothing more than a dry lesson in American history. They don't know what they're missing. The moving sounds of the Voices of Liberty choir in the lobby and the hall lined with flags and memorabilia chronicling almost 250 years of the United States as a country would be more than enough, but the show that follows is terrific. As the first audio-animatronics to climb a staircase and do other formerly impossible tasks, Ben Franklin and Mark Twain take guests through the highs and lows of America and its people, sending them out of the theater with a renewed appreciation for the can-do spirit of the American people.

LIVING WITH THE LAND (1982)

Riding a boat through a greenhouse could be described as the most ho-hum thing in the world to do, but this Epcot attraction—formerly known as Listen to the Land, with its own catchy theme song—is quite fascinating. It starts out as a classic Disney dark ride, complete with animatronics and sets depicting a variety of Earth's climates filled with the people, plants, and animals who live in them (plus glimpses of folks eating at the revolving restaurant that abuts the ride). The second half takes guests as close as possible to actual plants, fruits, and vegetables being grown indoors using methods developed by botanists and scientists working with Disney. For many, this ecologically themed attraction is just something to do while waiting for Soarin's nearby line to lessen, but it's actually one of the most interesting rides ever built by Disney.

MUPPET*VISION 3-D (1991)

Before Jim Henson's untimely death in 1990, he was planning a whole bunch of Muppet attractions for the Disney-MGM Studios theme park. Only one of them ever opened. Muppet*Vision 3-D, an interactive show that lives up to the spirit of the 1970s Muppet TV program, was the last project Henson worked on. It's his voice you hear as Kermit, the host. As the Hollywood Studios theme park mission has changed, the Muppets' presence there has gotten smaller and smaller. This attraction is showing its age a bit and is overlooked by guests who head for Rock 'n' Roller Coaster, Tower of Terror, Toy Story Mania!, or the nearby Star Tours, but the Muppets and their zany brand of gentle humor are definitely still worth a visit.

HONORABLE MENTION

TOM SAWYER ISLAND (1956)

Walt's sentimental favorite, because it reminded him of childhood adventures in Missouri. This little island in Disneyland's Rivers of America, with replicas in Florida and Tokyo, takes its inspiration from the stories of Mark Twain. Adults often skip this attraction, which is only accessible by raft, but kids love to spend hours there exploring the many caves, tunnels, forts, rock formations, and bridges. The Disneyland version was changed to a pirate theme in 2007.

CONSERVATION STATION/RAFIKI'S PLANET WATCH (1998)

The Kilimanjaro Safaris ride gets all of the attention at Animal Kingdom, but another attraction located nearby is just as much fun, even if less visited. With the help of *The Lion King*'s Rafiki, guests take a short train ride from the village of Harambe to Conservation Station, where they get to meet animal experts and discover how the park is committed to conserving the planet. They also get to spend time up close with some of the animals at the station. It closed for renovation in late 2018 and is scheduled to open again in the future.

INFORMATIVE BOOKS ABOUT THE DISNEY PARKS

THE BIRNBAUM GUIDES TO WALT DISNEY WORLD/ DISNEYLAND (1983 TO PRESENT)

For thirty-five years, these comprehensive Disney-sanctioned books—originally written by the late Stephen Birnbaum—have been the best-selling gold standard guides to the Disney parks.

MOUSEJUNKIES! TIPS, TALES, AND TRICKS FOR A DISNEY WORLD FIX: ALL YOU NEED TO KNOW FOR A PERFECT VACATION (2009) by Bill Burke

A guide to the Disney parks written from the perspective of a superfan; highly entertaining.

SINCE THE WORLD BEGAN: WALT DISNEY WORLD, THE FIRST 25 YEARS (1996) by Jeff Kurtti

A history of the Florida resort's first quarter century, with rare photos and illustrations.

THE IMAGINEERING FIELD GUIDES TO . . . (2006) by Alex Wright

Six compact guides, told from an Imagineering viewpoint, to all six Disney parks in the United States.

THE DISNEYLAND ENCYCLOPEDIA (2017) by Chris Strodder

The ultimate book about all things Disneyland, from 1954 to the present day.

PROJECT FUTURE: THE INSIDE STORY BEHIND THE CREATION OF DISNEY WORLD (2010) by Chad Denver Emerson

A thoroughly researched academic and interesting look at the evolution of Walt Disney World, from Walt's brain to the completed project.

DREAM IT! DO IT! MY HALF-CENTURY CREATING DISNEY'S KINGDOMS (2013) by Marty Sklar

The legendary Imagineer shares stories about the parks, from his fifty years at Disney.

LITTLE KNOWN FACTS ABOUT WELL-KNOWN PLACES: DISNEYLAND (2008) by David Hoffman

A book full of quick, bite-size facts about Disneyland. A follow-up book about Walt Disney World, written by Laurie Flannery, was released in 2011.

CLEANING THE KINGDOM: INSIDER TALES OF KEEPING WALT'S DREAM SPOTLESS (2015) by Lynn Barron

What's it like to clean up after millions at the Disney parks? This book has the answer.

MAPS OF THE DISNEY PARKS: CHARTING 60 YEARS FROM CALIFORNIA TO SHANGHAI (2016) by Vanessa Hunt

An amazing collection of the guide maps of Disney parks, from 1955 to 2016.